P9-EGL-183

HEALTHY COOKING

atHome with
THE CULINARY INSTITUTE OF AMERICA

HEALTHY COOKING

WILEY
JOHN WILEY & SONS, INC.

This book is printed on acid-free paper. ∞

Copyright © 2011 by The Culinary Institute of America. All rights reserved

Photography © 2011 by Ben Fink

Published by John Wiley & Sons, Inc., Hoboken, New Jersey

Published simultaneously in Canada

THE CULINARY INSTITUTE OF AMERICA

President	Dr. Tim Ryan '77
Vice President Dean of Culinary Education	Mark Erickson '77
Senior Director Continuing Education	Susan Cussen
Director of Publishing	Nathalie Fischer
Editorial Project Manager	Mary Donovan '83
Editorial Assistant	Erin Jeanne McDowell '08
Consulting Chef	David Kamen '88

No part of this publication may be reproduced, stored in a retrieval system, or transmitted in any form or by any means, electronic, mechanical, photocopying, recording, scanning, or otherwise, except as permitted under Section 107 or 108 of the 1976 United States Copyright Act, without either the prior written permission of the Publisher, or authorization through payment of the appropriate per-copy fee to the Copyright Clearance Center, Inc., 222 Rosewood Drive, Danvers, MA 01923, (978) 750-8400, fax (978) 646-8600, or on the web at www.copyright.com. Requests to the Publisher for permission should be addressed to the Permissions Department, John Wiley & Sons, Inc., 111 River Street, Hoboken, NJ 07030, (201) 748-6011, fax (201) 748-6008, or online at http://www.wiley.com/go/permissions.

Limit of Liability/Disclaimer of Warranty: While the publisher and author have used their best efforts in preparing this book, they make no representations or warranties with respect to the accuracy or completeness of the contents of this book and specifically disclaim any implied warranties of merchantability or fitness for a particular purpose. No warranty may be created or extended by sales representatives or written sales materials. The advice and strategies contained herein may not be suitable for your situation. You should consult with a professional where appropriate. Neither the publisher nor author shall be liable for any loss of profit or any other commercial damages, including but not limited to special, incidental, consequential, or other damages.

For general information on our other products and services or for technical support, please contact our Customer Care Department within the United States at (800) 762-2974, outside the United States at (317) 572-3993 or fax (317) 572-4002.

Wiley also publishes its books in a variety of electronic formats. Some content that appears in print may not be available in electronic books. For more information about Wiley products, visit our web site at www.wiley.com.

Library of Congress Cataloging-in-Publication Data:

Healthy cooking at home with the Culinary Institute of a America. — Consumer ed.

　　p. cm.

　Includes index.

　ISBN 978-0-470-05233-4 (cloth)

　1. Cooking.　I. Culinary Institute of America.

　TX714.H3935 2011

　641.5--dc22

　　　　　　　　　　　　　2010013098

Printed in China

10　9　8　7　6　5　4　3　2　1

Contents

Acknowledgments

We wish to acknowledge our faculty, past and present, who teach the material to our students and make it come to life for our guests: Dr. Tim Ryan, Mark Erickson, Robert Briggs, Jonathan Zearfoss, Ron DeSantis, Victor Gielisse, Greg Fatigati, Eve Felder, Morey Kanner, David Kamen, Mark Ainsworth, Fred Brash, Dan Turgeon, Thomas Kief, Steven Kolpan, Anthony Ligouri, Richard Vergili, Marjorie Livingston, Elizabeth Briggs, Catherine Powers, Lynn Gigliotti, Michael Garnero, and Joseba Encabo. The Worlds of Flavor and Worlds of Healthy Flavors conferences held each year on our St. Helena, California campus have added another level of excitement and, ultimately, resulted in our Principles of Healthy Menu Development. We wish to acknowledge Greg Drescher and John Barkley for their important contributions by creating a forum for thought-provoking conversations between food-service and nutrition experts as part of the on-going national discussion of what healthy cooking and eating means in the twenty-first century.

CHAPTER ONE

What Is Healthy Cooking?

Good healthy cooking is no different from good cooking of any kind. Good cooking is the art of producing the best flavor in any dish. By choosing to develop great flavor at every step along the way, cooks and chefs alike have changed the landscape of healthy cooking from one of unrelenting beige and brown foods with little in the way of flavor beyond the occasional squirt of lemon juice into one that practically vibrates with the colors, textures, and aromas of foods we've adopted into our daily lives.

Ruby red pomegranate seeds that crunch and pop when you bite into them, deep purple eggplant that becomes a silken purée spiked with garlic, brilliant orange squashes and pumpkins roasted until tender and paired with sage, peppery greens sautéed with garlic, and a rainbow of chiles paired with nuts and seeds in a rich mole sauce are just some of the food options that have become commonplace in the last five to ten years.

Healthy cooking leads to healthy eating. This book docs not address specific diets or dietary needs; if you are in need of information about diets for specific conditions or for weight loss, there are several excellent resources available in print and online. Throughout this book, we will keep two important keys to healthy eating in mind. Variety is one key to healthy cooking, as it is to healthy eating. Choosing an array of foods increases your chances of getting the various nutrients you need; most advice for healthier eating recommends that we seek out foods that are less processed, like fresh fruits and vegetables and whole grains. In addition, a variety of foods looks exciting and filling on the plate. You can see the riot of flavors before you even taste anything.

Portion control is the other key to healthy eating and healthy cooking. Adding some ingredients, for example salt, sugar, or fat, in large quantities to a dish can virtually blot out any positive nutritional benefits. Choosing to eat portions that are enough to satisfy hunger without overwhelming our bodies is one way to use portion control in healthy eating. The other is in budgeting and monitoring high-calorie, high-fat, and high-sodium foods when you add them to a dish or use them as a condiment.

The Importance of Flavor

Although flavor is the focus of this book, we have to acknowledge that flavor is nothing if not subjective. What one person thinks is delicious another thinks is anything but, and what one person perceives as much too salty or spicy may be "just right" to someone else.

FLAVOR PROFILES

Flavor profiles are a snapshot of the specific flavoring ingredients and combinations of ingredients you might find within a cuisine. An Asian flavor profile includes ginger, garlic, soy sauce, cilantro, and lemongrass, for instance; a Mexican flavor profile includes chiles, pumpkin seeds, cilantro, and cumin. The profiles are influenced by politics, economics, religion, and the environment. (For more about flavor profiles, see Select Spice Mixtures of the World, page 289.)

Despite our tendency to keep flavor and nutrition separate, they are inextricably linked. Sweet foods like fruits and honey supply calories and energy. Savory foods often have protein, vital for growth and development. Tart and sour foods are acidic and often have vitamins that are essential to health. And bitter (alkaline) foods are often poisonous or toxic in large quantities, unless tamed by cooking.

Flavor is composed of many elements, which makes it distinct in some ways from the related term, *taste*. Taste has to do with specific sensory experiences of food that occur primarily in the mouth, like sweet, sour, salty, bitter, umami, and possibly others, whereas flavor includes all of our sensory experience: taste, smell, texture, appearance, and touch.

EXPERIENCING FLAVOR

The taste receptors in the human mouth (including all areas inside the mouth, not just the tongue) recognize five basic tastes: sweet, sour, salty, bitter, and umami, a Japanese word that means "deliciousness." Researchers continue to examine how we perceive tastes, and some have proposed additional "tastes," including calcium, which is said to be bitter and metallic. Chemesthesis is the taste associated with chemical irritation in the mouth, the kind of thing that happens when ingredients like salt, lemon juice, or garlic are present in large enough quantities to stimulate a reaction that we perceive as a burning sensation. Free fatty acids may be yet another taste, influencing not only how we experience the flavor of the food (sour or pungent, for instance) but also the way it feels (slippery or thick). The different types of fatty acids are what make goat's milk taste different from cow's milk.

FLAVOR DYNAMICS

With *flavor dynamics*, two or more flavors have been blended in some way to produce a new flavor experience. Sometimes the dynamics are the result of mixing things together so that you can't easily recognize specific flavors. The term also applies when two or more flavors are put into an unexpected juxtaposition, so that one flavor acts to improve the way the second flavor is experienced. Pineapple, served hot with a caramel sauce, reveals its sweet-and-tart flavors even more dramatically when you add crack black peppercorns. The heat in the pepper noticeably enhances the other flavors.

In addition to continued discoveries of how many specific tastes there may be, humans are also capable of discerning subtle variations on an almost infinite number of combinations of those tastes. This is due in large part to the aromas of food. Lemon juice and distilled vinegar are both sour, and white sugar and maple syrup are both sweet, but no one would ever confuse lemon juice and vinegar or sugar and syrup—their aromas distinguish them from each other and from other foods (see Sensing Flavor, page 7).

Most foods have combinations of flavors, just as most foods contain more than one type of nutrient. The chemical composition of foods gives them their flavors—cruciferous vegetables like cabbage and Brussels sprouts contain sulfur compounds that give them a bitter, pungent taste, which is reduced a little, or destroyed, during cooking; the acids in citrus fruits make them sour, but the natural sugars in the fruit tame the sour taste.

COOKING FOODS AFFECTS THEIR FLAVORS

Preparation affects the flavor of foods as well. Foods like garlic and onions get their flavor from volatile oils, which are released when the food is cut. Finely minced or crushed garlic has more exposed surfaces to release these oils than sliced garlic, so crushing will impart a stronger garlic taste than slicing. Heat changes the chemical makeup of foods, too. Raw garlic is harsh and pungent. Sauté it quickly and it becomes palatable yet retains a strong, distinctive flavor, but roast it slowly and it becomes sweet and mellow.

If individual foods and ingredients have complicated flavors on their own, then combining ingredients and then cooking them can heighten or intensify a specific flavor, while blending them may make the flavors even more intricate.

Dry-heat cooking methods like grilling or roasting allow browning to occur. Steamed cauliflower has a much simpler, purer taste than roasted cauliflower, for example. A stew that is made without first browning the meat or sautéing aromatic vegetables will taste quite different from one that uses these techniques.

By adding ingredients in a certain sequence, you create layers of flavors. One fairly simple example is the addition of freshly minced chives to French onion soup (just before adding the crouton). The fresh chives impart another dimension of onion, and their sharp, pungent note contrasts dramatically with the sweet, mellow caramelized onions.

More intricate layering occurs when you combine several different ingredients in a dish. For example, consider what happens when you cook meat and then make a mushroom sauce: You may dry-sauté beef medallions or filets. After removing them from the pan, you deglaze it, adding a full-bodied dry red wine to dissolve the reduced juices from the meat to make them into a sauce. The mushrooms go in next and release their essence into the sauce. Finally, aromatic components—fortified wine, fresh herbs, and black pepper—are added just before serving so that their volatile compounds are not lost to prolonged cooking. The end result is a complex sensory experience gradually revealed as we enjoy the meal.

Developing Flavor

While every cook is limited by a variety of factors, including the seasons, availability, and cost, it is in the act of cooking that the cook takes control. A talented cook can turn ordinary or inexpensive ingredients into something fabulous.

COOKING TECHNIQUE

One of the biggest areas where cooks influence flavor is in choosing the cooking technique. Heat alters the chemical structure of food, breaking down cell walls, releasing flavor compounds and nutrients, and making the food more tender.

Dry-heat cooking techniques attain temperatures higher than moist-heat methods. These higher temperatures allow foods to brown and develop a crust. Moist-heat cooking methods are typically gentler. Because foods do not brown, their flavors tend to be simpler and purer. Compare the difference between grilled or roasted salmon and poached salmon.

TEXTURES

The foods' textures affect how their flavors are perceived as well. A silky-smooth bisque and a chunky potage may have the same ingredients, but the puréed soup's flavor may be subtler than the latter, where each ingredient remains distinct. Because all of our senses are involved in tasting (see Sensing Flavor, page 7), food that looks attractive on the plate is more appealing than a carelessly arranged dish.

TEMPERATURE

Even temperature can be used to add an unexpected element to a dish. Very hot and very cold foods tend to have less discernable flavors. Foods like ice cream, cheeses, and fruits have more developed flavors if they have been allowed to sit at room temperature for a while. Piping-hot foods and beverages can deaden the palate. When hot and cold foods are served together, an interesting contrast can be created. In cuisines where food is often spicy, this is a time-honored tradition. For example, in Indian cuisine, a mango lassi (mangoes, yogurt, spices) might be served as a beverage with a fiery pork vindaloo and spicy mango chutney. Some of the ingredients are similar, and several are the same (mango, spices), but the temperature and creamy quality of the chilled drink provide a cooling counterpoint to the hot and spicy pork dish.

Using Seasonings and Flavorings

The way you choose and use seasoning and flavoring ingredients determines the ultimate flavor of the dish. Some flavoring ingredients don't require any special monitoring. Toasted, parched, or freshly ground spices and chiles add rich smoky flavors without introducing sodium or fat. Fresh herbs and aromatic ingredients like garlic, lemongrass, ginger, or lime juice add flavor but not calories. High-sodium foods, such as salt, capers, anchovies, and olives, do call for strict measuring and proper handling. Sometimes, you may rinse away some of the brine or soak salty foods to reduce the sodium they add to a dish. You can often find low- or reduced-sodium versions of salty condiments like soy or tamari sauce. Salt itself should always be used properly and with care.

SALTING FOODS

Salt is a seasoning that is almost taken for granted. Nearly everyone notices when you leave it out of a dish, because foods taste a little dull and flat. As we continue to learn more about the potential health risks of a diet high in sodium, cooks and nutritionists alike are looking at salt more closely once again. Adding a little salt can have the effect of bringing out the best flavor in foods. Humans do crave salt because it is essential to the healthy functioning of our bodies, but it has become too easy to consume far more salt than we need. Too much sodium can have serious and negative effects on our health.

We do not advocate simply eliminating salt, unless there is a specific reason to do so, but we do encourage all cooks to use salt wisely. Use kosher salt, as we have done in our recipes, wherever salt is called for. The same volume of kosher salt has about half the sodium of table salt (for more information, see Types of Salt, page 8).

SENSING FLAVOR

We experience flavor with all of our senses. When a plate of food is set before you, you experience it in many ways: You see its colors, you smell its aromas, and you might hear sizzling. You might hear it crunch when you cut into it or when you chew it. In addition to tasting its flavors, you'll feel the temperature of the food, its texture or consistency, and perhaps whether it is cooling, like mint, or fiery from peppers.

Sight gives clues to flavor; for example, you expect vibrantly green sugar snap peas to taste from-the-garden fresh and slices of orange sweet potato bearing grill marks to have a sweet, slightly smoky taste and a dense, melting texture. Sight also adds to the appeal of food in far more subtle ways. Artfully presented, carefully arranged food is more tempting than food casually or even sloppily set on the plate.

We might not think of foods as making sounds, but they do, both as they cook and when we eat them. A sizzling platter of fajitas and a fizzing glass of Champagne send flavor cues before the food or beverage reaches the mouth. Some foods become audible when we eat them. When tucking into a crispy-looking, golden piece of herb-breaded baked chicken, you expect that first bite to be accompanied by a hearty crunch. If the coating turns out to be quietly soggy, you will most likely feel disappointed, even cheated somehow, regardless of the actual taste and aroma.

When you touch a food with your fingers or with a utensil, you receive a preview of its texture. A piece of poached salmon that softly flakes under the gentle prodding of a fork hints at the tenderness of the fish. A steak that resists your most insistent sawing tells you that it is going to be a lot of work for not much reward.

Smell plays an enormous role in our perception of flavor, as anyone who has ever had a head cold knows. In fact, aroma is a primary component of flavor. While we are able to perceive just a few basic tastes, we are able to distinguish among hundreds of aromas. For example, an orange and a tangerine share the same basic tastes of sweet and sour, but in a blind taste test most people are still able to tell the difference because each fruit has a distinct set of characteristic aromas and slightly different textures.

When you chew and swallow the first bite, you experience the full flavor of a dish. What we typically think of as "taste" or "flavor" is actually the interaction of taste and smell, combined with the feel of the food in the mouth. Our sense of taste comes from the chemical receptors on our tongues, our taste buds. Additionally, the insides of our mouths feel sensations such as the burn of hot chiles, the cooling effect of mint, the astringency of tannins in tea or wine, the numbing sensation of cloves, and the fizz of carbonated beverages.

HIDDEN SOURCES OF SODIUM

Salt isn't the only source of sodium in foods. Processed and prepared foods are often high in sodium, even when they don't actually taste salty. Look for low- or reduced-sodium versions of ingredients like soy sauce, prepared broths or stocks, and condiments.

TYPE	ROLE
MONOSODIUM GLUTAMATE (MSG)	Flavor enhancer
SODIUM BENZOATE	Preservative
SODIUM CASEINATE	Thickener and binder
SODIUM CITRATE	Buffer, used to control acidity in soft drinks
SODIUM NITRITE	Curing agent in meat
SODIUM PHOSPHATE	Emulsifier, stabilizer
SODIUM PROPIONATE	Mold inhibitor
SODIUM SACCHARIN	Noncaloric sweetener

TYPES OF SALT

Salt is found in several forms, each of which carries different qualities. However, all types of salt, with the exception of light salt, are composed of 40 percent sodium and 60 percent chloride. One teaspoon of table salt or 6 grams of any salt other than light salt contains 2,325 milligrams of sodium.

Table salt is most commonly used in cooking and as a table condiment. It consists of small, dense, granular cubes that adhere poorly to food, dissolve slowly in solution, and are difficult to blend.

Iodized salt is table salt to which iodine has been added as a preventative against goiter, an enlargement of the thyroid gland caused by iodine deficiency.

Kosher salt is granular salt that has been compressed to provide a greater surface area. It is flaky and, compared to table salt, lighter in weight, dissolves more readily, and adheres better to food. Diamond Crystal® kosher salt is formed through an evaporation process similar to that used in the production of sea salt. The size of a grain of Diamond Crystal kosher salt is larger than that of other kosher salt. This means that a teaspoon of Diamond kosher salt contains fewer grains of salt and weighs less than a teaspoon of other kosher salts. Although both types of kosher salt are typically more expensive than table salt, many chefs prefer to cook almost exclusively with kosher salts.

Sea salt and bay salt are collected through the evaporation of natural salt water and consist of thin, flaky layers. They adhere well to food and dissolve quickly. These salts also contain other trace minerals that occur naturally in the waters from which the salts are collected. As such, sea and bay salts from different areas of the world taste different. All are generally more complex in flavor than table and kosher salts. Sea and bay salts can be purchased in fine-grain and larger crystal forms.

A given volume of each type of salt weighs a different amount. Unless noted otherwise, recipes in this book calling for salt refer to kosher salt. To substitute a kosher or sea salt for table salt and achieve the same level of saltiness, 1½ to 2 times the volume may be necessary. However, you should always start with the original amount stated and taste before adding more.

Healthy Ingredients

From field to table, monitoring the U.S. food supply for wholesomeness and safety is a huge job. The way that food is grown and produced can have a profound effect on how safe, nutritious, and healthful it is. Cooks should consider a number of things when they decide what foods to buy and where to buy them. Quality, cost, and availability are some obvious considerations, but today, we have both the opportunity and the responsibility to think about how foods were raised or grown, the ways in which they were processed, and the consequences to our own health as well as that of the planet.

If healthy cooking is an important to you, you also need to be knowledgeable about some common practices: conventional farming, organic and sustainable farming, free-range animal husbandry practices, fish ranching, and aquaculture. Foods that have been genetically modified, bioengineered, or treated with hormones are very much on our minds these days.

Agriculture in the United States has changed dramatically in the last fifty or so years. Mechanized farming, synthetic chemicals for fertilization and pest control, improved irrigation methods, and seed stock that is both resistant to disease and produces greater yields are but some of the innovations. And while some people feel these modern methods, often referred to as "conventional" farming practices, are a necessity if there is to be enough affordable food for everyone, others believe they pose a threat to the health and well-being of society and the environment.

However, foods that are organic, hormone-free, free-range, and not genetically modified tend to be more expensive than foods produced by conventional farming methods. There are consequences for every choice that is made. The challenge is making the best possible choices for your particular situation.

ORGANIC FOODS

In keeping with the tenets of sustainable agriculture, many farmers endeavor to grow crops and raise livestock organically. Until recently, "organically grown" was generally understood to mean "grown without synthetic pesticides and herbicides." The trouble, however, was that no federal regulations pertaining to organic growing practices existed, making it difficult for consumers to be sure of exactly what they were buying.

In October 2002, the United States Department of Agriculture (USDA) established a set of national standards that food labeled "organic" must meet. Organic foods can only be produced on land that has been free of prohibited substances for at least three years. During the time that farmland is being changed from conventional to organic, it is called "transitional." This has become an impediment for some farmers, since the time and the costs involved in becoming certified organic are significant. Organic livestock is fed 100 percent organic agricultural feed (although vitamin and mineral supplements are acceptable). They must have access to the outdoors, and ruminants (such as cattle) must have access to pasturelands. Animals may not be given hormones to enhance or promote growth, or antibiotics. Vaccines and preventive management practices are used to maintain animals' health.

The USDA has also established standards for the labeling of organic foods, including processed foods and packaged goods containing organic ingredients. Foods labeled "100 percent organic" must contain only organically produced ingredients. Foods labeled "organic" must contain at least 95 percent organically produced ingredients, and the remaining 5 percent ingredients must either be on the National List or must be unavailable commercially in organic form.

Foods that contain at least 70 percent organic ingredients can use the phrase "made with organic ingredients." However, the USDA seal cannot appear on the package.

Although there is no scientific evidence that organic foods have a better nutrition profile, many people prefer them for their flavor and quality, or because they reduce the quantity of pesticides and herbicides on foods or in the soil or water. Organic foods are increasingly available and increasingly in demand. They can be an important part of an overall strategy for bringing healthy cooking into the kitchen, as long as you are aware of the standards for the use of the word on package labels or in advertisements.

SUSTAINABLE AGRICULTURE

History teaches that the decline of many ancient civilizations was in part due to nonrenewable farming methods. Many modern farming methods appear to be similarly depleting our natural resources. At the same time, the world's population is growing at an unprecedented pace. This raises serious questions about whether our present agricultural systems will be able to support so many people.

Sustainable agriculture attempts to choose agricultural practices according to their effects on society and the environment. Its goal is to secure for farmers the best crop yields and economic returns while considering the needs of society and the health of the environment in the present and the future. Economic profitability in the present is weighed against environmentally conservative farming methods of the future.

Sustainable agricultural practices stem from the concept of biodynamics, a system based upon the concept that all things in nature are interrelated. The methods that farmers employ on their individual fields eventually affect much larger local ecosystems and, over time, can have a global effect.

Among the problems sustainable agriculture seeks to address are topsoil depletion, water and energy overconsumption, groundwater contamination, overuse of chemical pesticides and herbicides, escalating production costs, and disintegrating economic and social conditions in rural farming communities.

Allergens and Toxins in Foods

The overwhelming majority of food in the United States is safe. While exceptions are real and may be of valid concern, steps to ensure the continued safety and wholesomeness of foods are in place. It is also important to recognize that some foods can cause an individual to suffer a reaction. Some reactions are caused by an intolerance; the classic example is lactose intolerance. The symptoms are similar to that for a food-borne illness. Others are caused by allergens. The reactions can range from mild, as in a case of hives, to extremely severe and potentially life threatening.

FOOD ALLERGIES

A food allergy is different from a dislike or an intolerance. When you dislike a food, you may feel like it is making you sick, even when you merely smell, see, or talk about it, but the reaction is more emotional than physical. When you cannot tolerate a food well, you usually experience symptoms like bloating or cramping.

If you have a true allergy, you may come to dislike the food because of the allergic reaction you experience, but a surprising number of food allergy sufferers long for the shrimp cocktail, omelet, or peanut butter sandwich that they can't eat.

The way your body reacts when you eat something to which you are truly allergic can be dramatic and dangerous. An allergic reaction to a food is usually rapid. The skin can become itchy and develop hives or welts. Some individuals report that their throats start to close up or that their tongues start to swell (anaphylactic shock). Severe reactions require immediate medical attention.

As of January 2006, all packaged foods that contain major food allergens (milk, eggs, fish, crustacean shellfish, tree nuts, wheat, peanuts, and soybeans) must be identified on the label. Many manufacturers let their customers know if foods that contain nuts are processed in the same plant as those that do not contain nuts. Depending on an individual's sensitivity, even the very small amount of allergen left on a piece of equipment and transferred to a food could be enough to set off a reaction.

MERCURY, PCBS, AND OTHER TOXINS IN SEAFOOD

Fish is full of beneficial nutrients, notably omega-3 fatty acids and good-quality protein, but depending on the waters it lived in, fish can be high in mercury or other heavy metals or pollutants like polychlorinated biphenyls (PCBs). Farm-raised fish may be high in antibiotics or other chemicals.

Nearly all fish and shellfish contain traces of mercury, but the risks from consuming it in very small amounts should not be a concern for most people, with the exception of pregnant or nursing women, children under twelve, the elderly, and people with compromised immune systems, who should limit their consumption of some types of fish. Mercury is of special concern for infants and unborn children because their nervous systems are still developing.

For most people, the risks depend on the amount of fish and shellfish eaten and the levels of mercury in the fish. Mercury accumulates in the body over time, so larger fish that have lived longer, and predatory fish, pose a greater risk.

The Food and Drug Administration (FDA) and the Environmental Protection Agency (EPA) have established the following guidelines to reduce exposure to mercury:

1. Avoid shark, swordfish, king mackerel, and tilefish; they all contain high levels of mercury.

2. Eat up to twelve ounces a week of a variety of fish and shellfish that are low in mercury. Five common varieties that are generally considered safe are shrimp, salmon, pollock, catfish, and canned light tuna. Albacore tuna has more mercury than light tuna, so it is recommended that canned albacore be limited to six ounces per week. Tuna steaks may also be high in mercury and should be limited to six ounces per week as well.

3. If you purchase fish from private sources or individuals, check advisories about the safety of local fish. If no information is available, limit consumption to six ounces per week and do not consume any other fish during that week.

Nutrition Labeling

Nutrition labels contain specific information about food products. Labeling can appear on packaged goods or on menus, or the information may appear in advertisements. The specific wording is created by the food manufacturer or restaurant, but any claims or promises must match the standards set by the FDA. Any type of nutrition claim is regulated by the FDA under the Nutrition Labeling and Education Act (NLEA) of 1990. The standards are updated frequently as new studies add to our share of information.

A BRIEF HISTORY OF FOOD LABELING IN THE UNITED STATES

Since 1906, the U.S. government has developed legislation to inform consumers about the safety and quality of foods by requiring information on food labels. In 1969, the White House Conference on Food, Nutrition, and Health recommended that a system be developed to deliver nutrition information to consumers. For nearly two decades, nutrition labeling was largely voluntary and minimally regulated unless a food contained added nutrients or included a claim about its nutrient content or usefulness in the daily diet. Because information was inconsistent, it was difficult for consumers to make accurate comparisons.

Until December 14, 2007, there were no rules governing what qualified as "light" or "healthy," and the terms were used indiscriminately. Today, all of those terms have been described and defined. In order to qualify for a nutrition claim, specific standards must be met. The term "light," for example, has been used in the past when the product really showed only a very slight reduction in calories, fat, or sodium. Sometimes, those reductions were nothing more than a manipulation of the serving size recorded on the label. If you see the term light on a label today, you can be sure that it was compared to a reference amount.

In 1990, Congress enacted the Nutrition Labeling and Education Act (NLEA), which required that standardized nutrition information be included on packaged food labels. Terms like *fat-free*, *low-sodium*, *light*, and *healthy* were clearly defined to ensure that nutrition and health claims were used responsibly and consistently by food producers.

Restaurant menu claims were originally not included in these regulations, but two public advocacy groups, the Center for Science in the Public Interest (CSPI) and Public Citizen, filed suit in 1993 to prevent this exclusion. In 1996, the U.S. District Court issued a ruling that agreed with the plaintiffs, and the court ordered the FDA to amend its regulations. These went into effect in 1997.

NUTRIENT CONTENT CLAIMS

The FDA established a specific list of words and phrases that may be used to describe the nutrient contents of foods that fit certain criteria. Nearly all of the criteria are based on standard serving sizes known as reference amounts. According to the FDA, three types of claims may be used to describe the nutrition profile of foods:

An absolute claim characterizes the exact amount or range of a nutrient in a particular food. Terms that indicate an absolute claim are *free*, *low*, *reduced*, and *less*. For example, to meet the definition of "low sodium," a food must contain 140 milligrams or less per reference amount.

A relative claim is a statement made that compares the nutrient content of one food to another food, known as the reference food. Words like *reduced* and *less* can also indicate a relative claim; *reduced*, as well as *added* and *light* or *lite*, may be used to compare products that are similar (such as cookies to cookies), whereas *more* and *less* can be used to compare foods within the same category that may be substituted for one another (such as cookies for cake). For example a soup labeled "light" must have at least one-third less sodium than the full sodium version of a similar type of soup.

An implied claim is a statement that highlights the presence or absence of an ingredient that is associated with the level of a nutrient. "High in oat bran" carries the implied claim that the food is high in fiber, so any food with this claim must meet the established criteria for high-fiber foods. Other ingredient-nutrient relationships include sugar and calories, oils and total fat, tropical oils and saturated fat, and whole grains or bran and dietary fiber.

Implied claims are difficult to define and can be confusing because it can be easy to unwittingly make an implied claim. Saying a pizza is "made with low-fat cheese" implies that the pizza is at least "reduced fat" compared to a similar pizza. Such a statement would be prohibited by the FDA if the pizza failed to meet the criteria for a "reduced-fat" food.

Some statements about ingredients are not considered nutrient claims. These are general statements that pertain to ingredients that are perceived to have value (e.g., "made with fresh fruit and honey"), that do not serve nutritive purposes (e.g., "no preservatives"), or that may need to be avoided for various reasons (e.g., "100% milk free"). Additionally, statements in which the ingredient is part of the identity of a food, such as whole wheat pasta or multigrain bread, are not considered nutrient claims.

HEALTH CLAIMS

A health claim defines the relationship between the nutrient content of a food and a disease or health-related condition. A nutrient content claim refers only to a level or range of a nutrient in a food, while a health claim includes two elements: a reference to the nutrient or substance and a reference to a disease or health-related condition. Generally, a health claim must:

1. Be complete, truthful, and not misleading.

2. Use "may" or "might" to express the relationship between nutrient and disease.

3. Indicate that the risk of disease depends on many factors.

Health claims may be expressed through statements, icons or symbols, or as a vignette. The form of the claim is not important as long as all the required elements are present. The FDA recognizes eleven nutrient-disease relationships that may be used in health claims:

1. Calcium and osteoporosis

2. Sodium and hypertension

3. Dietary fat and cancer

4. Dietary saturated fat and cholesterol and the risk of heart disease

5. Fiber-containing grain products, fruits, and vegetables and cancer

6. Fruits, vegetables, and grain products that contain fiber, particularly soluble fiber, and the risk of heart disease

7. Fruits and vegetables and cancer

8. Folate and neural tube defects

9. Dietary sugar alcohol and dental caries (cavities)

10. Dietary soluble fiber, such as that found in whole oats and psyllium seed husks, and risk of coronary heart disease

11. Soy protein and risk of coronary heart disease

CLAIMS ABOUT DIETARY GUIDELINES

In addition to nutrient and health claims, food-service operators also have the option of indicating that a particular food falls within dietary guidelines. A statement that a food or meal meets the dietary guidelines of a recognized dietary authority is not considered a nutrient content or health claim by the FDA, provided that the statement is limited to general dietary guidance and does not characterize the level of a nutrient in a food. A statement such as "Meets the National Cancer Institute recommendations for fiber" makes the food subject to nutrient content claim requirements because it characterizes the content of a specific nutrient.

A Healthy Kitchen

A healthy kitchen is a safe and clean kitchen. It is a place where foods can be stored and prepared in ways that keep them not only delicious but also wholesome and safe to eat.

Foods can be contaminated at a number of steps along the way from the farm to your table. Microorganisms are virtually everywhere, and most are helpful or harmless. Among those that are pathogenic, or responsible for causing illness, are fungi, viruses, parasites, and bacteria. Fungi, which include mold and yeast, are more often responsible for food spoilage than food-borne illness. Viruses such as hepatitis are introduced to foods when farm workers or food handlers don't follow proper hand-washing practices, but it is bacteria of various sorts that are responsible for the majority of food-borne illnesses. While there is not much you can do to protect against foods that you are buying, you can control what happens after you get them into your kitchen.

SAFE TEMPERATURES FOR FOODS

Keeping foods at safe temperatures is an important part of food safety. While it is true that different types of bacteria thrive at different temperatures, the most common, and the most dangerous, types of bacteria thrive at temperatures between 40° and 140°F.

Foods such as meats, poultry, seafood, tofu, and most dairy products are all potentially hazardous because they are provide a perfect environment for pathogens to thrive: moisture, the right pH level, and the protein they need to grow and reproduce. Cooked foods such as rice, beans, pasta, and potatoes, as well as sliced melons, sprouts, and garlic-and-oil mixtures, are also potentially hazardous.

PREVENTING CROSS-CONTAMINATION

Although cooking will destroy many of the microorganisms present, careless handling afterward can reintroduce pathogens. Cross-contamination occurs when disease-causing substances are transferred from one food or surface to another. Wash your hands thoroughly with soap and warm water before and after handling raw ingredients. Use separate cutting boards and knives for raw and cooked foods, or wash your space and equipment with hot, soapy water between uses. All food should be stored properly to prevent contact between raw and cooked items. Store raw ingredients below and away from cooked foods or foods that will be served fresh, in order to prevent cross-contamination by dripping juices.

Chilling will not kill most pathogens, but it can drastically slow their reproduction. In general, refrigerators should be kept between 36° to 40°F. The front of a refrigerator tends to be the warmest area and the back the coldest. Before being placed in a refrigerator, food should be cooled, stored in clean containers, and wrapped well.

Because microorganisms reproduce readily at temperatures between 40°F and 140°F, do not let food sit out in this range of warm temperatures for more than two hours.

FOODS SHOULD BE STORED AT THE FOLLOWING TEMPERATURES:

Meat and poultry	32° to 36°F / 0° to 2°C
Fish and shellfish	30° to 34°F / −1° to 2°C
Eggs	38° to 40°F / 3° to 4°C
Dairy products	36° to 40°F / 2° to 4°C
Produce	40° to 45°F / 4° to 7°C

COOLING FOODS BEFORE STORING

Cool cooked foods rapidly before you put them in the refrigerator. If a food is still hot when you store it, the center might stay warm long enough to support bacterial growth. To cool foods safely, bring them to 70°F within two hours, and to 40°F within four more hours as follows:

Place hot liquids like soups, stews, sauces, or stocks in metal containers (which conduct temperatures better than plastic or glass), then in an ice water bath. (To make an ice water bath, fill a large basin or your sink about half full with cold water and add enough ice to fill the container about three-fourths full.) Stir frequently to bring the temperature down more rapidly. Spread semisolid foods like rice or polenta in a shallow pan. Cut solid foods into pieces if necessary so they can cool down. Once a food is at room temperature (outside and in), you can wrap and store the food in your refrigerator.

To reheat foods safely, put them into pans over direct heat or, for smaller amounts, into the microwave. Heat foods completely according to the following standard:

Bring foods up to at least 165°F for at least 15 seconds.

CHAPTER TWO

Soups, Salads, and Appetizers

Soups, salads, and other small plates are the perfect way to begin a healthy meal. Among other things, they offer a simple way to introduce more fresh fruits and vegetables into your meals. When you have the time for a separate first course, it slows the entire pace of the meal down. A first course takes the edge off your appetite, which means you can more fully appreciate the rest of the meal without overindulging. A first course can add color and texture to a meal, especially if you base your selections on a rainbow of in-season vegetables and fruits.

Healthy Techniques for Soups

Many of the recipes in this chapter work perfectly as entrées for a light lunch or supper. Or, you could build a meal out of a selection of these recipes. You can choose from a variety of soups created from familiar and exotic ingredients in brilliant colors, from carrots to beets to fresh peas. Cutting back on the cream and butter, or eliminating them altogether, allows the flavors to truly shine. The salads and appetizers showcase bright, bold flavors—Vietnamese salad rolls redolent with fresh herbs, a bracing salad of avocado and grapefruit—that offer an array of colors, textures, temperatures, and tastes inspired by the ingredients they feature.

GARNISHING AND FINISHING SOUPS

When you decide to garnish a soup, you have a lot of options. Some garnishes are healthier than others. Before you resort to oyster crackers or sour cream, consider the possibilities.

1. ADD MORE INGREDIENTS THAN YOU SEE IN THE RECIPE LIST.

Soups have a special talent for "hiding" flavors. Mothers have been sneaking extra veggies and whole grains (including some of the least loved ones: okra, turnips, lima beans, and barley) for generations because it takes a truly dedicated individual to identify and pick out the offending vegetable.

If you are making a brothy soup, like *potage au pistou* or minestrone, go ahead and add more colorful vegetables. Whenever possible, pick brightly colored ingredients. Sometimes, adding a bit more of the main ingredient, but in a barely blanched or raw state, is highly effective from the standpoint of appearance, since soups tend to lose some of their vibrant colors as they cook. And of course, adding more vegetables, whole grains, or legumes increases nutrients in your soup, usually without a significant increase in calories.

2. USE A TINY AMOUNT OF HIGH-FAT, HIGH-FLAVOR INGREDIENTS, ADDED AT THE LAST POSSIBLE MOMENT.

Heavy or sour cream, grated cheese, flavored oils, and pesto are some of the most popular garnishes for soups. Whenever they can be used in truly small amounts and still deliver a significant amount of flavor, we've included them in some recipes. For instance, you can get a lot of impact from a much smaller amount by adding it to the soup as a small dollop or drizzle on each serving, rather than stirring cream into the whole batch of soup. Instead of sprinkling spoonfuls of grated cheese into your minestrone, simmer the rind of a piece of Parmesan cheese in the soup.

3. **REMEMBER THE CRUNCH.**
The reason we love crackers and other crunchy things is simple: Too much of one thing loses its appeal pretty quickly. Foods soft enough to spoon up from a bowl definitely benefit from some extra texture. In addition to croutons, you can try toasted nuts (chopped if they are large), or curls or strips of raw vegetables (carrots, fennel, celery, and radishes are excellent). Popcorn is another excellent option, plain or dusted with spices.

4. **ADD FINISHING INGREDIENTS WITHOUT INCREASING SODIUM.**
Quite often, recipes will ask you to add salt and pepper before the dish has finished cooking. And in some cases, adding a tiny amount while the soup simmers is essential to developing the best flavor. You should always take a careful taste of the soup before you add any more salt. But before sprinkling in the salt, try some of these options with very little to no added sodium: vinegar, citrus juice, wines (especially fortified wines like sherry or Madeira).

CREATING SOUP SAMPLERS

A soup sampler lets you serve a little bit of a two or three different soups. It is an elegant way to add variety to a dinner party menu. If you planning to create a sampler, think about the flavors of the soups and decide if you would enjoy them together. Next, consider whether you want to feature soups that are all the same basic texture (all purées, for instance) or whether you want some contrast. And finally, remember that the serving of each individual soup should be small enough that you don't end up with an overall serving of soup that is too large.

You might want to have a common "thread" as we do on page 29 with a selection of three cold puréed vegetable soups. Or you might use a flavor like onions or mushrooms to unite a collection of soups. Serving a selection of soups, especially when those soups feature fresh seasonal vegetables at their flavor peak, is a great way to add more vegetables to any meal.

Making a sampler of two or three soups does require some advance work. But if the soups are served chilled, then you have virtually no work to do when you plan to serve them besides checking the seasoning and adding the garnish.

PURÉEING SOUPS

Choose your puréeing technique according to the equipment you have in your kitchen or based upon the specific texture you want to achieve.

Immersion Blender
An immersion blender permits you to purée a soup or other preparation directly in the pot. First, remove any sachets, bay leaves, bones, or other inedible ingredients. Stir the soup slowly with the blender's motor running. Keep the head completely submerged while the blades are turning to prevent splatters.

Blender or Food Processor
To use a regular standing blender or a food processor to purée, cool the soup or other preparation slightly first. Fill the blender or the work bowl of the food processor no more than halfway full to avoid making a mess or, worse, scalding yourself. Like immersion blenders,

standing blenders and food processors produce a very fine, smoothly textured soup with just a small amount of air incorporated into the purée.

Food Mill

Food mills tend to make denser purées than blenders or food processors, as no air is whipped into the mixture. They will also strain out skins, seeds, and tougher fibers as they purée. If your food mill has more than one disk, fit it with a fine disk for a velvety smooth soup, or a coarse disk for a thicker, more textured purée. For the best consistency, pass the soup through the coarse disk first, then switch to the fine disk. (If you cannot change disks on your food mill, use the mill for the first pass and a blender for the second.) Work in batches, filling the food mill no more than halfway each time and discarding the accumulated solids between batches.

Sieve and Spoon

Rustic or home-style purées or purée soups can be relatively coarse and rely simply on pressing the cooked solids through a sieve using a wooden spoon. Use a circular motion and press firmly against the food with the rounded back of a wooden spoon. Be sure to collect the purée that clings to the outside of the sieve.

Wooden Spoons and Potato Mashers

Sometimes, you want a purée soup to retain a chunky texture. In such cases, you can choose to purée a portion of the soup by one of the methods outlined above, or you can simply use the time-honored technique of smashing the soup ingredients against the side of the pot with your wooden spoon as you stir it. Or you can smash the ingredients using a potato masher instead. Starchy ingredients like beans, squashes, or potatoes will thicken the soup and add body.

Healthy Techniques for Salads

Lettuces are sold in a host of different ways: bins or baskets of mixed greens at the market, whole heads—with or without packing material—and, most recently, bags of greens that are prewashed (sometimes "triple" washed). Baby spinach, mixes including radicchio and frisée, and lesser known greens from the Mediterranean and Asia are making their way into the market, no matter where you live.

No one should ever be tempted to skip the washing and drying step when using prepared, bagged lettuces and greens, no matter how many times the bag claims it's been washed already. The flurry of news reports about food-borne outbreaks related to fresh spinach and lettuce have brought more attention to the problems of keeping foods safe, an important issue that came through loud and clear after stringent investigations. In more than one instance, the source of the contamination occurred before the produce arrived at grocery stores and kitchens. Foods became contaminated either in the field or during harvesting, often before they ever reached the processing plant. Scrupulous food processors do all they can to assure that foods stay safe at each step of processing, but the fact is, large-scale operations have the potential to spread a food-borne disease rapidly over a wide area. Once foods have come in contact with pathogens like E. coli, there is nothing you can do to make them safe again. Washing, even cooking, will not remove or inactivate all types of pathogens.

This does not mean that you should not eat these delicious, healthy vegetables. It does mean that we encourage you to find clean and reliable markets in your town and, whenever possible, to check the country of origin in the markets where you shop. Other countries do not have the same standards regarding safe food handling and processing procedures as the United States. It may be in your interest to opt for locally grown and processed foods.

GARNISHING SALADS

Fresh or dried fruits, nuts, and cheeses are just some of the ways you might want to garnish a salad. Some garnishes can be included with abandon, since they add virtually no extra calories, sodium, or fat. Others demand a little more care, and count as "controlled indulgences."

1. ADD FRUIT.

Fresh fruits, including apples, pears, peaches, watermelon, berries, grapes, and citrus fruits, give salads a wide array of extra benefits. Pomegranate seeds are a great addition, as are tropical fruits like star fruit (carambola), kiwi, lychee nuts, or bananas. Fresh fruits add moisture and juiciness, along with their nutritional benefits. Remember to cut and add apples and pears at the last minute so they won't turn brown.

Dried fruits, like apricot, prunes, cherries, raisins, currants, or dates, also have a place as a healthy salad garnish. As fruits dry, they lose water and get smaller in size, but they do not lose calories. One grape weighs about 6 grams and contains about 7 calories. One raisin is much smaller than 1 grape, weighing only 2 grams, but it still has all 7 calories. Calories in dried fruits are in a smaller volume than in fresh, so you should measure them to keep overall calories under control. Remember that their flavors are concentrated, too, so you get a noticeable effect from a small amount.

2. ADD NUTS AND SEEDS.

Nuts are a rich source of some important nutrients. More to the point, though, they give substance to salads. Many nuts benefit from being toasted first, as described on page 290.

3. ADD (A LITTLE) CHEESE.

If you enjoy cheese, adding a bit to your salad is a great way to indulge without going overboard. Choose among fresh soft cheeses, like goat cheese and or mozzarella; blue cheeses like Roquefort or Stilton; or grating cheeses like Parmesan or Romano. Certain cheeses have noticeable affinity with certain fruits, so if you've followed our fruit suggestion and chose apples or pears, a salty, pungent blue cheese like Stilton is a classic choice. A few large curls of freshly shaved Parmesan pack a lot of flavor; since the pieces are paper thin, you may end up adding an amount equivalent to less than a teaspoon, but it will look like a lot more.

CREATING A SALAD SAMPLER

One of the key components of healthy eating is enjoying a variety of foods. When you put together a variety of salads and other marinated dishes, you not only have a great-looking and great-tasting plate, but you are also making it that much easier to get a wider array of nutrients. Serve salad sampler plates as appetizers or entrées.

1. BUILD IN SOME CONTRAST.

A large part of the pleasure we take in a meal has to do with the way it looks. A variety of bright colors is more attractive than a monotone plate. The same is true of textures and flavors. A sampling of salads might run the gamut from crisp to tender, moist to dry, spicy to subtle.

Cut the ingredients for salads into different shapes. Leave small items whole when possible and cut others into slices or wedges that take advantage of their natural shapes. Add a bed of greens for contrast and height.

2. CREATE A FLAVOR BRIDGE.

You might like to include a few things that make "bridges" from one dish to another. This will give a bit more cohesion and clarity to the dish. If you have decided to make a sampler that includes a lemon, garlic, and tahini dressing for one dish, you might consider adding sesame seeds as a garnish for another selection in your sampler. If you have fresh tomatoes in one salad, use dried tomatoes in another to keep your selections connected to each other.

ASPARAGUS SOUP

By rinsing the just-cooked asparagus with cold water—a technique known as refreshing vegetables—you stop the asparagus from continuing to cook from its own residual heat. The sudden chill will also help set a vivid green color.

MAKES 8 SERVINGS

1 lb asparagus (about 20 spears)

2 tbsp butter

⅓ cup diced onion

2 garlic cloves, minced

1 tbsp minced shallot

¼ cup all-purpose flour

4 cups Chicken Broth (page 294)

1 tsp grated lemon zest

½ tsp kosher salt

½ cup evaporated fat-free milk

2 tbsp heavy cream, whipped

1. Bring a large pot of salted water to a rolling boil over high heat. Snap off and discard the woody stem ends of the asparagus. Cut away the tips and cook in boiling water until tender, about 3 minutes. Drain the tips in a colander, rinse with cold water until cool to the touch, and drain once more. Set aside for garnish. Peel the stalks and cut into 1-inch-long pieces.

2. Melt the butter in a large soup pot over low heat. Add the onion, garlic, and shallot and cook, stirring frequently, until limp and translucent, 4 to 5 minutes.

3. Add the flour and cook about 5 minutes, stirring frequently.

4. Add the sliced asparagus, broth, and zest and simmer until the asparagus is tender, 6 to 8 minutes.

5. Purée the soup in a food processor or blender until smooth. Strain the soup through a medium-mesh sieve and discard the asparagus fibers.

6. Stir in the salt and evaporated fat-free milk. Ladle the soup into heated bowls and garnish each portion with some of the whipped cream and asparagus tips.

ZESTING CITRUS (284), **BOILING, BLANCHING, AND PARBOILING VEGETABLES** (123), **PURÉEING SOUPS** (21)

CARROT CONSOMMÉ with Lemongrass, Ginger, Spicy Asian Grilled Shrimp, and Bean Thread Noodles

This refreshing soup gets great flavor from fresh herbs, lemongrass, and lime leaves. To get the same flavor, you can substitute strips of lime zest for the lime leaves and fresh sweet basil for the Thai basil. Use rice sticks or cellophane noodles in place of the bean thread if you like.

MAKES 8 SERVINGS

5 large egg whites, lightly beaten

3 cups julienned carrots

½ stalk lemongrass, thinly sliced

1 tbsp chopped ginger

5 kaffir lime leaves, chopped

8 cups fresh carrot juice

½ tsp kosher salt

½ tsp white peppercorns, crushed

1⅓ cups cooked and cooled bean thread noodles

¾ cup carrot curls

1¼ pounds Spicy Asian Grilled Shrimp (page 195)

2 tbsp shredded Thai basil

2 tbsp shredded mint

3 tbsp chopped cilantro

1 tbsp white sesame seeds

1 tbsp black sesame seeds

1. Combine the egg whites, julienned carrots, lemongrass, ginger, and lime leaves in a medium soup pot over low heat. Add the carrot juice and mix well. Bring the mixture to a simmer over medium-low heat, stirring frequently until the egg whites cook enough to make a semisolid mass that rises to the top of the pot, about 12 minutes. Reduce the heat to low and simmer just until clear, about 20 minutes.

2. Strain through a fine-mesh sieve lined with cheesecloth. Season with the salt and pepper.

3. To serve the consommé, place a tight ball of noodles into heated bowls, top with carrot curls, and surround with some grilled shrimp. Ladle the hot consommé over and top with the basil, mint, cilantro, and sesame seeds.

JULIENNE AND BATONNET (119), **SHREDDING OR CHIFFONADE** (119), **PREPARING GINGER** (284)

CURRIED APPLE–SQUASH SOUP

This thick and creamy chilled soup gets a hint of warmth from the curry powder. Top the finished soup with more apples and fresh chives for additional flavor and texture.

MAKES 8 SERVINGS

4 cups Chicken Broth (page 294)

6 garlic cloves, minced

2⅔ cups diced celery

⅔ cup diced onion

¾ cups diced leeks, white and light green parts only

2 tsp Curry Spice Blend (page 291)

Few grains freshly grated nutmeg (optional)

½ tsp ground cinnamon

2½ cups chopped butternut squash

1⅓ cups peeled, cored, and diced Golden Delicious apples

¼ tsp kosher salt

1½ cups heavy cream

GARNISHES

½ cup Greek-style yogurt (low- or nonfat)

2 tbsp chopped chives

1. Heat 2 tablespoons of the broth in a large soup pot over low heat. Add the garlic, celery, onion, and leek and cook, stirring frequently, until the onions are translucent, 4 to 5 minutes.

2. Add the remaining broth, curry, nutmeg (if desired), and cinnamon and bring to a boil over medium-high heat.

3. Reduce the heat to medium low, add the squash, and simmer until the squash is tender, about 8 minutes.

4. Add the apples and continue to simmer until all the ingredients are tender, about 5 minutes.

5. Purée the soup in a blender or food processor until smooth. Add the salt and cream. Chill completely.

6. Ladle the soup into chilled bowls and garnish with the yogurt and chives.

CLEANING LEEKS (120)

Sampler of cold soups: Asparagus Soup (page 25), Beet-Fennel-Ginger Soup (page 30), and Curried Apple-Squash Soup

BEET-FENNEL-GINGER SOUP

Puréeing this soup gives it a smooth texture that complements its deep, earthy flavor. Serve the soup cold in chilled bowls or cups.

MAKES 8 SERVINGS

2½ cups chopped red beets

4 cups chopped savoy cabbage

2 cups chopped fennel

1 garlic clove, chopped

⅓ cup chopped ginger

6 cups Vegetable Broth (page 295)

½ tsp kosher salt

¼ tsp freshly ground black pepper

½ cup nonfat yogurt

2 tbsp chopped fennel sprigs

1. Combine the beets, cabbage, fennel, garlic, ginger, and broth in a large soup pot and bring to a boil. Cover, reduce the heat to medium low, and simmer until the vegetables are tender, about 25 minutes.

2. Strain the soup through a large-mesh sieve. Purée the vegetables in ½ cup of the broth in a food processor or blender until smooth. Add enough of the remaining broth to reach a pourable consistency. Chill the soup at least 2 hours before serving.

3. Season with the salt and pepper. Ladle the soup into chilled bowls and top with some of the yogurt and fennel sprigs.

PREPARING GINGER (284), **PURÉEING SOUPS** (21)

THAI HOT AND SOUR SOUP

Some of the ingredients for this soup—rice vermicelli, lemongrass, Thai fish sauce, and pickled chile—may require a trip to an Asian grocery or specialty market. Once you have all your ingredients assembled, the soup goes together quickly.

MAKES 8 SERVINGS

¼ lb small shrimp, peeled, butterflied, and deveined

2 oz thin rice noodles (rice vermicelli)

8 cups Fish or Chicken Broth (page 294)

1 stalk lemongrass, cut into 2-inch pieces and smashed

¼ cup Thai fish sauce (*nam pla*)

2 tbsp chili oil

1 tbsp lemon juice

1 tbsp lime juice

2 tsp grated lime zest

½ pickled chile

Kosher salt and freshly ground black pepper

⅓ cup rinsed and drained canned straw mushrooms

¼ cup chopped cilantro

1. Bring a pot of water to a boil. Add the shrimp and boil until cooked through, about 3 minutes. Transfer the shrimp to a colander and rinse the shrimp with cold water until cool. Drain once more and set aside.

2. Add the rice noodles to the reserved pot of boiling water add and cook until tender, 2 to 3 minutes. Drain, rinse with cold water, and drain again. Set aside.

3. Combine the broth, lemongrass, fish sauce, chili oil, lemon juice, lime juice, lime zest, and pickled chile in a soup pot. Bring to a simmer over low heat and cook for 10 minutes. Use tongs to remove the lemongrass. Taste and season with salt and pepper.

4. Divide the shrimp, rice noodles, mushrooms, and cilantro among heated bowls. Ladle the broth over and serve.

PEELING AND DEVEINING SHRIMP (188), **ZESTING AND JUICING CITRUS FRUITS** (284), **BUTTERFLYING SHRIMP** (189)

MINESTRONE

There is no one right way to make minestrone. Recipes vary from cook to cook according to individual preferences, so feel free to improvise with other vegetables, beans, or pasta shapes to suit your taste. Pancetta, a type of Italian bacon, is a traditional ingredient to add some fat and flavor to the soup. Look for it in delis and butcher shops.

MAKES 8 SERVINGS

2 tbsp olive oil

2 slices pancetta, chopped

1½ cups chopped green cabbage

1 cup chopped onion

1 cup sliced carrot

½ cup chopped celery

2 garlic cloves, minced

8 cups Chicken Broth (page 294)

½ cup diced peeled potato

One 3-inch-square piece Parmesan cheese rind

½ cup vermicelli or angel hair pasta, broken into 2-inch pieces

½ cup chopped plum tomatoes (peeled and seeded)

½ cup cooked chickpeas (page 94)

⅓ cup cooked kidney beans (page 94)

⅓ cup Pesto (page 299)

½ tsp kosher salt, or as needed

¼ tsp freshly ground black pepper, or as needed

Freshly grated Parmesan cheese, as needed

1. Heat the oil in a soup pot over medium heat. Add the pancetta and cook until its fat melts, 3 to 5 minutes. Do not allow the pancetta to brown.

2. Add the cabbage, onion, carrot, celery, and garlic and cook until the onions are translucent, 6 to 8 minutes.

3. Add the broth, potatoes, and cheese rind, bring to a boil, and simmer until the vegetables are tender, about 30 minutes. Do not overcook.

4. Meanwhile, prepare the vermicelli. Bring a large pot of salted water to a boil. Add the pasta and stir to separate. Cook until tender. Cooking time may vary by brand; follow package directions. Drain immediately.

5. When the vegetables are tender, add the vermicelli, tomatoes, chickpeas, and kidney beans. Remove and discard the cheese rind.

6. Season the soup with the pesto, salt, and pepper. Ladle the soup into heated bowls and sprinkle with grated cheese.

PEELING AND SEEDING TOMATOES (121), **COOKING LEGUMES** (94)

FARRO AND CHICKPEA SOUP

Farro is a Tuscan wheat that is often served in combination with beans, traditionally cannellini. In the United States, farro is known as emmer and can be found in most health food stores, or in gourmet food shops specializing in Italian products. We use the whole berry for this dish.

MAKES 6 SERVINGS

1½ cups dried chickpeas, soaked for 4 to 12 hours and drained

1 Spice Sachet (page 285), including 2 garlic cloves and zest of 1 orange

1 carrot, cut in half, plus ½ cup diced carrot

Kosher salt

Ground cayenne

1 cup farro

½ yellow onion, plus 1 cup diced onion

1 sprig thyme

1 bay leaf

¼ cup olive oil *or* vegetable oil

½ cup diced celery

GARNISHES

1 tbsp julienned orange zest

1 tbsp chopped rosemary

1 tbsp coarsely chopped parsley

1. Combine the beans, sachet, and 1 carrot half in a soup pot. Add water to cover by 3 inches and bring to a boil over high heat. Reduce the heat to medium and simmer, stirring occasionally and adding water as necessary to keep the beans completely covered, until the beans are barely tender to the bite, 60 to 75 minutes. Add salt and cayenne as needed and continue simmering until the beans are very tender, about 60 minutes more. Drain, reserving the cooking liquid. Discard the carrot half and the sachet.

2. Meanwhile, rinse the farro in several changes of cool water. Remove any black kernels.

3. Combine 4 cups of water, the onion half, the remaining carrot half, the thyme, and bay leaf in a medium saucepan. Bring to a boil over high heat. Reduce the heat to low and simmer for 5 minutes. Add the farro and ½ teaspoon salt and simmer, uncovered, until the farro pops open and is soft enough to bite but still noticeably chewy, 45 to 60 minutes. Drain the farro; reserve the cooking liquid and discard the vegetables and herbs. Set aside and cover to keep warm.

4. Purée about two-thirds of the beans with 2½ cups of their cooking liquid until smooth. Return the purée and whole beans to the soup pot. Add more cooking liquid as needed to thin the consistency.

5. Heat the oil in a medium sauté pan over medium heat. Add the diced carrot, the diced onion, and the celery and sauté until tender but not brown, 5 to 6 minutes. Stir into the beans. Return the soup to a simmer, taste, and season as needed with salt and cayenne. Ladle the soup into heated bowls and top with 2 tablespoons of the farro. Scatter the orange zest over the top and garnish with the rosemary and parsley.

DICING (119), **ZESTING CITRUS** (284), **JULIENNE AND BATONNET** (119)

CHILLED GAZPACHO

Originally from southern Spain, gazpacho is the perfectly refreshing way to enjoy summer's best tomatoes. Finish it with cucumbers and croutons for crunch and some good extra-virgin olive oil for richness.

MAKES 8 SERVINGS

2 jalapeños, diced

2¼ cups chopped tomato (peeled and seeded)

1 cup diced green pepper

¾ cup thinly sliced green onion

1 cup diced cucumber (peeled and seeded)

½ cup diced celery

3 tbsp chopped basil

1 tbsp chopped tarragon

4 cups Chicken or Vegetable Broth (page 294)

2 tbsp extra-virgin olive oil, plus more for garnish

2 tbsp balsamic vinegar

½ tsp kosher salt

¼ tsp ground white pepper

½ tsp Tabasco sauce

2 tsp Worcestershire sauce

1 cup Garlic Croutons (page 206)

1. Purée the jalapeños, tomato, pepper, green onion, cucumber, celery, basil, tarragon, broth, oil, the balsamic, salt, pepper, Tabasco, and Worcestershire in a food processor or blender until smooth. Cover and chill for 8 to 12 hours to allow the flavor to develop.

2. Ladle the soup into chilled bowls and top each portion with some croutons and a few drops of the remaining oil.

SERVING NOTE Add a teaspoon of small-dice vegetables (cucumbers, tomatoes, and/or peppers) for some texture, in addition to croutons. Add a small piece of fennel frond or dill. Some seafood, like crayfish or shrimp, adds some substance to the soup.

DICING (119), **PEELING AND SEEDING TOMATOES** (121), **PURÉEING SOUPS** (21)

FRESH CORN CHOWDER with Green Chiles and Monterey Jack

This chowder is best made with fresh corn on the cob, since you can only get corn milk from the whole ear. After you cut the kernels away, hold the cob over a bowl, and then use the spine of your knife to scrape out the flavorful juices. Add the corn milk with the cream when you purée the corn kernels. For some extra crunch and corn flavor, garnish the soup with thin strips of corn tortilla that you've toasted until crisp in a dry skillet.

MAKES 8 SERVINGS

6 ears of corn, shucked

1 cup heavy cream

2 slices bacon, minced

1¼ cups minced onion

1 cup minced red pepper

½ cup minced celery

½ tsp minced garlic

6 cups Chicken Broth (page 294)

2 cups diced yellow or white potatoes

2 cups chopped tomato (peeled and seeded)

One 4-ounce can chopped green chiles, drained

½ cup grated Monterey Jack cheese

Kosher salt and freshly ground black pepper

Tabasco sauce

1. Cut the corn kernels from the cobs with a sharp knife, capturing as much of the milk as possible. Reserve ¾ cup of the kernels. Purée the remaining kernels with the heavy cream in a food processor or blender. Set aside.

2. Cook the bacon in a soup pot over medium heat until crisp, about 8 minutes. Add the onion, pepper, celery, and garlic. Reduce the heat to low and cover. Cook, stirring occasionally, until the vegetables are tender, 10 to 12 minutes.

3. Add the broth, potatoes, and tomatoes and bring to a simmer. Cook, covered, until the potatoes are tender, about 20 minutes. Skim off and discard any fat from the surface of the soup.

4. Add the puréed corn mixture, the reserved corn kernels, the chiles, and cheese and cook on low heat just until the corn is warmed, about 5 minutes. Season as needed with salt, pepper, and Tabasco. Ladle the chowder into heated bowls.

WORKING WITH CORN ON THE COB (121), **DICING** (119), **PEELING AND SEEDING TOMATOES** (121)

SWEET ONION–RADISH SOUP

Because radishes have a sharp and peppery taste, herbs with strong flavors best complement the soup. Use freshly chopped chives, cilantro, mint, thyme, or basil to accentuate the flavors of the soup. You can also whip the cream and pipe it over the soup.

MAKES 8 SERVINGS

2 tbsp butter

2 garlic cloves, minced

¾ cup diced celery

⅔ cup diced leeks, white and light green parts only

1⅔ cups diced sweet onion

4 cups Chicken Broth (page 294)

2 medium all-purpose potatoes, peeled and quartered

2½ cups grated plus ½ cup thinly sliced red radish

¼ cup heavy cream

½ tsp kosher salt

¼ tsp freshly ground black pepper

2 tbsp lemon juice

¼ cup chopped herbs (chives, cilantro, mint, thyme, or basil)

1. Melt the butter in a large soup pot over low heat. Add the garlic, celery, leeks, and onion and cook, stirring frequently until the leeks and onion are limp and translucent, 5 to 6 minutes.

2. Add the broth and potatoes and bring to a boil. Reduce the heat to medium low and simmer until the potatoes are tender, about 20 minutes.

3. Add the grated radishes and continue to simmer for 5 minutes more.

4. Purée the soup in a food mill or with an immersion blender until smooth.

5. Just before serving, bring the cream to a boil. Stir the cream, salt, pepper, lemon juice, and herbs into the soup. Ladle the soup into heated bowls and garnish with the thinly sliced radishes.

DICING (119), **CLEANING LEEKS** (120), **ZESTING AND JUICING CITRUS** (284)

TORTILLA SOUP

Try warming this soup up with some additional spice—adding a pinch of cayenne or a dash of Tabasco will make a slightly spicier soup.

MAKES 8 SERVINGS

4 garlic cloves, minced

1⅓ cups diced onion

8 cups Chicken Broth (page 294)

Five 6-in corn tortillas, cut into strips

2 tbsp chopped cilantro

1 cup tomato purée

1 tbsp ground cumin

2 tsp chili powder

2 bay leaves

GARNISHES

1 cooked chicken breast half, cut into strips

⅔ cup diced avocado

⅔ cup shredded cheddar cheese

1. Preheat the oven to 200°F.

2. Cook the garlic and onion in 2 tablespoons of the broth in a medium skillet over low heat, stirring frequently, until translucent, 4 to 5 minutes. Purée the mixture in a food processor or blender until smooth.

3. Lightly toast the tortillas strips on a rack on a baking sheet in the oven until crisp and dry, about 12 minutes. Reserve about ⅓ cup of the toasted strips to garnish the soup and crush the remaining strips.

4. Combine the crushed tortillas, onion and garlic purée, cilantro, and tomato purée in a large soup pot. Bring to a simmer over medium-low heat.

5. Add the remaining broth, the cumin, chili powder, and bay leaves and continue to simmer for about 15 minutes. Remove the bay leaves.

6. Purée the soup in a food processor or blender until smooth. Serve the soup in heated bowls and garnish with the reserved toasted tortilla strips and some chicken, avocado, and cheese.

GRILLED GARLIC SHRIMP with Radish Salad

A simple, quick marinade of garlic and fresh lime juice gives the shrimp great flavor that pairs perfectly with the peppery taste of the radishes.

MAKES 6 SERVINGS

GRILLED SHRIMP
¾ lb shrimp, peeled, deveined, shells reserved

2 garlic cloves, minced

Juice of 1 lime

Bamboo skewers, as needed

VINAIGRETTE
1 cup Chicken Broth (page 294)

1 tsp cornstarch

1 tbsp olive oil

5 oz shrimp shells (reserved from above)

2 garlic cloves, minced

1 tbsp diced shallot

⅓ cup tomato paste

2½ tsp brandy

2 tbsp apple cider vinegar

2 tbsp rice wine vinegar

1 tbsp tahini

1 tbsp reduced-sodium soy sauce

2 tbsp minced ginger

½ minced jalapeño

2 tsp sesame oil

1 tbsp peanut oil

½ tsp kosher salt

¼ tsp freshly ground black pepper

RADISH SALAD
¾ cup thinly sliced daikon

¾ cup thinly sliced radish

¾ cup finely julienned carrot

1 tbsp finely julienned celery

3 oz green or soba noodles

GARNISHES
2 cups cilantro leaves

¼ tsp black sesame seeds

¼ tsp white sesame seeds

1. Toss the shrimp, garlic, and lime juice in a medium bowl. Thread 4 shrimp each onto the bamboo skewers. Refrigerate until needed.

2. For the vinaigrette, combine 2 tablespoons of the broth with the cornstarch and stir to make a smooth paste (known as a slurry). Set aside.

3. Heat the olive oil in a medium saucepan over medium heat. Add the shrimp shells and sauté until opaque, 3 to 4 minutes. Add the garlic and shallots and cook, stirring frequently, over low heat, until the shallots are limp and translucent, 2 to 3 minutes more.

4. Add the tomato paste and sauté until rust colored, about 5 minutes more. Add the brandy to the pan and stir well to release any drippings. Simmer over medium-low heat until almost cooked away, 3 to 4 minutes. Add the remaining broth and stir to combine. Strain the broth.

5. Stir the cornstarch slurry to recombine it, if necessary. Gradually add the slurry to the broth and bring the mixture back to a boil over medium heat, whisking constantly, until thickened.

6. Remove from the heat, add the vinegars, and cool completely. Stir in the tahini, soy sauce, ginger, and jalapeño. Gradually whisk in the sesame and peanut oils. Season with the salt and pepper.

7. For the salad, combine the daikon, radish, carrot, and celery in a medium bowl and toss with ⅓ cup of the vinaigrette. Set aside to marinate while preparing the noodles.

8. Bring a pot of salted water to a boil. Add the noodles and boil until tender to the bite, 7 to 9 minutes. Drain and cool slightly. Gently toss the noodles with ¾ cup of the vinaigrette.

9. Preheat a grill for a hot fire.

10. Grill the shrimp skewers until pink and cooked through, about 3 minutes on each side. Serve with the dressed noodles and radish salad. Garnish with the cilantro and sesame seeds.

PEELING AND DEVEINING SHRIMP (188), **PREPARING GINGER** (284), **JULIENNE AND BATONNET** (119)

CARPACCIO OF BEEF with Fresh Artichoke and Tomato Salad

Carpaccio is a dish of thinly sliced raw meat, usually served as an appetizer, but it makes a perfect light lunch when paired with this artichoke and tomato salad.

MAKES 6 SERVINGS

7 oz beef tenderloin, trimmed

2 cups quartered artichoke hearts

1 cup chopped tomato (peeled and seeded)

3 tbsp minced shallot

2 tbsp chopped basil

½ cup Balsamic Vinaigrette (page 293)

3 cups loosely packed mixed salad greens

Freshly ground black pepper

6 tbsp Anchovy-Caper Dressing (page 294)

1. Line a baking sheet with parchment paper. Chill the beef thoroughly so that it is firm enough to slice easily. Slice it very thinly with a sharp knife. Lay the slices out on parchment paper as they come off the blade. Do not stack them on top of one another. Cover with plastic wrap and refrigerate.

2. Place the artichoke hearts, tomato, shallot, basil, and ¼ cup of the vinaigrette in a medium bowl and toss to coat evenly.

3. Place the mixed greens and the remaining ¼ cup vinaigrette in a large bowl and toss to coat lightly. Arrange the dressed greens on chilled plates and top with the artichoke-tomato mixture. Place the beef slices over the top and season with a generous amount of pepper. Drizzle the dressing over the beef and serve immediately.

PREPARING ARTICHOKES (121), **PEELING AND SEEDING TOMATOES** (121), **PREPARING SPINACH AND LEAFY GREENS** (121)

MEDITERRANEAN-STYLE MUSSELS

As the mussels cook, they release their own aromatic juices into
the simmering white wine, creating a flavorful broth.

MAKES 6 SERVINGS

2 tsp butter

2 garlic cloves, minced

⅔ cup dry white wine

2 tbsp heavy cream

Few threads saffron

⅓ cup thinly sliced green onion

⅔ cup chopped tomato (peeled and
seeded)

2 tbsp lemon juice

1¼ cups Jus Lié (page 296)

80 mussels, cleaned and debearded (about
3 pounds)

1 tbsp chopped chives, for garnish

1. Melt the butter in a large soup pot over medium heat. Add the garlic and sauté until aromatic, about 1 minute. Add the wine, cream, and saffron and simmer over medium-low heat about 5 minutes.

2. Add the green onion, tomato, lemon juice, and jus lié and continue to simmer, 5 minutes more.

3. Add the mussels, cover, and steam until their shells open, about 4 minutes. Serve the mussels with the sauce and garnish with chives.

PEELING AND SEEDING TOMATOES (121), **JUICING CITRUS** (285), **MUSSELS** (188)

ARTICHOKE SEVICHE in Belgian Endive

In this dish, the lime juice is important both for its flavor and its ability to keep the artichokes from turning brown when exposed to air.

MAKES 4 SERVINGS

2 cups large-dice artichoke hearts

1 cup diced plum tomato, peeled and seeded

½ cup julienned red onion

1 green onion, thinly sliced on the diagonal (split lengthwise)

2 tbsp chopped cilantro, or as needed

2 tsp minced garlic

½ tsp minced jalapeño, or as needed

2 tbsp extra-virgin olive oil

1 tbsp lime juice, or as needed

Kosher salt and freshly ground black pepper, as needed

12 Belgian endive spears

1. Place the artichokes, tomato, red onion, green onion, cilantro, garlic, and jalapeño in a medium bowl and toss. Drizzle the oil and lime juice over the seviche and season generously with salt and pepper. Toss to coat evenly. Cover the bowl and marinate the seviche in the refrigerator at least 2 and up to 12 hours.

2. Taste the seviche just before serving and adjust the seasoning with salt, pepper, cilantro, and lime juice as needed. Spoon the seviche into the endive spears and serve on a chilled platter or individual plates.

PREPARING ARTICHOKES [121]

SPINACH SALAD with Marinated Shiitakes and Red Onions

Sautéed shiitake mushrooms add an earthy flavor and heartiness
to this salad, making it perfect for an autumn lunch.

MAKES 8 SERVINGS

2 tbsp peanut oil

3 cups sliced shiitake mushrooms

2 tsp reduced-sodium soy sauce

1 tbsp cider vinegar

⅛ tsp kosher salt, or as needed

⅛ tsp freshly ground black pepper, or as
needed

Dash Tabasco sauce

2 tsp olive oil

½ cup diced red onion

6 cups trimmed, washed, and torn spinach

2 cups radicchio chiffonade

¼ cup **Balsamic Vinaigrette** (page 293)

1. Heat the peanut oil in a sauté pan over medium heat until it shimmers.

2. Add the mushrooms and sauté for 2 minutes. Add the soy sauce and cook until the soy sauce is nearly cooked away, about 2 minutes. Remove from the heat and place the mushrooms in a bowl. Add the vinegar, salt, pepper, and Tabasco. Cool completely.

3. Heat the olive oil in the pan over low heat. Add the onion and cook, stirring frequently, until limp and translucent, 5 to 7 minutes. Remove from the heat and cool to room temperature.

4. Place the mushrooms, onions, spinach, radicchio, and vinaigrette in a large bowl and toss. Adjust the seasoning with salt and pepper as needed. Serve immediately.

CLEANING MUSHROOMS (122), **SHREDDING OR CHIFFONADE** (119), **PREPARING SPINACH AND LEAFY GREENS** (121)

MOROCCAN CARROT SALAD

This unusual carrot salad gets its mysteriously rich flavor from
cooking dates together with onions to a soft purée.

MAKES 8 SERVINGS

2 lb carrots, peeled and thinly sliced

2 garlic cloves, peeled

4 tbsp olive oil

Juice of 1 lemon

1 tbsp ground cumin

Pinch cayenne

1 tsp minced cilantro

1 tsp minced parsley

2 onions, finely chopped

1 cup chopped dates

1. Combine the carrots and garlic in a medium saucepan and add water to cover by 1 to 2 inches. Bring to a simmer over low heat and cook until tender, about 5 minutes. Transfer the carrots to a bowl with a slotted spoon. Remove and discard the garlic cloves and reserve the cooking liquid.

2. Cook the cooking liquid over medium heat until reduced to ½ cup. Whisk in 2 tablespoons of the oil and all of the lemon juice. Pour the mixture over the carrots. Add the cumin, cayenne, cilantro, and parsley. Set aside.

3. Heat the remaining 2 tablespoons oil in a medium saucepan over medium heat. Add the onions and sauté until translucent, about 5 minutes. Add the dates and cook until softened. Toss the onion-date mixture with the carrots. Cool to room temperature. Cover and refrigerate for 1 to 2 hours before serving.

WARM CABBAGE SALAD

This salad makes a great accompaniment for sandwiches as well as a
delicious bed for grilled or roasted meats, poultry, or fish.

MAKES 6 SERVINGS

2 tsp olive oil

½ cup diced red onion

1 garlic clove, minced

¼ cup Vegetable Broth (page 295) *or* water

2 tsp tarragon vinegar

2 tbsp dry white wine

2 tsp sugar

4 cups shredded savoy cabbage

¼ tsp caraway seeds

1 tbsp chopped parsley

1. Heat the oil in a large skillet over medium heat until it shimmers. Add the onion and garlic and cook, stirring frequently, until the onion is tender and the garlic smells sweet, 5 to 6 minutes.

2. Combine the broth, vinegar, wine, and sugar in a small bowl and stir to dissolve the sugar. Add the broth mixture, cabbage, and caraway seeds to the skillet and cook, stirring occasionally, until the cabbage is tender, 8 to 10 minutes. Remove from the heat and stir in the parsley.

3. Serve warm or at room temperature.

SHREDDING OR CHIFFONADE (119)

MEDITERRANEAN SALAD

This simple salad combines classic Mediterranean flavors. The briny and acidic flavors
of the anchovies and olives give extra richness to the artichokes and cheese.

MAKES 6 SERVINGS

1 cup Vinaigrette-Style Dressing (page 292; see Note)

6 anchovy fillets, minced

6 cups mixed baby greens

⅓ cup cooked and quartered artichoke hearts

⅔ cup shelled peas

¾ cup julienned carrots

⅓ cup picholine olives, pitted

⅓ cup Niçoise olives, pitted

GARNISHES

⅔ cup grated Asiago cheese

⅔ cup chopped parsley

1. Combine the vinaigrette and anchovies in a small bowl.

2. Place the mixed greens, artichoke hearts, peas, carrots, and olives in a large bowl and toss. Add the anchovy vinaigrette and toss again to coat. Garnish with the cheese and parsley and serve.

NOTE Use red wine vinegar in the recipe for Vinaigrette-Style Dressing.

PREPARING ARTICHOKES (121), **JULIENNE AND BATONNET** (119)

CHINESE LONG BEAN SALAD with Tangerines and Sherry-Mustard Vinaigrette

Chinese long beans are also known as yard-long beans, though they are seldom left to grow to this length. They are part of the same plant family as the black-eyed pea. Green beans may be substituted if Chinese long beans are unavailable.

MAKES 6 SERVINGS

1½ cups Chinese long beans, trimmed, cut into 1½-inch lengths

3 tangerines, peeled, cut into sections, juice reserved

½ cup thinly sliced Vidalia onion

⅓ cup sunflower seeds, toasted

¼ tsp kosher salt

Pinch freshly ground black pepper

SHERRY-MUSTARD VINAIGRETTE

¾ tsp cornstarch

⅓ cup Vegetable Broth (page 295)

2 tbsp olive oil

2 tbsp sherry vinegar

2 tbsp tangerine juice (from tangerines above)

1 tbsp Dijon mustard

1 tbsp light brown sugar

¼ cup minced shallot

1 garlic clove, minced

¼ tsp kosher salt

Pinch freshly ground black pepper

1. Bring a pot of water to a boil. Add the beans and boil until barely tender, 3 to 5 minutes. Drain and cool slightly.

2. Combine the beans, tangerine sections, onion, and sunflower seeds in a large bowl. Season with the salt and pepper.

3. For the vinaigrette, combine the cornstarch with 2 tablespoons of the broth to form a paste. Bring the remaining broth to a boil in a small pot over medium-high heat. Remove from the heat.

4. Gradually add the cornstarch slurry to the broth and bring the mixture back to a boil over medium heat, whisking constantly, until it has thickened. Remove from the heat and cool completely.

5. Combine the remaining vinaigrette ingredients in a small bowl and whisk into the thickened broth.

6. Toss the bean mixture with the vinaigrette in a large bowl and serve.

TOASTING SPICES, NUTS, AND SEEDS (290)

ROMAINE AND GRAPEFRUIT SALAD with Walnuts and Stilton

In this refreshing combination, the deep, rich flavors of the walnuts and Stilton are amplified by the brightness of the grapefruit.

MAKES 6 SERVINGS

½ tsp cornstarch

2 tbsp ruby port

⅓ cup Vegetable Broth (page 295)

1 tbsp red wine vinegar

1 tbsp grapefruit juice

1 tbsp olive oil

3 cups romaine, cut in wide shreds

GARNISHES

1¼ cups white and pink grapefruit sections

½ cup crumbled Stilton cheese

½ cup chopped walnuts

1. Combine the cornstarch and port in a small bowl to form a paste. Bring the broth to a boil in a small pot over medium-high heat. Remove from the heat.

2. Gradually add the cornstarch slurry to the broth and bring the mixture back to a boil over medium heat, whisking constantly, until it has thickened.

3. Remove from the heat and stir in the vinegar and grapefruit juice. Cool completely. Slowly whisk in the oil.

4. Place the romaine in a large bowl and toss with the dressing. Garnish with the grapefruit sections, cheese, and walnuts and serve.

JUICING CITRUS (285), **SHREDDING OR CHIFFONADE** (119), **TOASTING SPICES, NUTS, AND SEEDS** (290)

ASPARAGUS with Lump Crabmeat and Sherry Vinaigrette

This simple salad is fresh and delicious, highlighting the flavors of good springtime asparagus with juicy crabmeat. Use a combination of white and green asparagus for greater visual impact.

MAKES 6 SERVINGS

2¾ cups sliced asparagus (trimmed and peeled)

¾ cup Vinaigrette-Style Dressing (page 292; see Note)

6 oz lump crabmeat, picked over

1 cup julienned tomato

GARNISH

1 tbsp chopped chives

1. Bring a large pot of water to a boil. Add the asparagus and boil until barely tender, about 1 minute. Drain the asparagus in a colander, rinse with cold water until the asparagus feels cool to the touch, and drain once more. Transfer to a bowl.

2. Add the vinaigrette and toss gently. Marinate for at least 1 and up to 4 hours before serving.

3. Arrange the asparagus on a plate and top with the crabmeat and tomato. Reserve the remaining vinaigrette in the bowl.

4. Drizzle the salad with the reserved vinaigrette. Scatter the chives over to garnish.

NOTE Use sherry vinegar in the preparation of the dressing.

JULIENNE AND BATONNET (119), **BOILING, BLANCHING, AND PARBOILING VEGETABLES** (123)

WARM SALAD of Wild Mushrooms and Fennel

Warm salads are a deliciously satisfying alternative to simple mixed greens. Make sure to clean the mushrooms well.

MAKES 6 SERVINGS

⅔ cup peeled garlic cloves

3 tbsp extra-virgin olive oil

5 cups wild mushrooms, sliced or quartered

2 cups Chicken Broth (page 294)

3 tbsp capers (drained and rinsed)

3 tbsp sliced Kalamata olives

⅔ cup chopped sun-dried tomatoes

2 tbsp minced sage

3 cups thinly sliced fennel

1¼ cups shredded radicchio

⅓ cup lemon juice

1 tbsp freshly ground black pepper

⅓ cup julienned red pepper, for garnish

1. Place the garlic cloves in a small saucepan and add water to cover by 1 inch. Bring to a boil over high heat and drain. Repeat and reserve the garlic cloves.

2. Heat the oil in a large sauté pan over medium heat. Add the garlic and sauté until golden brown, 2 to 4 minutes. Add the mushrooms and sauté until tender, 3 to 4 minutes. Add the broth to the pan and stir well to release any drippings. Continue to simmer until the broth is nearly cooked away, 12 to 15 minutes. Stir in the capers, olives, tomatoes, and sage and keep warm.

3. Bring a pot of water to a boil. Add the fennel and boil until barely tender, 3 to 5 minutes. Drain and set aside.

4. Combine the fennel and radicchio in a large bowl and top with the warm mushroom mixture. Drizzle the salad with the lemon juice. Sprinkle with black pepper and garnish with red pepper.

CLEANING MUSHROOMS (122), **SHREDDING OR CHIFFONADE** (119), **JULIENNE AND BATONNET** (119), **JUICING CITRUS** (285)

STUFFED CHERRY TOMATOES with Minted Barley-Cucumber Salad

The barley salad can be prepared up to two days in advance. You may want to double the ingredients for the filling to have on hand as an accompaniment to grilled or broiled salmon. The tomatoes can be stuffed up to six hours before they are served.

MAKES 8 SERVINGS

½ cup pearl barley

¼ cup diced tomato

¼ cup diced cucumber

⅓ cup chopped parsley

2 tbsp chopped mint

1 tbsp thinly sliced green onion, white portion only

2 tsp extra-virgin olive oil

1 tsp lemon juice

Kosher salt and freshly ground black pepper, as needed

16 cherry tomatoes

1. Place the barley in a large saucepan and add cold water to cover. Soak for 30 minutes. Drain well.

2. Add enough water to cover the barley and bring to a boil over high heat. Reduce the heat to low and simmer until tender, about 40 minutes. Strain through a sieve, transfer the sieve to a bowl of ice water, and let cool for 1 minute. Set the sieve over a bowl and let the barley drain.

3. Combine the barley, tomato, cucumber, parsley, mint, and green onion in a large bowl. Stir in the olive oil, lemon juice, salt, and pepper.

4. Cut the core from the cherry tomatoes and make two cuts into each tomato to open it out like a flower. Stuff with some of the salad. Serve on a chilled platter or individual plates.

VIETNAMESE SUMMER ROLLS

These refreshing rolls are light, easy, and delicious, with great colors and textures.
Try other dipping sauce combinations, such as soy-ginger or sweet chili sauce.

MAKES 6 SERVINGS

DIPPING SAUCE

¼ cup sugar

2 tbsp fish sauce

1 tbsp lemon juice

1 tbsp rice wine vinegar

2½ tsp water

1 garlic clove, minced

1 tsp chili sauce

FILLING

2½ oz rice noodles

6 shrimp, peeled and deveined

⅔ cup shredded carrot

¾ tsp kosher salt

⅔ cup shredded iceberg lettuce

1 tbsp plus ½ tsp sugar

2 tbsp lemon juice

⅓ cup warm water

6 rice paper wrappers

¼ cup cilantro leaves

1. For the dipping sauce, whisk together all the ingredients in a small bowl. Cover and chill.

2. For the filling, bring a pot of water to a boil. Add the rice noodles and boil until tender, 4 to 6 minutes. Drain the noodles in a colander, rinse with cold water until the noodles feel cool to the touch, and drain once more. Transfer to a bowl.

3. Bring a pot of water to a boil. Add the shrimp and boil until cooked through, about 3 minutes. Drain the shrimp in a colander, rinse in a bowl of ice water until cool to the touch, and drain once more. Slice the cooled shrimp in half lengthwise.

4. Toss the carrots with ½ teaspoon of the salt and marinate for 10 minutes. Drain any excess moisture from the carrots. Combine the noodles, carrots, lettuce, ½ teaspoon sugar, the lemon juice, and the remaining ¼ teaspoon salt in a large bowl.

5. Combine the 1 tablespoon sugar and the warm water in a large bowl.

6. To assemble the spring rolls, moisten one wrapper in the sugar water and place on a clean, flat-weave cloth. Place some of the noodle mixture, 2 shrimp halves, and a few cilantro leaves in the center of each wrapper. Fold each end of the wrapper in and roll to completely enclose the filling. Refrigerate until needed. Serve with the dipping sauce.

ZESTING AND JUICING CITRUS FRUITS (284), **PEELING AND DEVEINING SHRIMP** (188), **SHREDDING OR CHIFFONADE** (119)

MEDALLIONS OF LOBSTER with Shaved Vegetable Salad

This dish is made even more flavorful with a pesto that includes fresh spinach, cilantro, and mint in addition to basil. To shave the vegetables for this salad, use a Japanese-style mandoline if you have one. If not, slice them as thin as you can, or use a vegetable peeler to shave them.

MAKES 6 SERVINGS

2 lobsters, about 1 pound each

2½ cups Fish Broth (page 295)

SHAVED VEGETABLE SALAD

½ cup shaved carrot

½ cup shaved celery

½ cup shaved daikon

1 tbsp shredded pickled ginger

¼ cup Ginger-Sesame Vinaigrette (page 293)

SPINACH-HERB PESTO

1¼ cups packed spinach leaves

1 tbsp chopped basil

1 tbsp chopped cilantro

2 tsp chopped mint

1 garlic clove, minced

½ tsp extra-virgin olive oil

⅓ cup Vegetable Broth (page 295)

⅓ cup Tomato Coulis (page 298)

1. For the lobster, bring a large pot of water to a boil. Add the lobsters and poach until they are bright red, about 5 minutes. Remove the meat from the shells, reserving the shells. Slice the tail meat into 18 even medallions, dice the claw meat, and reserve separately until needed.

2. Place the lobster shells in a large soup pot with the broth over medium heat. Cover and simmer over medium-low heat for 30 minutes. Strain the broth, discarding the shells, and return the broth to the pot. Reduce the liquid to about ¼ cup. Set aside.

3. For the vegetable salad, combine the carrot, celery, daikon, ginger, and vinaigrette with the diced lobster claw meat in a bowl and toss to coat evenly. Set aside. (The salad can be prepared up to 8 hours before serving the dish.)

4. For the pesto, purée the spinach, basil, cilantro, mint, and garlic in a food processor or blender until a coarse paste forms. With the machine still running, gradually add the oil and vegetable broth and continue to purée until the paste is smooth.

5. Serve the lobster medallions on a bed of the salad with the tomato coulis and pesto drizzled over the top. Pour the reduced lobster broth over the salad.

BOILING WHOLE LOBSTER AND HARD-SHELL CRAB (189), **PREPARING SPINACH AND LEAFY GREENS** (121)

HUMMUS (Chickpea Spread)

This popular Middle Eastern dip makes a wonderful sandwich filling for pita with sliced cucumbers, onions, tomatoes, and lettuce. You can also try adding a pinch of cumin or some freshly chopped parsley for a different flavor. Look for tahini in natural foods stores or in the ethnic foods section of your supermarket.

MAKES 1½ CUPS

1½ cups cooked chickpeas (drained and rinsed if canned)

1 tbsp tahini paste

1 tbsp extra-virgin olive oil, or as needed

1 tbsp lemon juice, or as needed

½ tsp kosher salt

¼ tsp freshly ground black pepper

1. Purée the chickpeas, tahini, oil, and lemon juice in a food processor or blender until a paste forms. Continue to purée until the mixture has a light, spreadable consistency, similar to mayonnaise.

2. Transfer the hummus to a bowl, taste, and season with the salt, pepper, and more lemon juice as needed. Drizzle a little additional oil over the surface, if desired.

COOKING LEGUMES [94], **JUICING CITRUS** [285]

GUACAMOLE

This recipe simply uses a fork to mash the avocados and combine the other ingredients; food processors and blenders make the mixture too smooth.

MAKES 2¼ CUPS

2 large ripe avocados, halved, pitted, and peeled

1 green onion, minced

1 garlic clove, minced

2 tbsp lime juice

¾ tsp seeded and minced jalapeño

¾ tsp chopped cilantro

¾ tsp kosher salt

¼ tsp freshly ground black pepper

1. Mash the avocado flesh with a fork in a bowl to a chunky consistency.

2. Add the green onion, garlic, lime juice, jalapeño, cilantro, salt, and pepper. Fold to combine.

3. Press plastic wrap directly on the guacamole's surface to prevent discoloring. Allow the flavors to blend for 1 hour, and serve.

JUICING CITRUS [285]

CHAPTER THREE

Pasta, Pizza, and Sandwiches

These three staples of the American diet may not always be the first things that come to mind as part of a healthy diet, but there is no reason to eliminate them from your repertoire. In this chapter, we offer a number of ways to incorporate healthy techniques into their preparation.

Pasta can be a great choice for any meal. Making it a healthy choice is actually very easy. A classic tomato sauce is always a great choice, of course, not only for its flavor but also for its supply of vitamins, minerals, and fiber. Despite a general impression of pizzas as loaded with calories in the form of cheese and pepperoni, there is no magic involved in turning out delicious pizzas that are as much a part of a healthy diet as a salad. Sandwiches made from fresh vegetables and flavorful spreads, rather than sliced cheese and mayonnaise, are perfect to eat at home or to take with you to work or school for healthy lunches.

Healthy Techniques for Pasta

Instead of sauces made with lots of cheese, meat, butter, or cream, opt for fresh vegetable ragoûts and coulis. Ravioli and tortellini are classic stuffed pasta dishes. Fillings for pastas should have bold flavors, and there are several options beyond the familiar three-cheese filling. White beans cooked into a savory purée, a vegetable ragoût, or something a bit more luxurious, like lobster, are some of the options you'll discover here.

MIXING THE DOUGH FOR FRESH PASTA

Remember that pasta, whether a first course or a main dish, should be enjoyed in moderately sized portions.

Fresh egg pasta can be prepared quickly by hand or by machine. Using some whole wheat flour gives the pasta a bit more nutritional value. You can also add vegetable purées or spices to the dough for added flavor and color.

Mixing and Kneading Pasta Dough by Hand

To mix pasta by hand, mound the flour and salt on a clean work surface and make a well in the center. Place the eggs, flavoring ingredients, and oil in the well. Using a fork and working as rapidly as possible, incorporate the flour into the liquid ingredients little by little, until a shaggy mass forms. You may need to use one hand to hold the "wall" of flour up as you mix, so the liquids don't run out as you work. Once the dough is moist enough to press together, gather it into a ball. Knead the dough, dusting the dough, your hands, and the work surface with flour as necessary to keep it from sticking. Use the heel of one hand to push the dough away from you and the fingertips to pull it back into a ball. Turn the dough as you knead it. It takes about 10 minutes to properly knead the dough. It should have a uniform texture and no longer feel tacky.

Mixing Pasta Dough in a Food Processor

To use a food processor with a blade, add the ingredients to the bowl of the food processor, cover the lid, and process until the dough looks very crumbly but is moist enough to hold together when you press it into a ball. Turn the dough out onto a floured work surface and knead it until smooth and elastic.

Mixing Pasta Dough in a Stand Mixer

To use a stand mixer with a dough hook attachment, add the ingredients and mix on low speed for about 2 minutes, or until the dough forms a ball. Increase the speed and continue mixing for another 2 to 3 minutes. The dough is ready to roll out now (see below).

SHAPING FRESH PASTA

There are so many options for shaping pasta dough that we simply can't name them all. Fresh pasta is primarily cut into long strips or ribbons, or used to make stuffed pastas like ravioli. No matter what shape your pasta is intended to be, you begin by rolling out the dough.

Rolling Pasta Dough by Hand

Immediately after kneading, the dough can be difficult to roll out. Let the dough rest for about 30 minutes. As you work with the dough, dust the dough and the work surface with a little flour so that it doesn't stick and tear, but not so much that the pasta begins to stiffen and dry out. Flatten the dough into a disk and start rolling the dough from center to the edge. Try to keep the pressure on the dough even. It will stretch as you work until you get it to the desired thickness. Once the pasta is rolled out, you can cut it into sheets or strips by hand.

Making fresh pasta

Rolling the Dough with a Pasta Machine

To work with a pasta machine, cut off a piece of dough about the size of an egg, and flatten it into a rectangle. Set the rollers to the widest opening, and guide the flattened dough through the machine as you turn the handle. Roll the dough to form a long, wide strip. Fold the dough in thirds, like a letter, and pass it through the same setting two or three times. Reduce the opening of the rollers and pass the pasta through until it is as thin as you need it.

Cutting the Dough

Most pasta machines have a cutting attachment that produces two different widths of noodles, and you can acquire additional attachments for different sizes. Roll the pasta through the cutting attachment, and catch it in a loose "nest" as it falls from the machine.

You can also use knives or pastry wheels to cut the dough. To make long strips, roll up the pasta and make crosswise cuts. There are special tools that crimp, seal, and separate ravioli, but it is just as easy to cut them yourself with a pastry cutter or a cookie cutter.

After you've cut the dough, transfer it to a sheet pan that has been dusted with a bit of flour and scatter a bit more on the top. If you are cooking the pasta soon, you can let it sit uncovered. Pasta dough will keep in the refrigerator for a day or two, loosely covered with plastic wrap; try not to keep it longer than two days, otherwise the texture will not be quite as good.

Healthy Techniques for Pizza

Pizza is without doubt one of our favorite foods. It's also very simple to adapt to a healthy eating lifestyle, with the addition of vegetable toppings and healthy tomato sauces, which have plenty of vitamins and nutrients. Our recipe is nearly 50 percent whole grain (in the form of whole wheat flour) to make it a healthier part of your pizza.

SHAPING PIZZA

To shape pizza dough, press the dough into a disk, stretching and turning the dough as you work. You may finish stretching the dough by flipping it: With the dough resting on the backs of your hands, simultaneously spin the dough and toss it into the air. As it falls back down, catch it on the backs of your hands once more. Continue until the crust is evenly thick, ⅛ to ¼ inch. If you prefer, you can pull and stretch the dough directly on a lightly floured work surface until it has an even thickness.

TOPPINGS FOR PIZZA

Some healthy topping options you'll find include vegetables like fresh or roasted tomatoes, mushrooms, squashes, onions, spinach; pickled foods like capers or olives; thick ragùs with a variety of vegetables or dried legumes; or herb purées. Mozzarella, though a classic topping, can easily be dispensed with in favor of other ingredients like a pungent herb purée or a drizzle of olive oil. Choose whatever healthy foods whatever appeals to you, from seafood to poultry or apples to artichokes.

BAKING PIZZA

A crisp crust depends upon a hot oven. Ovens in pizzerias can reach much higher temperatures than home ovens, but there are steps you can take to mimic the effect.

1. PREHEAT THE OVEN.
    Our recipes call for the oven to reach a temperature of 500°F. Bringing an oven to that temperature can take some time, so plan accordingly. Oven temperatures this high can set off home fire alarms; if you have a hood or fan, turn it on to help avoid tripping the alarm unnecessarily, but do not take out the batteries (it is much too easy to forget to put them back in).

2. USE A BAKING STONE OR TILES.
    A ceramic baking stone helps keep the bottom of the crust crisp and dry as it bakes. Another option is to line a baking rack with unglazed tiles. Tiles and stones should be in the oven as it preheats so they are very hot before you put the pizza on them.

3. USE (OR CREATE) A PEEL TO TRANSFER THE PIZZA TO THE STONE.
    If you bake the pizza on a baking sheet, it will taste great, but the crust won't be quite as crisp as it would have been if baked on a stone or tiles. Getting the pizza onto the stone involves sliding it off a flat surface and onto the pizza stone. Peels look like large wooden paddles. Their handles are long enough to permit you to get the pizza right onto the stone in the oven without endangering your hands. Use a quick, jerking motion and a flick of the wrist to slide the pizza from the peel onto the tiles. If you don't have a peel, you can improvise with a baking sheet that has edges on only two or three sides.

Healthy Techniques for Sandwiches

If pizza is one of our favorite indulgences, then sandwiches are surely our favorite quick meal. We eat them at breakfast, lunch, and dinner. They show up in miniature versions as hors d'oeuvres. We've taken to international favorites as well, including tacos, quesadillas, wraps, and pitas.

VARY THE BREAD

Whole-grain breads, including whole wheat and rye breads, are sandwich classics, but you can expand your repertoire. Sandwich wraps are the perfect way to shift the balance in your sandwich away from the bread and toward the filling. Burritos are really nothing more than a wrap—or perhaps wraps are nothing more than burritos—and you can readily find whole-grain wraps, such as tortillas and lavash. Toast them first in a dry skillet over medium heat or over an open flame. This makes the wrap easier to roll and fold and adds flavor.

CHOOSE A FLAVORFUL SPREAD

The purpose of the sandwich's spread is to keep the filling inside the sandwich, to keep the bread from getting soggy, and to add some moisture, richness, and flavor. Sometimes the spread does double duty, both as part of the filling and as a binding agent for a filling such as tuna or chicken salad. You can get taste and binding effects from a range of options. Mayonnaise is a traditional choice, but we prefer a dairy-based spread made from ricotta cheese and yogurt. Like mayonnaise, the spread has a creamy texture, but it is more nutrient dense than mayonnaise. Consider less traditional "spreads" too, like chutney or guacamole.

OPT FOR HEALTHIER FILLINGS

Sandwiches built entirely from fresh, roasted, grilled, baked, or even stewed vegetables can be substantial enough to make into a satisfying meal, if you want a break from sliced meats. The filling can be cold or hot, according to your preference. If your filling is already high flavor, high fiber, and low calorie, you may be able to add a few discretionary calories in the form of some crumbled goat cheese or a thin slice of aged cheddar or provolone. In sandwiches especially, a little goes a long way.

BASIC PASTA DOUGH

If stored in an airtight container, this dough may be stored for up to two days, or frozen for up to a month. Thaw frozen dough, still wrapped, overnight in the refrigerator. Bring chilled dough to room temperature before using.

MAKES 1 POUND, ENOUGH FOR 6 SERVINGS

1¼ cups all-purpose flour, plus more as needed for dusting pasta

¾ cup whole wheat flour

2 large eggs

1 to 2 tbsp water, if needed

1. Mound the flours on a clean surface. Create a well in the center and place the eggs in the center. Using a fork, whisk the eggs together to blend them, and slowly start dragging the flour into the mixture and combining it to make a rough dough. If the dough will not hold together when pressed into a ball, add ½ teaspoon of water at a time until the dough is moist enough to knead.

2. Once the flour is evenly moistened, knead well by hand on a well-floured work surface until all the ingredients are well combined and the dough seems smooth and elastic. Wrap the dough in plastic wrap or place it in a covered bowl and let it rest for at least 30 minutes.

3. Divide the dough into pieces about the size of a large egg. Working with one piece at a time, roll the pasta through the largest opening of your pasta machine. Fold the dough into thirds and roll it through the largest opening once more. Change the setting to the next narrowest, and roll the pasta through the machine once more. Continue to roll the pasta, dusting it with more flour to keep the pasta from sticking to the machine, to itself, or to the work surface, until it is about ⅛ inch thick. If you are making filled pasta shells, add the filling and cut them as directed in your recipe. If you are cutting the pasta into ribbon shapes, let the sheet dry a little as you roll out the remaining pieces of dough.

4. To cut fresh pasta into ribbons, either run the pasta through the cutting attachment of your pasta machine or cut the sheets into the desired shape. Gather the cut pasta into nests and hold them on a tray or baking sheet lined with parchment. Dust the nests with a little more flour. The pasta can be left to dry at room temperature for about 1 hour, then held in the refrigerator for up to 2 days or in the freezer for up to 4 weeks. (For hand-rolling and cutting instructions, see page 61.)

5. To cook fresh pasta, bring a large pot of lightly salted water to a rolling boil over high heat. Add the pasta, stir to separate the strands, and continue to boil until tender to the bite, 3 to 5 minutes. Drain the pasta in a colander, and serve at once with a sauce.

MIXING THE DOUGH FOR FRESH PASTA (60)

FETTUCCINE with Corn, Squash, Jalapeño, Yogurt, and Cilantro

Greek-style yogurt has a rich, creamy texture and a full flavor. We've used it here instead of either sour cream or crème fraîche. It works well in dishes like this one as long as the yogurt is not brought to a boil, which can cause the sauce to separate.

MAKES 6 SERVINGS

1 lb Basic Pasta Dough (opposite page)

1 tsp butter

1½ cups diced onion

2¼ cups diced zucchini

2½ cups corn kernels

2 tbsp diced jalapeño

2 garlic cloves, minced

1¾ cups Vegetable Broth (page 295)

½ tsp kosher salt

Pinch freshly ground black pepper

⅓ cup Greek-style yogurt

2 tbsp chopped cilantro

1. Roll out the pasta and cut into fettuccine with a pasta machine or a knife. Set the fettuccine aside on a lightly floured tray or baking sheet. Bring a large pot of lightly salted water to a rolling boil over high heat.

2. Melt the butter in a large sauté pan over medium heat. Add the onion and zucchini and cook, stirring frequently, until the onions are limp and translucent, 4 to 5 minutes. Add the corn, jalapeños, and garlic and cook until the corn is tender, 2 to 3 minutes. Add the vegetable broth and season with the salt and pepper. Keep the sauce warm over low heat while you cook the fettuccine.

3. Add the fettuccine to the boiling water and stir to separate the strands. Cook until the pasta is just tender, about 5 minutes. Drain the fettuccine in a colander and shake off the excess water.

4. Add the fettuccine and the yogurt to the sauce and toss them together off the heat until the pasta is evenly coated. Serve at once on heated plates, topped with the cilantro.

DICING (119), **DICING ONIONS** (120), **WORKING WITH CORN ON THE COB** (121)

OPEN-FACE BUCKWHEAT RAVIOLI with Vegetable Ragoût

Buckwheat is rich in iron and protein, making it a healthy and delicious substitute to traditional pasta. These "ravioli" are made by mounding a delicious vegetable ragoût on top of squares of hearty buckwheat pasta.

MAKES 6 SERVINGS

1 lb Buckwheat Pasta Dough (see Note)

VEGETABLE RAGOÛT

3 tbsp olive oil

2 garlic cloves, minced

1½ tsp minced shallot

1 large zucchini, diced

1 large yellow squash, diced

1 green pepper, diced

1 red pepper, diced

1½ cups sliced shiitake mushrooms

1½ cups chopped tomatoes (peeled and seeded)

¾ cup Chicken or Vegetable Broth (page 294)

2 tbsp chopped herbs (chives, tarragon, and/or parsley)

½ tsp kosher salt

¼ tsp freshly ground black pepper

¾ cup shaved Parmigiano-Reggiano

2 tbsp balsamic vinegar

1 tbsp extra-virgin olive oil

1. Preheat the oven to 350°F.

2. Working with half of the dough at a time, roll the pasta dough into thin sheets about 6 inches wide (the width of a standard pasta machine). Cut the pasta into 3-inch squares. You should have between 30 and 36 squares. Set the squares aside on a lightly floured tray or baking sheet.

3. Combine the olive oil, garlic, shallot, squashes, peppers, and mushrooms in a large bowl and toss. Place in a large roasting pan and roast in the oven until lightly brown and tender, 20 to 30 minutes. Add the tomatoes and broth and continue roasting for 10 to 15 minutes more. Toss the ragoût with the herbs in a large bowl and season with the salt and pepper. Keep warm while you prepare the pasta.

4. Bring a large pot of lightly salted water to a simmer over medium heat. Add the buckwheat pasta squares to the simmering water and stir to separate them. Cook until they are tender to the bite, 5 to 6 minutes. Drain the pasta in a colander to let the water drain away.

5. Assemble the open-face ravioli in individual bowls by topping warm pasta squares with the vegetable mixture. Top with some cheese and drizzle with a little balsamic vinegar and extra-virgin olive oil.

NOTE To make buckwheat pasta, replace the whole wheat flour with buckwheat flour in the Basic Pasta Dough (page 64).

MIXING THE DOUGH FOR FRESH PASTA (60), **CLEANING MUSHROOMS** (122), **DICING** (119)

TOP: *Mix the buckwheat dough until it comes together when pressed.*

BOTTOM: *Use a pizza wheel to cut the pasta.*

WHITE BEAN RAVIOLI

White beans have an incredibly creamy texture that makes them an excellent filling for this pasta. Top the finished ravioli with a drizzle of Basil Oil (page 294) or a simple but flavorful sauce, such as Roasted Red Pepper Coulis (page 299).

MAKES 6 SERVINGS

⅔ cup dried cannellini beans, soaked

2¼ cups Vegetable Broth (page 295)

1 bay leaf

3 sprigs thyme

3 tbsp extra-virgin olive oil

6 garlic cloves, minced

¼ tsp lemon juice

Pinch kosher salt

Pinch freshly ground black pepper

½ recipe Basic Pasta Dough (page 64)

1 tbsp Basil Oil (page 294, optional) *or* ¾ cup Roasted Red Pepper Coulis (page 299, optional)

1. Combine the beans, broth, bay leaf, and thyme in a large soup pot. Bring to a simmer over medium-low heat and cook until tender, about 45 minutes. Drain the beans, reserving the broth and discarding the bay leaf and thyme. Transfer the beans to a large bowl and mash with a fork.

2. Heat the oil in a small sauté pan over medium heat. Add the garlic and cook, stirring frequently, over low heat until the garlic is tender, about 1 minute. Add the garlic, lemon juice, salt, and pepper to the mashed beans. Adjust the mixture's consistency with the reserved cooking liquid, if needed. Refrigerate the bean mixture for at least 1 hour.

3. Roll the pasta dough into thin sheets about 6 inches wide (or the width of a standard pasta machine). Mound about 1 teaspoon of filling approximately 1 inch from the long edge of the strip, spacing the filling about 2 inches apart. Lightly brush the edges of the pasta as well as between the mounds of filling with water. Fold the sheet in half lengthwise and gently press down around the filling to release any trapped air in the pasta. Use a knife or a pasta wheel to cut the ravioli apart, or use a 2-inch round cutter for round ravioli. Seal the edges. You should have 30 to 36 ravioli. Set the filled ravioli aside on a lightly floured tray or baking sheet.

4. Bring a large pot of lightly salted water to a simmer over medium heat.

5. Add the ravioli to the simmering water and cook until they rise to the surface and are tender to the bite, 4 to 5 minutes. Drain the ravioli in a colander. Serve in heated bowls drizzled with basil oil or red pepper coulis.

COOKING LEGUMES (94)

LINGUINE with Olives, Basil, and Red and Yellow Tomatoes

Olives are known for their fruity, briny flavor. Kalamata, or calamata, olives are extremely fruity and have a delightfully meaty texture.

MAKES 6 SERVINGS

2 tbsp olive oil

2 garlic cloves, minced

4½ cups red and yellow cherry tomatoes (cut larger tomatoes into halves or quarters)

1 pound dried linguine

⅔ cup green onion, finely sliced

½ cup pitted Kalamata olives, sliced

2 tbsp Vegetable Broth (page 295; optional)

⅓ cup shredded basil

Pinch freshly ground black pepper

⅓ cup shaved Parmigiano-Reggiano (optional)

1. Heat the oil in a large sauté pan over medium heat. Add the garlic and sauté until aromatic, about 1 minute. Add the tomatoes and cook just until heated, 1 to 2 minutes. Keep the tomatoes warm over low heat while you cook the pasta.

2. Bring a large pot of lightly salted water to a rolling boil over high heat. Add the pasta and stir a few times to separate the strands. Cook the linguine until tender to the bite, 9 to 10 minutes. Drain the linguine through a colander, reserving about ½ cup of the pasta water.

3. Add the green onion, olives, and the pasta to the tomato mixture and lift and toss to combine the ingredients over low heat. Add enough of the reserved pasta water to evenly and lightly coat the linguine (the pasta should look creamy, not oily or dry).

4. Remove the pan from the heat and add the basil and pepper. Serve the pasta in a heated bowl or individual plates. Top the pasta with shaved Parmigiano-Reggiano, if desired.

SHREDDING OR CHIFFONADE (119)

TOP: *Use a paring knife to peel the broccoli rabe stems.*

BOTTOM: *Sauté broccoli rabe until bright green.*

FEDELINI with Broccoli Rabe, Pancetta, Parmigiano-Reggiano, and Toasted Bread Crumbs

Sautéeing the broccoli rabe softens its bitterness and infuses it with some of the flavor of the pancetta.

MAKES 6 SERVINGS

1¼ oz pancetta, julienned

1 cup diced onion

3 garlic cloves, minced

1 tbsp chopped thyme

1 tsp red pepper flakes

1 bunch broccoli rabe, trimmed and chopped

1¾ cups Chicken Broth (page 294)

1 tbsp lemon juice

1¾ lb dried fedelini

GARNISHES

¾ cup toasted bread crumbs (see Note)

⅓ cup grated Parmigiano-Reggiano

2 tbsp chopped parsley

1. Cook the pancetta in a large sauté pan over medium heat until it the pancetta bits are crisp and the fat has rendered, about 2 minutes. Add the onion and garlic and sauté, stirring frequently, until the onions are golden brown, about 4 minutes. Add the thyme and red pepper flakes and cook just long enough to heat them, about 1 minute.

2. Add the broccoli rabe and sauté, stirring frequently, until it is bright green and hot, about 3 minutes. Add the broth and simmer over low heat until the broccoli rabe is tender and the broth has nearly cooked away, about 5 minutes. Taste and season with lemon juice and red pepper. Keep the broccoli rabe warm while you cook the pasta.

3. Bring a large pot of lightly salted water to a rolling boil over high heat. Add the fedelini and boil until tender to the bite, 7 to 9 minutes. Drain the fedelini through a colander, reserving about ½ cup of the pasta water.

4. Add the fedelini to the broccoli rabe and lift and toss to combine the ingredients over low heat. Add enough of the reserved pasta water to evenly and lightly coat the fedelini if needed (the pasta should look creamy, not oily or dry).

5. Serve the pasta in a heated bowl or individual plates. Top with the toasted bread crumbs, Parmesan, and parsley.

JULIENNE AND BATONNET (119), **JUICING CITRUS** (285)

TOASTED BREAD CRUMBS Remove the crust from 4 or 5 slices of peasant-style bread and let the slices air-dry for 1 day. Cut the bread into large dice and process in a food processor until medium-size crumbs form. Spread the crumbs on a baking sheet and spray with oil. Bake in a 350°F oven, turning frequently, until golden brown, about 10 minutes.

GRILLED ASPARAGUS with Morels, Bowtie Pasta, and Spring Peas

This recipe showcases the very best spring has to offer, highlighting plump fresh asparagus by grilling and pairing it with delicate morels and tender peas. If necessary, dried morels can be used; rehydrate them in warm water first. Use the rehydrating liquid in the preparation to replace an equal amount of the vegetable broth.

MAKES 6 SERVINGS

5 cups sliced asparagus (peeled and trimmed)

2 tsp olive oil

1 cup sugar snap peas

2 tsp butter

2 tbsp minced shallot

2¾ cups fresh morel mushrooms, halved

3¼ cups shelled peas

1 cup snow peas

⅓ cup Vegetable Broth (page 295)

2 tbsp chopped marjoram

½ tsp kosher salt

Pinch freshly ground black pepper

1¾ lb dried bowtie pasta

GARNISHES

1 cup green onion, split lengthwise and thinly sliced

½ cup grated dry Jack cheese

1. Prepare a grill for a medium fire. Toss the asparagus in the oil. Using a roasting rack, grill the asparagus until tender, turning the asparagus once, about 2 minutes on each side. Slice into 1-inch pieces.

2. Bring a large pot of water to a rolling boil over high heat. Meanwhile, trim the ends and pull the strings from the snap peas. Add the snap peas to the water and boil until tender, 2 to 3 minutes. Drain and set aside.

3. Melt the butter in a large sauté pan over medium heat until it begins to turn brown. Add the shallot and morels and cook, stirring frequently, over low heat until the shallots are limp and translucent, 2 to 3 minutes.

4. Add the asparagus, shelled peas, snow peas, broth, marjoram, salt, and pepper. Steam until the vegetables are tender and the liquid has almost evaporated, 4 to 5 minutes. Keep them warm over low heat while you cook the pasta.

5. Bring a large pot of lightly salted water to a simmer over medium heat. Add the bowtie pasta to the simmering water, stirring a few times to separate the pieces, and cook until almost tender, 6 to 7 minutes (or about 2 minutes less than the recommended cooking time on the package). Add the snap peas and continue to cook until the pasta is tender and the snap peas are hot, another 2 minutes. Drain the pasta and snap peas through a colander, reserving a few tablespoons of the pasta cooking water.

6. Add the pasta and snap peas to the vegetables, and lift and toss to combine the ingredients over low heat. Add enough of the reserved pasta water to evenly and lightly coat the linguini (the pasta should look creamy, not oily or dry). Serve the pasta at once in a large heated bowl or individual plates, topped with green onion and cheese.

CLEANING MUSHROOMS (122)

LOBSTER CAPPELLETTI with Ginger Sauce

Creamy lobster filling is perfectly complemented by the sweet and sour ginger sauce.

MAKES 6 SERVINGS

LOBSTER FILLING

½ lb cooked lobster meat

1 large egg white

2 tbsp heavy cream

1 tbsp minced shallot

2 garlic cloves, minced

2 tsp chopped chives

1 pound Basic Pasta Dough (page 64)

2¼ cups Ginger Sauce (page 296)

GARNISH

12 pieces shelled cooked lobster claw meat

2 tbsp grated lime zest

1. Purée the lobster, egg white, and heavy cream in a food processor or blender until a smooth paste forms. Place the purée in a metal bowl over an ice bath. Fold in the shallots, garlic, and chives. Leave the lobster filling over the ice bath while rolling out the pasta.

2. Working with half of the dough at a time, roll the pasta dough into thin sheets about 6 inches wide (the width of a standard pasta machine). Cut the dough into 3-inch squares or rounds. Mound 1 teaspoon of the filling in the center of each piece. Lightly brush the edges of the pasta with water and fold it in half. Seal the edges by pressing them with the tines of a fork. Overlap the two tips and press them to seal the pasta into a cappelletti shape. You should have 30 to 32 cappelletti. Set the filled cappelletti aside on a lightly floured tray or baking sheet.

3. Gently heat the ginger sauce in a small saucepan over low heat while you cook the cappelletti.

4. Bring a large pot of lightly salted water to a simmer over medium heat. Add the cappelletti and simmer until they rise to the surface and are tender to the bite, 7 to 9 minutes.

5. Drain the cappelletti in a colander and then combine them with the ginger sauce. Garnish each serving with 2 lobster claw pieces and lime zest.

BOILING WHOLE LOBSTER AND HARD-SHELL CRAB (189), **ZESTING CITRUS** (284)

FALL HARVEST PASTA SALAD

This pasta salad can be prepared with additional or alternate vegetables and fruits, if desired. Pumpkin can be substituted for the squash, and pears can be substituted for the apples. Try a number of combinations that feature seasonal products of fall.

MAKES 6 SERVINGS

1 cup diced butternut squash

½ cup pearl onions (peeled)

1 ear of corn, shucked

1 cup quartered mushrooms

2 apples, cored and cut into eighths

1 cup dry green or pigeon peas

DRESSING

¼ cup apple cider

2 tsp Dijon mustard

1 tbsp maple syrup

¼ cup cider vinegar

1 tbsp chopped chives, or as needed

1 tbsp chopped parsley, or as needed

½ tsp kosher salt, or as needed

¼ tsp freshly ground black pepper, or as needed

½ cup canola oil

1 cup halved cooked green beans

1 pound whole wheat pasta, cooked

1. Preheat the oven to 400°F.

2. Toss the squash, pearl onions, corn, mushrooms, and apples in a large roasting pan and roast until nicely browned and cooked through, 8 to 10 minutes. Cool completely. Cut the kernels from the ear of corn.

3. For the dressing, combine the cider, mustard, maple syrup, vinegar, chives, parsley, salt, and pepper in a large bowl. Slowly add the oil while whisking constantly.

4. Toss the roasted vegetables, beans, and pasta in a large bowl to combine. Add the dressing and toss to coat. Season with chives, parsley, salt, and pepper, if desired.

CLEANING MUSHROOMS (122), **BOILING, BLANCHING, AND PARBOILING VEGETABLES** (123)

ASIAN BUCKWHEAT NOODLE SALAD with Spicy Sesame Chicken

Sesame oil is a deeply flavored oil pressed from sesame seeds. It can be found
in specialty markets and the international section of most grocery stores.
Some varieties are flavored with chili, and a little goes a long way.

MAKES 6 SERVINGS

SPICY SESAME CHICKEN

1 tsp peanut oil

1 tsp sesame oil

Pinch red pepper flakes

¼ tsp minced ginger

1⅓ lb cooked chicken breast, shredded

BUCKWHEAT NOODLE SALAD

1 tsp peanut oil

2½ cups sliced shiitake mushrooms

2 tsp tamari

Pinch coarsely ground black pepper

10 oz dried buckwheat noodles (soba noodles)

1 tsp sesame oil

1⅓ cups bean sprouts

1 cup thinly sliced green onion

1 cup julienned carrot

¾ cup julienned snow peas

¾ cup Asian Vinaigrette (page 294)

1¼ cups mixed greens, loosely packed

⅔ cup frisée, loosely packed

GARNISHES

⅔ cup pickled ginger

1 tsp black sesame seeds, toasted

1 tsp white sesame seeds, toasted

1. For the chicken, combine the peanut oil, sesame oil, red pepper flakes, and ginger in a small bowl. Add the chicken and toss to coat. Refrigerate until needed.

2. For the salad, heat the peanut oil in a large sauté pan over medium heat. Add the shiitakes and sauté until tender, 3 to 4 minutes. Season with the tamari and pepper. Remove from the heat and cool completely.

3. Bring a large pot of lightly salted water to a boil over high heat. Add the buckwheat noodles and boil until tender to the bite, 7 to 9 minutes. Drain the noodles, rinse in cold water until cool to the touch, and drain once more. Toss with the sesame oil in a large bowl.

4. Combine the shiitakes, noodles, bean sprouts, green onion, carrot, snow peas, and half the vinaigrette in a large bowl and toss.

5. Combine the mixed greens, frisée, and remaining vinaigrette in another large bowl and toss to coat. Top with the noodle salad and chicken. Garnish with the pickled ginger and sesame seeds.

CLEANING MUSHROOMS (122), **JULIENNE AND BATONNET** (119), **PREPARING SPINACH AND LEAFY GREENS** (121), **PREPARING GINGER** (284), **TOASTING SPICES, NUTS, AND SEEDS** (290)

BASIC PIZZA DOUGH

This dough will keep, refrigerated, for two days or frozen for up to one month. Thaw frozen dough, still wrapped, overnight in the refrigerator. Bring chilled dough to room temperature and allow to rise before using.

MAKES 1¼ POUNDS

1¾ tsp honey

1½ tsp instant dry yeast

1 cup water, or as needed

1¼ cups whole wheat flour

1¼ cups bread flour

½ tsp kosher salt

¼ cup cornmeal

1. Mix the honey, yeast, ½ cup of the water, ½ cup of the whole wheat flour, and ½ cup of the bread flour in a large bowl and stir to make a thin batter. Place the batter in a warm area and cover with plastic wrap or a damp towel. Allow the batter to rest for 1 hour, or until it becomes frothy and increases in bulk.

2. Add the remaining ½ cup of the water, the remaining flours, and the salt to the batter. Knead in a stand mixer with a dough hook attached on medium speed or by hand, adding more water as needed until a smooth, elastic dough forms, 8 to 10 minutes. The dough should cleanly pull away from the sides of the bowl.

3. Place the dough in a warm area and cover with plastic wrap or a damp towel. Allow the dough to rise until it has doubled in bulk and holds an impression for a few seconds when pressed with a finger, about 1 hour.

4. Turn the dough out on a lightly floured work surface and release the gas in the dough by kneading briefly. For individual pizzas, divide the dough into 6 equal pieces and shape into balls. For large pizzas, divide the dough in half. Cover the dough with plastic wrap and allow to rise a second time, about 1 hour. (If you wish, you can freeze the balls of dough before the second rise; they will keep for about 6 weeks.)

5. Flatten each dough ball into a circle (about 7 inches wide for individual pizzas or 14 inches wide for larger pizzas). Place each circle on a sheet pan sprinkled with the cornmeal. Garnish as desired and bake as directed in your recipe.

NOTE To thaw pizza dough, take it from the freezer and leave it in the refrigerator until it softens, usually about 6 hours. Unwrap the dough and place it on a floured work surface. Cover loosely. Let it come to room temperature and relax for about 1 hour before shaping and baking the dough.

USING YEAST (259)

PIZZAS with Roasted Tomatoes and Mozzarella

This classic combination is amplified by using roasted tomatoes
to give these pizzas a richer, smokier flavor.

MAKES 6 SERVINGS

2 tsp olive oil

2 tbsp chopped basil

1 tsp chopped oregano

3 garlic cloves, minced

1 recipe Basic Pizza Dough (page 77)

3¼ cups sliced roasted plum tomatoes

10½ oz part-skim mozzarella, thinly sliced

¾ cup Tomato Coulis (page 298)

¼ cup grated Parmigiano-Reggiano

1 tsp freshly ground black pepper

3 cups loosely packed mixed greens

¼ cup Balsamic Vinaigrette (page 293)

1. Preheat the oven to 500°F.

2. Combine the oil, 1 tablespoon of the basil, the oregano, and garlic.

3. Roll out the dough for individual pizzas as directed in the dough recipe. Transfer one piece to a peel, if available, or place it on a baking sheet. Spread 1½ teaspoons of the basil-oregano mixture over the dough. Overlap the tomatoes and the mozzarella slices around the outer edge of the pizza. Spoon some tomato coulis in the center of the pizza. Sprinkle the pizza with a small amount of the Parmigiano-Reggiano and a pinch each of the remaining basil and the pepper. Repeat with the remaining dough balls to make 6 pizzas. (Or make two large pizzas, dividing the topping ingredients between them.)

4. Bake the pizzas until the crust is golden brown and crisp, about 10 minutes. Toss the greens with the vinaigrette and serve with the pizza at once.

ROASTING AND BAKING VEGETABLES (124)

BARBECUED CHICKEN PIZZAS with Tomato Salsa

Add a little Tabasco and some roasted jalapeños to bring a bit of kick to these pizzas. Or top with grilled vegetables like corn, peppers, or onions to amplify the smoky flavor.

MAKES 6 SERVINGS

1¼ lb skinless, boneless chicken breast

1¾ cups Barbecue Sauce (page 300)

1 recipe Basic Pizza Dough (page 77)

1¼ cups grated Monterey Jack cheese

¾ cup Tomato Salsa (page 304)

1. Prepare a grill for a medium fire. Coat the chicken with half of the barbecue sauce. Grill on the first side until marked, 4 minutes. Turn over and grill until browned on the outside and cooked through, 5 to 7 minutes. Cool, slice thinly, and refrigerate until needed.

2. Preheat the oven to 500°F.

3. Roll out the dough for individual pizzas as directed in the dough recipe. Transfer one piece to a peel, if available, or place it on a baking sheet. Brush with some of the remaining barbecue sauce. Place cheese around the outer edge of the dough. Arrange some of the sliced chicken on top of the cheese. Spread the salsa in the center of the pizza. Repeat with the remaining dough balls to make 6 pizzas.

4. Bake the pizzas until the crust is golden brown and crisp, about 10 minutes. Serve at once.

GRILLING (157)

LOBSTER AND JALAPEÑO PIZZAS

Arugula is a peppery green that is excellent on pizzas or sandwiches. You can also serve these pizzas with a side salad of lightly dressed arugula to complement the flavors of the finished pizza.

MAKES 6 SERVINGS

1 recipe Basic Pizza Dough (page 77)

2 tbsp extra-virgin olive oil

6 oz thinly sliced part-skim mozzarella

12 oz chopped, cooked lobster

1½ cups coarsely chopped arugula (blanched)

1 tbsp lemon juice

⅓ cup grated Parmigiano-Reggiano

3 tbsp minced shallot

1 jalapeño, seeded and minced

3 tbsp chopped cilantro

1. Preheat the oven to 500°F.

2. Roll out the dough for individual pizzas as directed in the dough recipe. Transfer one piece to a peel, if available, or place it on a baking sheet. Brush with some of the olive oil. Overlap the mozzarella around the outer edges of the dough. Top with some of the lobster, arugula, a sprinkling of lemon juice, and a small amount of the Parmigiano-Reggiano. Sprinkle with some of the shallots, jalapeño, and cilantro. Repeat with the remaining dough balls to make 6 pizzas.

3. Bake the pizzas until the crust is golden brown and crisp, about 10 minutes. Serve at once.

BOILING WHOLE LOBSTER AND HARD-SHELL CRAB (189), **BOILING, BLANCHING, AND PARBOILING VEGETABLES** (123), **JUICING CITRUS** (285)

BLACK BEAN BURGERS

Burgers made with beans are incredibly satisfying. Garnish these with a selection of Mexican-inspired toppings, as we do here, to make the most of these savory "burgers." We like whole wheat pita to hold the fillings together, but you could certainly opt for a whole wheat bun or serve them on a bed of greens with no bread at all.

MAKES 6 SERVINGS

⅔ oz chorizo, diced

2 garlic cloves, minced

⅓ cup diced onion

½ jalapeño, seeded and minced

½ tsp cumin seeds, toasted and ground

½ tsp chili powder

1 large egg white, lightly beaten

1 tbsp lime juice

¼ cup chopped cilantro

½ tsp kosher salt

1½ cups cooked black beans (page 94)

½ cup cornmeal

2 tbsp olive or canola oil

2 tbsp nonfat yogurt

2 tbsp sour cream

⅓ cup Tomato Salsa (page 304)

6 pitas, split

1. Cook the chorizo in a medium sauté pan over low heat. When a small amount of fat has rendered, add the garlic, onion, and jalapeño and sauté until the onions have browned, 5 to 6 minutes.

2. Add the cumin and chili powder and sauté until aromatic, about 1 minute.

3. Combine the chorizo mixture, egg white, lime juice, cilantro, salt, and beans in a large bowl.

4. Form the mixture into 12 small patties and dust lightly with cornmeal. Heat the oil in a large sauté pan over medium heat. Sauté the burgers until golden brown on each side, 3 to 4 minutes.

5. Combine the yogurt and sour cream. Place the burgers inside the pita pockets, add a little salsa and a dollop of the yogurt mixture, and serve.

TOASTING SPICES, NUTS, AND SEEDS (290)

GRILLED GARDEN SANDWICHES with Warm Cabbage Salad

Draining the ricotta cheese gives it a thicker, spreadable texture, which gives this grilled sandwich an excellent creaminess. Try using other vegetables, or even fruits, to make other versions of this sandwich.

MAKES 6 SERVINGS

1 cup part-skim ricotta cheese

1 medium red onion, sliced about ¼ inch thick

12 slices whole wheat bread

2 tbsp Vegetable Broth (page 295)

1¾ cups sliced mushrooms

¾ cup julienned red peppers

¾ cup julienned yellow peppers

¼ tsp kosher salt

Pinch freshly ground black pepper

2 tbsp shredded basil

2½ cups thinly sliced Granny Smith apples (peeled and cored)

¾ cup thinly sliced plum tomato

¾ cup thinly sliced cucumber

⅔ cup thinly sliced zucchini

1½ cups Warm Cabbage Salad (page 47)

1. Drain the ricotta in a sieve lined with cheesecloth in the refrigerator for 8 to 10 hours.

2. Prepare a grill for a medium fire. Grill the onion slices and wheat bread on the first side until marked, 2 minutes. Turn them over and grill until very hot and browned on the second side, 2 minutes more, and reserve.

3. Preheat the oven to 350°F.

4. Heat the broth in a large sauté pan over medium heat. Add the mushrooms and peppers and cook, stirring frequently, over low heat until the vegetables are slightly tender and the broth has completely reduced, about 5 minutes. Season with the salt and pepper.

5. Spread one side of the bread slices with ricotta. Sprinkle basil over the ricotta. Layer the grilled onions, pepper mixture, apples, tomato, cucumber, and zucchini on top and press together firmly with another slice of bread. Place on a sheet pan and bake until very hot, 20 to 25 minutes, turning 2 or 3 times while heating. Serve with the warm salad.

CLEANING MUSHROOMS (122), **JULIENNE AND BATONNET** (119), **SHREDDING OR CHIFFONADE** (119)

GRILLED MAHI MAHI SALAD SANDWICHES

Bitter greens and a briny dressing are the perfect complement to the freshness of the mahi mahi, sometimes called dolphin fish. While all fish appear to have some level of mercury, it is thought that smaller species, like mahi mahi, have less than larger ones.

MAKES 6 SERVINGS

⅓ cup Anchovy-Caper Dressing (page 294)

¾ lb mahi mahi, grilled and cooled

1¼ cups diced roasted red and yellow peppers

6 slices whole wheat bread

6 Belgian endive spears

⅓ cup thinly sliced red onion

6 radicchio leaves

½ cup frisée, loosely packed

1. For the dressing, whisk together the vinaigrette, anchovies, olives, mustard, garlic, basil, thyme, oregano, and chives in a medium bowl.

2. Break the mahi mahi into chunks in a large bowl by hand and combine with the peppers. Add the dressing and toss gently until combined.

3. Toast the bread and cut the slices in half on the diagonal.

4. Top half of the slices of bread with endive spears, red onion slices, and the mahi mahi mixture. Place a second piece of toast on top of the fish so that the corners of the second toast point opposite those of the base piece. Top with a radicchio leaf, some frisée, and more fish.

SHREDDING OR CHIFFONADE (119), **GRILLING** (157), **ROASTING AND PEELING PEPPERS** (120)

WHOLE WHEAT QUESADILLAS with Roasted Chicken, Ancho Chile Caciotta, and Mango Salsa

Caciotta is a cow's milk cheese whose rind is rubbed with tomato paste to produce a rustlike color and a deep, earthy flavor. It can be found in gourmet stores and specialty cheese shops.

MAKES 6 SERVINGS

1 fryer chicken (2½ to 3 lb)

½ tsp kosher salt

¼ tsp freshly ground black pepper

MANGO SALSA

2 medium mangoes, peeled, seeded, and diced

½ medium papaya, peeled, seeded, and diced

½ canned chipotle, minced

3 tbsp fresh orange juice

Juice of 2 limes

Twelve 8-in whole wheat flour tortillas

1⅓ cups thinly sliced green onion (split lengthwise)

⅓ cup pine nuts, toasted

1½ cups grated ancho chile caciotta

1. Preheat the oven to 350°F.

2. Season the chicken with the salt and pepper and roast to an internal temperature of 165°F, 1 to 1½ hours. Cool, remove all meat from the bones, and shred. Reduce the oven heat to 225°F.

3. For the salsa, combine the mangoes, papaya, chipotle, orange juice, and lime juice in a medium bowl and toss. Set aside.

4. Cover the tortillas with a damp towel and warm in the oven until soft.

5. To assemble the quesadillas, place shredded chicken, green onion, pine nuts, and cheese in the center of a tortilla. Top with another tortilla and place in a heated, oil-sprayed sauté pan.

6. Lightly brown on both sides over medium heat, making certain that the cheese is melted in the middle before removing from the heat. Cut the quesadilla into quarters. Serve with mango salsa. Repeat steps 5 and 6 with the remaining ingredients.

TOASTING SPICES, NUTS, AND SEEDS (290), **JUICING CITRUS** (285)

CRABMEAT AND SHRIMP SANDWICHES

Using fresh, not frozen, seafood makes all the difference in this sandwich. Make it during spring and summer, with ripe, juicy tomatoes, and soft, creamy avocados as the topping. Try grilling the pita slightly before you fill it to add a little warmth to the sandwich.

MAKES 6 SERVINGS

YOGURT-MUSTARD DRESSING

¾ cup mayonnaise

1 cup part-skim ricotta cheese

1 cup nonfat yogurt

2 tbsp white wine vinegar

1 garlic clove, minced

3 tbsp minced shallot

2 tsp Worcestershire sauce

½ tsp Tabasco sauce

2 tsp Dijon mustard

½ tsp kosher salt

CRABMEAT AND SHRIMP FILLING

½ lb shrimp, cooked and peeled

½ lb crabmeat, cooked

6 pitas, split

¾ cup thickly sliced tomato

⅓ cup thinly sliced avocado (pitted and peeled)

½ cup thinly sliced red onion

1 cup alfalfa sprouts

1. Combine the dressing ingredients in a large bowl. Add the shrimp and crabmeat and toss to coat evenly.

2. Fill each pita with the seafood mixture, tomato, avocado, onion, and alfalfa sprouts and serve immediately.

PEELING AND DEVEINING SHRIMP (188)

CHAPTER FOUR

Grains and Legumes

Grains and dried legumes like beans, lentils, and peas are staple foods used throughout the world as the nutritious foundation of many meals. Most have relatively subtle flavors, making them eminently useful as palate cleansers and heat tamers. Since grains and legumes carry other flavors well, they are often paired with small amounts of intensely flavored foods to bring those foods into balance. Grains and legumes absorb flavors as they cook, responding well to an array of aromatics and seasonings, and they reward you with soothing, soul-satisfying sustenance.

At one time, dried beans, lentils, and peas had all but disappeared from many kitchens across our nation—with the exception of the baked beans that almost invariably accompanied a baked ham dinner or hamburgers and hot dogs at summer barbecues. When Tex-Mex and Southwestern cooking became popular, beans came into their own. Our love affair with Middle Eastern and Mediterranean cuisines has introduced us to lentils, chickpeas, and fava beans. Any country or region with a rich peasant tradition has at least one or two bean dishes that grace the dinner table. In some countries, those dishes represent more than a national favorite—they are part of the very fabric of the country's history.

Since we Americans were first able to find heretofore unknown grains, our brown-and-white boxes of converted rice have been crowded out by a rainbow of other rices—starchy round-grained Arborio for risottos; long-grain and fragrant rices such as basmati, jasmine, popcorn, and pecan rice for steaming or for pilafs; and black rice, brown rice, red rice, and wild rice to add a robust flavor and color. But rice isn't the only grain that's available to us. Pearl barley, cracked wheat and bulgur, kasha, quinoa, millet, and teff are turning up on menus and supermarket shelves. One of the best ways to make an ethnic meal taste authentic is to include the appropriate grains. Even if you typically stick to one cooking style, substituting other grains for rice adds new flavors, textures, and colors to your meals.

When you are planning a meal, use the recipes in this chapter as the main course, as an accompaniment to a meat or vegetable dish, or as a starter course for a more elegant meal. In addition to such favorite dishes as pilafs and risottos, grains and legumes are featured in salads, fritters, and pancakes. There is something honest and sustaining about these foods. Preparing them with care and attention is an excellent way to get back to basics in the kitchen.

Selecting Grains and Legumes

When purchasing grains and legumes, look for stores with plenty of business and a rapid turnover of inventory, especially if you prefer to purchase in small quantities from bulk bins. Grains and legumes do have a long shelf life, but the older they are, the longer they take to cook and the more liquid they may require. And, as they age, their flavor can turn musty and stale. Keep whole grains in the refrigerator or freezer if you won't be using them within a few weeks of purchase, or their natural oils may become rancid. They can be cooked directly from the freezer without thawing. Beans, lentils, and dried peas can be stored in plastic bags or other airtight storage containers for a few months and don't require refrigeration.

COOKING RATIOS AND TIMES FOR SELECTED GRAINS

TYPE	RATIO OF GRAIN TO LIQUID (CUPS OF GRAIN: CUPS OF LIQUID)	APPROXIMATE YIELD (IN CUPS)	COOKING TIME
Barley, pearl	1:2	4	35 to 45 minutes
Barley groats	1:2½	4	50 minutes to 1 hour
Buckwheat groats (kasha)	1:1½ to 2	2	12 to 20 minutes
Couscous†		1½ to 2	20 to 25 minutes
Hominy, whole‡	1:2½	3	2½ to 3 hours
Hominy grits	1:4	3	25 minutes
Millet	1:2	3	30 to 35 minutes
Oat groats	1:2	2	45 minutes to 1 hour
Polenta	1:3 to 3½	3	35 to 45 minutes
Rice, Arborio (for risotto)	1:3	3	20 to 30 minutes
Rice, basmati	1:1½	3	25 minutes
Rice, converted	1:1¾	4	25 to 30 minutes
Rice, long-grain, brown	1:3	4	40 minutes
Rice, long-grain, white	1:1½ to 1¾	3	18 to 20 minutes
Rice, short-grain, brown	1:2½	4	35 to 40 minutes
Rice, short-grain, white	1:1 to 1½	3	20 to 30 minutes
Rice, wild	1:3	4	30 to 45 minutes
Rice, wild, pecan	1:1	4	20 minutes
Wheat berries‡	1:3	2	1 hour
Wheat, bulgur, soaked§	1:4	2	2 hours
Wheat, bulgur, pilaf	1:2½	2	15 to 20 minutes
Wheat, cracked	1:2	3	20 minutes

† Grain should be soaked briefly in tepid water and then drained before it is steamed.

‡ Grain should be soaked overnight in cold water and then drained before it is cooked.

§ Grain may be cooked by covering it with boiling water and soaking it for 2 hours or cooking it by the pilaf method.

STONE-GROUND AND WHOLE-GRAIN MEALS AND FLOURS

Stone-ground processing means that the grains, often with the bran intact, are milled between stone wheels rather than steel rollers. The water-powered wheels seldom reach the high temperatures of steel rollers. Therefore, stone-ground flours and meals have higher levels of many vitamins, minerals, fiber, and natural oils. These flours and meals should be stored away from heat, light, air, and moisture to prevent them from going stale. Whole grains or meals have the bran intact before milling. The bran gives whole-grain flours a darker appearance, and items baked with whole-grain flours will have a nuttier and more pronounced flavor than those made from white wheat flour. The texture produced by whole-grain flours is also chewier and denser.

Healthy Techniques for Cooking Grains

Grains have a substance and a subtle flavor that make them excellent accompaniments to a wide variety of foods. They can stand on their own, or they can readily adapt to a supporting role, carrying the flavors of other ingredients.

STEAMING GRAINS

Simple steamed grains are an easy way to add texture, flavor, and nutrition to any meal. They make a great accompaniment to stews and stir fries, of course. We also love to use grains like brown rice, bulgur, or farro as the major component of a flavorful filling for stuffed vegetables. It is a good idea to rinse any whole grain under running cold water before starting to cook, but, with only a few exceptions, grains do not require soaking.

As grains steam, they should absorb all of the liquid they are cooking in. If they absorb just enough, the grains are plump and tender, with a bit of chewiness or "bite." To determine how much liquid you need for the grain you want to cook, consult the chart on page 91.

How to Steam Grains

1. COMBINE THE GRAIN AND COLD WATER (SEE TABLE ON PAGE 91 FOR AMOUNT OF WATER) IN A HEAVY SAUCEPAN.

2. BRING THE WATER TO A FULL BOIL AND STIR ONCE OR TWICE TO SEPARATE THE GRAINS.
Reduce the heat to medium and simmer, uncovered, until most of the water has been absorbed. Cover the pan tightly, reduce the heat to low, and continue cooking the grain without stirring it until tender to the bite and fluffy (cooking times can be found in individual recipes or in the chart on page 91). Remove the pan from the heat and let it stand, still covered, for 10 minutes. Fluff with a fork before serving.

COOKING PILAF

Preparing a grain by the pilaf method results in a different texture than a steamed grain. The differences are the result of the way the dish is cooked. Pilafs almost always include an aromatic vegetable (onions or leeks, for instance) that is cooked in a bit of oil. The grain is also cooked in the oil before you add the liquid.

How to Cook Pilaf

1. HEAT OIL IN A LARGE, HEAVY, OVENPROOF PAN.
If the recipe calls for aromatics such as minced onion, add to the pan and cook until translucent before adding the grain. Stir in the grain and sauté, stirring frequently, until coated with oil and heated through.

2. **ADD THE COOKING LIQUID.**

   You can make a pilaf with water, but a broth will result in a richer flavor. Heating the broth before you add it to the pilaf has two benefits: It reduces overall cooking time for the grain and it produces a better texture. Carefully pour in hot broth and bring to a simmer, stirring the grains once or twice to prevent them from sticking to the bottom of the pan.

3. **COVER THE POT AND COOK UNDISTURBED.**

   Once the liquid is simmering and you've added any seasonings, cover the pot and finish cooking the pilaf either over very low heat or in a 325°F oven. Cook until the grains are tender but still slightly firm. Remove pilaf from the heat and let it rest, still covered, for about 5 minutes. Fluff gently with a fork.

PREPARING CEREALS AND MEALS

Polenta and grits are simply hot cereals. They can be served soft or hard, with virtually no adornment or embellished with a wide array of extra ingredients. Once cooked and cooled, polenta and grits can be broiled, baked, or grilled for a whole new rendition. One important point about cooking cereals like polenta or grits (as well as oatmeal, farina, or other hot breakfast cereals) is to choose the right pot. It should be taller than it is wide, with a heavy bottom. A whisk is helpful as you add the cereal to the pot, but use a wooden spoon to stir the cereal as it cooks. Constant stirring gives cereals a creamier, richer texture.

1. **ADD THE CEREAL TO THE LIQUID.**

   Cereals and meals can be cooked in water, broth, or milk. Bring the liquid to a full boil, along with any desired seasonings or aromatics. Use one hand to add the measured cereal a little at a time, or pour it slowly and gradually into the simmering liquid. Whisk or stir constantly with the other hand as you add the cereal to keep it from clumping together.

2. **SIMMER AND STIR THE CEREAL.**

   Once you have added all the cereal, continue to cook over low to medium heat, stirring often. The more you stir, the creamier the finished dish will be. While it cooks, the cereal thickens and craterlike bubbles break the surface. When they are fully cooked, some cereals may even start to pull away from the sides of the pot as you stir.

3. **SERVING THE CEREAL.**

   The more grain you add to a cooked cereal dish, the stiffer it will be. Soft polenta or grits are loose enough to run a bit when they are put on a plate. Stiffer versions are perfect to cool and then cut into portions. Spread the cooked grain into an even layer in a shallow baking dish, cover, and chill thoroughly. Once it is properly chilled, you can cut it into pieces and then layer it with a filling and sauce to bake like lasagna, or serve it grilled or broiled until golden and crisp on the outside, accompanied with a flavorful stew.

Healthy Techniques for Cooking Legumes

Beans, peas, and lentils are not difficult to cook, although some of them do require a bit of advance planning. If you want to take advantage of the simplicity of canned beans, just remember to rinse them well to remove the canning liquid before you add them to a recipe. The liquid is often quite high in sodium. If you've made the beans yourself, you are in control of how much salt to add. Cooked beans hold well in their cooking liquid for a few days.

SOAKING AND COOKING TIMES FOR SELECTED DRIED LEGUMES

TYPE	SOAKING TIME	COOKING TIME
Adzuki beans	4 hours	1 hour
Black beans	4 hours	1 hours
Black-eyed peas*	—	1 hour
Chickpeas	12 hours	2 to 2½ hours
Fava beans	12 hours	3 hours
Great Northern beans	4 hours	1 hour
Kidney beans (red or white)	4 hours	1 hour
Lentils*	—	30 to 40 minutes
Lima beans	4 hours	1 to 1½ hours
Mung beans	4 hours	1 hour
Navy beans	4 hours	2 hours
Peas, split*	—	30 minutes
Peas, whole	4 hours	40 minutes
Pigeon peas*	—	30 minutes
Pink beans	4 hours	1 hour
Pinto beans	4 hours	1 to 1½ hours
Soybeans	2 hours	3 to 3½ hours

*Soaking is not necessary.

COOKING DRIED LEGUMES

There is a noticeable difference in taste between favas and limas, black beans and kidney beans, and navy beans and black-eyed peas, but in general, it is certainly fine to substitute one bean for another in many recipes as long as you take into account that different types of beans require different cooking times. Lentils and split peas cook in 30 to 45 minutes. Garbanzo beans (chickpeas) and lima beans can take up to 2 hours. Consult the chart on page 94 for more information. If time is short, use canned beans instead of cooking dried beans from scratch, but be sure to drain the beans and rinse them to remove the "tinny" flavor of the canning liquid and, more importantly, to reduce the sodium level.

SORTING AND RINSING LEGUMES

Pour the legumes onto a baking sheet and, working methodically from one end to the other, carefully sort through them, removing discolored or misshapen pieces. Pour the sorted beans into a bowl filled with cold water. Stir them once or twice. Let the beans settle and then remove and discard any that float to the surface. Drain the remaining legumes in a colander and rinse them well with cold running water.

SOAKING LEGUMES

There are two methods for soaking legumes: the long soak and the short soak.

The Long-Soak Method
Place the sorted and rinsed legumes in a large bowl and add enough cool water to cover them by a few inches, about four times the volume of water to beans. Transfer the bowl to the refrigerator and soak for the amount of time given on the chart on page 94 for specific beans.

The Short-Soak Method
Place the rinsed and sorted legumes in a pot and add enough water to cover by a few inches. Bring the water to a simmer. Remove the pot from the heat, cover, and let the legumes steep for 1 hour.

COOKING LEGUMES

You can buy canned beans, but the flavor, texture, and variety of beans you cook yourself is much better. Beans, dried peas, and lentils do require time to cook properly, but they don't demand your undivided attention.

1. DRAIN THE SOAKED LEGUMES.

Place in a large pot and add enough water to cover the beans by about 2 inches. Bring the liquid to a full boil and reduce the heat to a simmer. Stir the beans occasionally as they cook, and add more liquid if the level starts to drop.

2. ADD SEASONINGS AT THE APPROPRIATE TIME.

Most recipes tell you when to add various seasonings and flavorings, but the general rule is to add salt and any acidic flavoring ingredients, such as tomatoes, vinegar, or citrus juices, only after the beans are nearly tender. Adding them any earlier can toughen the skins, which might mean that the beans never get the soft, creamy consistency you want.

3. SIMMER THE BEANS UNTIL TENDER ENOUGH TO MASH EASILY.

Stir the beans occasionally as they cook, and add more liquid if the level starts to drop. Keep the heat low enough to maintain a gentle simmer; a rapid boil is not necessary. To check the beans for doneness, either bite into a bean or see if you can mash it easily. If the inside of the bean is fully cooked, it will look creamy, almost like a purée. If it isn't completely done, the inside may look white and granular.

LEMON-DILL RICE

Fresh lemon juice and zest brighten this simple rice dish and highlight the flavor of the fresh dill.

MAKES 6 SERVINGS

3 tbsp diced onion

2 cups Chicken Broth (page 294)

2½ cups dry white wine

1 bay leaf

2 tbsp fresh lemon juice

½ tsp grated lemon zest

¾ cup long-grain brown rice

2 tsp chopped dill

1. Preheat the oven to 350°F.

2. Cook the onions in ¼ cup of the broth in a medium ovenproof saucepan over low heat, stirring frequently, until the onions are limp and translucent, 3 to 4 minutes. Add the remaining 1¾ cups broth, the wine, bay leaf, lemon juice, lemon zest, and rice and bring to a boil.

3. Cover the pot tightly and cook in the oven until the rice is tender and has absorbed all the liquid, about 40 minutes.

4. Remove and discard the bay leaf. Fluff the rice with a fork and fold in the dill.

ZESTING AND JUICING CITRUS (284)

QUINOA PILAF with Red and Yellow Peppers

Try adding other vegetables based on seasonality. Fold in mushrooms, leeks, or tomatoes instead of bell peppers.

MAKES 6 SERVINGS

2 tbsp minced shallot

1 garlic clove, minced

1¾ cups Vegetable Broth (page 295)

1¼ cups quinoa, rinsed

¼ tsp kosher salt

¼ tsp freshly ground pepper

1 bay leaf

1 sprig thyme

¾ cup diced roasted red and yellow peppers

1. Preheat the oven to 350°F.

2. Cook the shallots and garlic in 2 tablespoons of the broth in a medium ovenproof saucepan over low heat, stirring frequently, until the shallots are limp and translucent. Add the quinoa, the remaining broth, the salt, pepper, bay leaf, and thyme and bring to a boil.

3. Cover the pot tightly and cook in the oven until the quinoa is tender and has absorbed all the liquid, about 15 minutes.

4. Remove and discard the bay leaf and thyme. Fluff the quinoa with a fork and fold in the peppers.

ROASTING AND PEELING PEPPERS (120), **COOKING PILAF** (92)

BARLEY AND WHEAT BERRY PILAF

Wheat berries are the entire wheat kernel with only the hull removed. They are an excellent source of fiber and can be found in health food stores or in gourmet markets.

MAKES 6 SERVINGS

⅔ cup wheat berries

3½ cups Vegetable Broth (page 295)

1 tbsp butter

1 tbsp minced shallot

⅔ cup diced leeks, white and light green parts

⅓ cup diced carrot

⅓ cup diced celeriac

1⅓ cups pearl barley

1¼ cups amber beer

¼ tsp kosher salt

Pinch freshly ground pepper

3 cups chopped collard or mustard greens

1. Soak the wheat berries in three times their volume of water for 8 to 10 hours. Drain the berries and combine with 2⅔ cups of the broth in a large soup pot. Cover and simmer over medium-low heat until tender, about 30 minutes. Drain and discard any excess broth, reserving the berries.

2. Preheat the oven to 325°F. Melt the butter in a medium ovenproof saucepan over medium heat. Add the shallot, leeks, carrot, and celeriac and cook, stirring frequently, over low heat until the vegetables are tender, 3 to 4 minutes. Add the barley, the remaining broth, the beer, salt, and pepper and bring to a boil. Cover the pot tightly and cook in the oven until the barley is tender and has absorbed all the liquid, about 45 minutes.

3. Meanwhile, bring a medium pot of salted water to a boil. Add the greens and boil until deep green and tender, about 7 minutes. Drain very well.

4. Combine the wheat berries, barley, and greens in a large bowl. Toss to combine.

DICING (119), **CLEANING LEEKS** (120), **PREPARING SPINACH AND LEAFY GREENS** (121)

WILD AND BROWN RICE PILAF with Cranberries

Use unsweetened cranberries in this dish. Or try substituting other dried fruits: Apricots, apples, cherries, blueberries, or mango would all be delicious. Dice larger fruits into small pieces.

MAKES 6 SERVINGS

⅓ cup dried cranberries

2 tbsp dry white wine

BROWN RICE

3 tbsp diced onion

⅔ cup brown rice

1⅓ cups Chicken Broth (page 294)

WILD RICE

½ cup apple cider

2 cups Chicken Broth (page 294)

⅔ cup wild rice

1. Preheat the oven to 350°F.

2. Plump the cranberries in the wine in a small bowl for about 20 minutes. Drain the cranberries, reserving the liquid.

3. For the brown rice, cook the onion in the reserved cranberry liquid in a small ovenproof pot over low heat, stirring frequently, until the onion is limp and translucent, 3 to 4 minutes. Add the brown rice and broth and bring to a boil. Cover the pot tightly and cook in the oven until the rice is tender and has absorbed all the liquid, about 40 minutes.

4. For the wild rice, combine the cider, broth, and wild rice in a medium ovenproof pot and bring to a boil. Cover the pot tightly and cook in the oven until the rice is tender and has absorbed all the liquid, about 35 minutes.

5. Combine both rices and the plumped cranberries in a large bowl.

FARRO

Farro is a Tuscan wheat that is also sold as emmer in the United States. It can be found in most health food stores, or in gourmet shops specializing in Italian products. Cooking times for farro can vary widely. If you use the whole grain, with the bran intact, you can choose to soak the grain first for about 8 hours and then simmer for another 40 to 45 minutes. But if you skip the soaking step, increase the cooking time to 1 to 1½ hours. Pearled farro has some of the bran removed and cooks in 30 minutes without soaking. Cracked farro cooks in about 10 minutes.

MAKES 6 SERVINGS

¾ cup whole-grain farro

4 to 5 cups cold water

¼ tsp kosher salt

1. Sort and rinse the farro, removing and discarding any bits of chaff or debris. Rinse well in a colander. If desired, soak the farro in a bowl with enough cold water to cover the grain by about 2 inches for 8 hours in the refrigerator. Drain.

2. Combine the farro, 4 cups of the water, and the salt in a medium saucepan. Bring to a full boil over medium-high heat. Stir the farro once or twice to separate the grains.

3. Cover and simmer, stirring occasionally, until the farro has absorbed all the liquid and is tender to the bite but still rather chewy, 40 to 45 minutes. (Note: If the farro is still undercooked and has already absorbed all the water, add a little more water and continue to cook until tender. If the farro is tender but has not absorbed all the water, drain the excess water away.)

4. Fluff with a fork.

FARRO with Vegetable Ragoût and Parsley and Toasted Almond Salsa

Cut the vegetables into attractive, bite-size pieces. The addition of
this unusual "salsa" brings a fresh flavor to the dish.

MAKES 6 SERVINGS

1½ cups broccoli florets

1½ cups cauliflower florets

1 cup sliced turnips

1 cup cubed carrot

¾ cup Vegetable Broth (page 295)

½ cup diced onion

2 garlic cloves, minced

1 tbsp fresh lemon juice

¼ tsp kosher salt

Pinch freshly ground pepper

2¾ cups cooked Farro (page 99)

¼ cup Parsley and Toasted Almond Salsa
(page 305)

1. Steam the broccoli, cauliflower, turnips, and carrots separately until they are partially cooked, 3 to 5 minutes each. (You can prepare these vegetables up to 3 days ahead and keep them refrigerated.)

2. Heat the broth in a large saucepan over medium heat. Add the onions and garlic and cook, stirring frequently, over low heat until the onions are limp and translucent, 4 to 5 minutes. Add the broccoli, cauliflower, turnips, and carrots and heat completely, 2 to 3 minutes. Season with the lemon juice, salt, and pepper.

3. Mound the farro in the center of a large soup plate. Arrange the vegetables around the farro and garnish with the salsa.

STEAMING AND PAN STEAMING VEGETABLES (123), **JUICING CITRUS** (285)

BUCKWHEAT POLENTA

Using buckwheat flour in addition to cornmeal gives this polenta
a nutty flavor while maintaining its silky texture.

MAKES 8 SERVINGS

2 tsp butter

2 garlic cloves, minced

4½ cups Chicken Broth (page 294)

1¼ cups nonfat milk

¼ tsp kosher salt

¼ tsp freshly ground pepper

⅔ cup yellow cornmeal

⅓ cup buckwheat flour

2 tbsp grated Romano cheese

1. Melt the butter in a large saucepan over medium heat. Add the garlic and sauté until aromatic, about 1 minute. Add the broth, milk, salt, and pepper and bring to a boil. Gradually add the cornmeal and buckwheat flour to the broth, whisking constantly. Reduce the heat to low and simmer, stirring frequently, for about 45 minutes. Remove from the heat and stir in the cheese.

2. Brush a sheet pan with water and pour the polenta into it. Cool, cover with plastic wrap, and refrigerate until firm.

3. Cut the polenta into 8 portions. Grill or reheat the polenta in the oven before serving.

CURRIED TEFF

Teff is an Ethiopian grain similar to quinoa, but it is smaller in size and has
a slightly sour taste that is enhanced by the curry in this recipe.

MAKES 6 SERVINGS

3 cups Chicken Broth (page 294)

1 tbsp butter

1 tbsp Ethiopian Curry Powder (page 291)

1 slice ginger

1 tbsp minced onion

1 garlic clove, minced

2⅓ cups teff

2 tsp shredded basil

2 tsp chopped oregano

1. Heat the broth in a small saucepot over medium heat.

2. Melt the butter in a large saucepan over medium heat. Stir in the curry powder. Add the ginger, onion, and garlic and cook, stirring frequently, over low heat until the onions are limp and translucent, about 4 minutes. Remove the ginger and discard. Add the teff and stir to coat.

3. Add the hot chicken broth and simmer until tender, about 10 minutes. Stir in the basil and oregano before serving.

SHREDDING OR CHIFFONADE (119)

COUSCOUS

Couscous is actually a type of semolina pasta; however, it is cooked and served much like other grains.

MAKES 6 SERVINGS

⅓ cup diced onion

1 garlic clove, minced

1¼ cups Chicken Broth (page 294)

1⅔ cups couscous

2 tsp chopped mint

1 tbsp chopped parsley

1 tsp coriander seeds

1. Preheat the oven to 350°F.

2. Cook the onion and garlic in ½ cup of the broth in a medium saucepan, over low heat until the onions are limp and translucent, 3 to 4 minutes. Add the remaining ¾ cup broth and bring to a boil.

3. Combine the onions, garlic, and broth with the couscous in an ovenproof pan. Cover tightly and cook in the oven until the couscous has absorbed all of the broth, about 3 minutes. Stir in the mint, parsley, and coriander just before serving.

NOTE An alternate method for cooking couscous is to simply put the couscous in a bowl and then bring the broth to a boil, pour it over the couscous, cover the bowl with plastic wrap, and allow it to sit until the couscous absorbs all of the broth and is tender, 3 to 5 minutes.

CORN, WILD RICE, AND QUINOA CAKES

Cornmeal and cornflake crumbs bind these cakes together while not sacrificing the texture of the wild rice and quinoa. Serve the cakes with an assortment of heirloom beans that have been sautéed with garlic and Jus Lié (page 296). Steamed seasonal vegetables also make a nice accompaniment.

MAKES 6 SERVINGS

½ cup quinoa

⅓ cup wild rice

4 cups Vegetable Broth (page 295)

½ tsp kosher salt, or as needed

Freshly ground pepper, as needed

1⅓ cups yellow cornmeal

½ tsp ground toasted cumin

Pinch cayenne

¾ cup cornflake crumbs

1. Rinse the quinoa several times in cold water. Drain.

2. Cook the wild rice and quinoa separately in two small pots in ¾ cup of the broth each until tender, about 40 minutes for the rice and 15 minutes for the quinoa. Fluff the grains with a fork when they are fully cooked and pour them into a shallow pan (the grains can be mixed at this point). When the grains are cool, season them with the salt and pepper.

3. Bring the remaining 2½ cups of broth to a boil. Gradually add ⅔ cup of the cornmeal to the broth, whisking constantly. Reduce the heat to medium low and simmer for 30 minutes, stirring constantly. Remove from the heat and stir in the wild rice, quinoa, cumin, and cayenne. Season with salt and pepper. Pour into a baking dish to cool. When cool enough to handle, form the mixture into 12 cakes.

4. Preheat the oven to 350°F. Combine the remaining ⅔ cup cornmeal with the cornflake crumbs. Dredge the cakes in the cornmeal mixture and spray lightly with vegetable oil spray. Place the cakes on a sheet pan and bake until heated through and golden brown on the outside, 15 to 20 minutes.

TOASTING SPICES, NUTS, AND SEEDS (290), STEAMING GRAINS (92)

VEGETARIAN DIRTY RICE

For even more flavor, trying folding grilled or roasted bell peppers into the finished dirty rice. The corn can also be roasted for sweeter, more intense flavor.

MAKES 6 SERVINGS

1 cup cranberries

½ cup minced onion

1 garlic clove, minced

1 cup **Vegetable Broth** (page 295)

⅔ cup long-grain brown rice

1 tbsp tomato paste

2 tsp cider vinegar

1 tsp minced jalapeño

½ tsp cumin seeds, toasted and crushed

½ tsp freshly ground black pepper

½ tsp mild or hot paprika

Pinch cayenne

⅓ cup grated cheddar cheese

¼ cup corn kernels

1. Preheat the oven to 350°F.

2. Bring a small pot of water to a boil over high heat. Add the cranberries and turn the heat down to low. Simmer until tender, about 5 minutes. Drain, transfer to a small bowl, and mash with a fork. Set aside.

3. Cook the onions and garlic in 2 tablespoons of the broth in a medium ovenproof saucepan over low heat, stirring frequently, until the onions are limp and translucent, 3 to 4 minutes. Add the rice and cook briefly, about 1 minute. Add the remaining broth, the tomato paste, vinegar, jalapeño, cumin, pepper, paprika, and cayenne and bring to a boil.

4. Cover the pot tightly and cook in the oven until the rice is tender and has absorbed all the liquid, about 40 minutes.

5. Fold in the mashed cranberries, cheese, and corn. Serve at once.

WORKING WITH CORN ON THE COB (121)

WILD RICE SALAD

Wild rice is high in fiber and protein and has a lightly nutty flavor. This salad and others made with wild rice are delicious served chilled, at room temperature, or even warm.

MAKES 6 SERVINGS

¾ cup wild rice

2 cups Chicken Broth (page 294)

¼ cup Vinaigrette-Style Dressing (page 292; see Note)

2 garlic cloves, minced

1½ tsp minced shallot

2 tbsp apple cider

¾ cup julienned Granny Smith apple

¾ cup julienned red pepper

¼ tsp chopped sage

GARNISH

⅓ cup chopped toasted walnuts

1. Preheat the oven to 350°F.

2. Combine the wild rice and broth in a medium saucepan. Bring to a boil over medium heat. Cover the pot tightly, and cook in the oven until the rice is tender, about 45 minutes. Drain any excess liquid.

3. Transfer the rice to a large bowl. While the rice is still hot, add the vinaigrette and toss well.

4. Cook the garlic and shallot in the apple cider in a small sauté pan over low heat, stirring frequently, until the shallots are limp and translucent, 2 to 3 minutes. Add the mixture to the rice.

5. Gently fold the apple, pepper, and sage into the rice. Serve at room temperature, garnished with the walnuts.

NOTE Use walnut oil and cider vinegar in the Vinaigrette-Style Dressing recipe.

JULIENNE AND BATONNET (119), **TOASTING SPICES, NUTS, AND SEEDS** (290)

BARLEY SALAD

Citrus, currants, Thai bird chiles, and curry powder give this salad an array of delicious flavors not usually associated with barley to create a sweet, light, nutty salad.

MAKES 6 SERVINGS

1²/₃ cups pearl barley

6 cups Vegetable Broth (page 295)

½ cup peeled cipollini onions

¼ cup ramps or green onions cut into ¼-inch lengths

½ cup currants

½ cup golden raisins

1½ Thai bird chiles

1 cup blood orange juice

2 tbsp Curry Spice Blend (page 291)

2 tbsp fresh lemon juice

2 tbsp honey

¼ tsp kosher salt

2 navel oranges, peeled, segmented, and cut into quarters

¾ cup chopped roasted pistachios

1. Preheat the oven to 450°F.

2. Combine the barley and broth in a medium saucepan. Bring to a simmer over medium heat and cook until the barley is tender, 35 to 40 minutes. Drain the liquid and cool the barley completely.

3. Roast half of the onions in the oven until dark brown, 20 to 25 minutes. Cool completely. Dice both the roasted and raw onions.

4. Cook the ramps or green onions in boiling water for 2 minutes. Remove from the water and set aside.

5. Combine the currants, raisins, chiles, and blood orange juice in a medium saucepan. Bring to a boil over high heat and remove from the heat. Steep for at least 30 minutes. Remove the chiles, mince, and return to the juice.

6. Stir together the curry, lemon juice, honey, and salt in a large bowl. Add the barley, onions, ramps, orange segments, and blood orange juice mixture. Toss to combine and marinate for 1 hour before serving. Top the finished salad with pistachios.

JUICING CITRUS (285), **TOASTING SPICES, NUTS, AND SEEDS** (290)

BASIC BEANS

Cooking beans in Chicken Broth (page 294) or Vegetable Broth (page 295) will make them more flavorful than if they were cooked in water alone. Any type of bean can be used in this recipe. Refer to the table on page 94 for soaking and cooking times.

MAKES 6 SERVINGS

1 cup dried black beans

4¾ cups water, Chicken Broth, or Vegetable Broth (pages 294 and 295)

1 Bouquet Garni (page 285)

2 garlic cloves

1. Soak the beans for 8 to 12 hours in enough cold water to cover by 3 inches. Drain the beans and rinse with cold water.

2. Combine the beans, water, bouquet garni, and garlic cloves in a large soup pot. Simmer over medium-low heat until the beans are tender, 45 minutes to 1 hour.

3. Remove and discard the bouquet garni and garlic cloves. Allow the beans to cool in their cooking liquid. Drain and use as desired.

COOKING DRIED LEGUMES (95), **PREPARING GARLIC** (284)

BRAISED BLACK-EYED PEAS

The bacon gives this dish a smoky flavor. Substitute smoked tofu and Vegetable Broth (page 295) for a vegetarian version of this flavorful side.

MAKES 6 SERVINGS

½ cup dried black-eyed peas

2½ cups Chicken Broth (page 294), or as needed

1 slice bacon, diced

1¾ medium onions, thickly sliced

2 tbsp chopped tomato (peeled and seeded)

1 bay leaf

1 sprig thyme

1. Preheat the oven to 350°F.

2. Place the black-eyed peas in a medium pot and add enough broth to cover by 1 inch. Bring to a simmer over medium heat until tender, about 40 minutes. Drain, reserving the cooking liquid.

3. Cook the bacon in a large ovenproof saucepan over medium heat until the fat begins to render and the bacon crisps. Add the onions and sauté until they begin to brown, 4 to 5 minutes.

4. Add the peas, tomato, bay leaf, thyme, and just enough of the cooking liquid to moisten the mixture and bring to a simmer over medium-low heat.

5. Cover the pot and braise in the oven until the peas have absorbed the liquid and are tender, about 30 minutes. Discard the bay leaf and thyme. Serve the peas very hot.

PEELING AND SEEDING TOMATOES (121), **STEWING AND BRAISING VEGETABLES** (125)

LENTIL RAGOÛT

Lentils can be found in a variety of colors and sizes. For this recipe, look for the commonly available brown lentils, or try substituting the smaller green lentils, also known as French lentils or *lentilles de Puy*. They maintain their shape quite well, which prevents the sauce from becoming too thick. Add lemon zest and caraway seeds to the sachet for a richer, more complex flavor.

MAKES 4 SERVINGS

1 slice bacon, diced

¼ cup diced onion

⅓ cup diced leeks, white and light green parts only

¼ cup diced carrot

¼ cup diced celery

1 garlic clove, minced

1 tbsp tomato paste

1 cup Chicken Broth (page 294)

¼ cup lentils

1 Spice Sachet (page 285)

2 tbsp sweet white wine

1½ tsp sherry vinegar

¼ tsp kosher salt

Pinch ground white pepper

2 tbsp Jus Lié (page 296)

1. Cook the bacon in a medium soup pot over medium heat until the fat renders. Add the onion, leeks, carrot, celery, and garlic and cook, stirring frequently, over low heat until the onions are limp and translucent, 4 to 5 minutes.

2. Add the tomato paste and sauté until rust colored, about 5 minutes more.

3. Add the broth, lentils, and sachet and simmer over medium-low heat until the lentils are tender, about 45 minutes.

4. Remove and discard the sachet. Add the wine, vinegar, salt, pepper, and jus lié. Cool completely. The ragout can be stored for up to 1 week refrigerated. Heat before serving.

DICING (119), **DICING ONIONS** (120), **CLEANING LEEKS** (120)

CHICKPEA STEW

For more flavor, replace the water with Chicken Broth (page 294) or Vegetable Broth (page 295). For a similar stew in less time, use canned chickpeas. Since they are already cooked, they will only need to be stewed until the flavors come together, ten to fifteen minutes. Serve with Farro (page 99) and a selection of seasonal vegetables for a meatless entrée.

MAKES 6 SERVINGS

SACHET

1 bay leaf

1 sprig thyme

3 garlic cloves, crushed

Zest of 2 oranges

½ cup chopped carrot

STEW

2⅓ cups dried chickpeas, soaked

1 tsp kosher salt

¼ tsp cayenne

2 tsp olive oil

1 cup diced onion

1¼ cups diced carrot

1 cup diced celery

2 tbsp chopped rosemary

3 tbsp chopped parsley

1. Make the sachet (see page 285).

2. Combine the sachet and the chickpeas in a large soup pot with enough water to cover by 3 inches. Bring to a simmer over medium-low heat until the peas are tender, 1 to 1½ hours.

3. Remove the sachet and add the salt and cayenne. Reserve about one-third of the peas and about 1 cup of the cooking liquid. Purée the rest of the chickpeas in a food processor or blender with enough of the cooking liquid to make a thick but smooth purée. Add the purée back to the reserved chickpeas.

4. Heat the oil in a large skillet over medium heat. Add the onion, carrot, and celery and cook, stirring frequently, until the onions are limp and translucent, 4 to 5 minutes. Stir the vegetable mixture, rosemary, and parsley into the stew.

ZESTING CITRUS (284), **COOKING DRIED LEGUMES** (95), **STEWING AND BRAISING VEGETABLES** (125), **DICING** (119), **DICING ONIONS** (120)

THREE-BEAN STEW

Choose any selection of beans; refer to the table on page 94 for approximate cooking times. A variety of bean colors produces the most attractive finished dish. To make the stew into a vegetarian entrée, add vegetables such as pumpkin, zucchini, corn, peas, and peppers and serve with a grain like rice, quinoa, or barley.

MAKES 6 SERVINGS

2 tsp olive oil

1 garlic clove, minced

1 tsp minced shallot

⅓ cup diced celery

⅓ cup diced carrot

⅓ cup diced onion

½ cup chopped tomatoes (peeled and seeded)

1 tsp Curry Spice Blend (page 291)

½ tsp cumin seeds, toasted and ground

1 cup cooked chickpeas (page 94)

1 cup cooked navy or great Northern beans (page 94)

1 cup cooked black or kidney beans (page 94)

1⅓ cups Vegetable Broth (page 295)

½ tsp freshly ground black pepper

2 tsp chopped parsley

2 tsp chopped cilantro

2 tsp chopped mint

1. Preheat the oven to 350°F.

2. Heat the oil in a large ovenproof sauce pot over medium-high heat. Add the garlic, shallot, celery, carrot, and onion and sauté, stirring frequently, until the onions begin to brown, 8 to 10 minutes.

3. Add the tomato, curry, and cumin and sauté until aromatic, about 2 minutes.

4. Add the beans and broth and bring the liquid to a simmer over low heat. Cover and stew in the oven or over low heat until the carrots and celery are tender, about 30 minutes.

5. Stir in the pepper, parsley, cilantro, and mint just before serving.

DICING (119), **PEELING AND SEEDING TOMATOES** (121), **TOASTING SPICES, NUTS, AND SEEDS** (290), **COOKING DRIED LEGUMES** (95), **STEWING AND BRAISING VEGETABLES** (125)

Purée of Yellow Split Peas

SOUTHWEST WHITE BEAN STEW

Try using a mix of colored peppers for this stew. Green peppers, which are unripe,
will be less sweet than the fully ripened orange, red, or yellow peppers.

MAKES 6 SERVINGS

3 cups cooked navy beans, rinsed and drained (page 94)

1 tsp safflower oil

½ cup diced red onion

½ cup diced assorted bell peppers

2 jalapeños, seeded, diced

3 garlic cloves, minced

2 tbsp sherry vinegar

⅓ cup chopped tomato (peeled and seeded)

1 tbsp chopped cilantro

1. Purée half of the beans until smooth. Combine the puréed beans with the whole beans.

2. Heat the oil in a soup pot over medium heat. Add the onion, peppers, jalapeños, and garlic and sauté until the onions are translucent, 4 to 5 minutes.

3. Add the bean mixture, stirring constantly, until the beans are heated through, 3 to 4 minutes.

4. Add the vinegar and tomato and remove from the heat when hot. Stir in the cilantro just before serving.

COOKING DRIED LEGUMES (95), **DICING** (119), **PEELING AND SEEDING TOMATOES** (121), **STEWING VEGETABLES** (125)

PURÉE OF YELLOW SPLIT PEAS

This dish would also be delicious made with other legumes, such as lentils, chickpeas, or beans.

MAKES 6 SERVINGS

2 tsp olive oil

1¼ cups minced red onion

1⅓ cups yellow split peas, rinsed

6 cups Vegetable Broth (page 295), or as needed

½ tsp kosher salt

1 bay leaf

2 tbsp red wine vinegar

1 tbsp extra-virgin olive oil

⅓ cup chopped green onion

1. Heat the olive oil in a medium sauce pot over medium heat. Add the red onion and sauté until tender and translucent, about 6 minutes. Add the split peas and stir to coat evenly with the oil. Pour in enough broth to cover the split peas by 2 inches. Season with the salt, add the bay leaf, and bring the broth to a boil.

2. Reduce the heat to low, cover, and simmer slowly until the split peas completely disintegrate, 1 to 1½ hours. (Add more broth or water during cooking as needed to keep the mixture from sticking.)

3. Remove the pan from the heat and remove and discard the bay leaf. Re-cover and let the peas stand until set and thickened, about 30 minutes. The mixture should have the consistency of mashed potatoes. Stir in the vinegar.

4. Drizzle on the extra-virgin olive oil and sprinkle with the green onions. Serve immediately.

VEGETARIAN REFRIED BEANS

The starchiness of the pinto beans combined with a little bit of vegetable broth is what makes this dish so smooth and creamy.

MAKES 6 SERVINGS

1⅓ cups pinto beans, soaked

1¼ cups Vegetable Broth (page 295), or as needed

1 tsp vegetable oil

½ cup diced onion

1 tbsp minced garlic

1 plum tomato, diced

¼ tsp kosher salt

¼ tsp cracked toasted cumin seeds

¼ tsp chili powder

1. Place the beans in a medium soup pot and add just enough broth to cover the beans. Bring to a simmer over medium-low heat until the beans are tender, 45 minutes to 1 hour. Drain, reserving the beans and broth separately.

2. Heat the oil in a large sauté pan over medium heat. Add the onions and garlic and cook, stirring frequently, until the onions are limp and translucent, 4 to 5 minutes.

3. Add the beans and simmer, stirring and mashing occasionally, until the beans are very hot and creamy, about 10 minutes. Add the tomato, salt, and just enough of the reserved broth to keep the beans moist. Simmer another 2 or 3 minutes to heat the tomatoes.

4. Season with the cumin and chili powder. Serve at once.

COOKING DRIED LEGUMES (95), **PREPARING GARLIC** (284), **TOASTING SPICES, NUTS, AND SEEDS** (290)

BLACK BEAN AND CORNMEAL TRIANGLES

Serve this loaf with sour cream and Tomato Salsa (page 304). It makes an excellent side dish or even light lunch, served with a salad.

MAKES 6 SERVINGS

2 tbsp vegetable oil

½ cup diced red pepper

½ cup diced green pepper

½ cup diced onion

5 garlic cloves, minced

1 cup diced sun-dried tomatoes

1 cup cooked black beans (page 94)

1 tbsp chopped cilantro

Dash Tabasco sauce

2½ cups Vegetable Broth (page 295)

½ tsp kosher salt

¼ tsp freshly ground black pepper

¾ cup cornmeal

¼ cup all-purpose flour

2 tsp olive oil, or as needed

1. Heat the vegetable oil in a large skillet over medium heat. Add the peppers, onions, and garlic and cook, stirring frequently, until the onions are limp and translucent, 4 to 5 minutes. Remove from the heat and stir in the tomatoes, beans, cilantro, and Tabasco.

2. Bring the broth, salt, and pepper to a simmer in a medium sauce pot over medium heat. Gradually add the cornmeal, stirring constantly. Reduce the heat to low and simmer, stirring constantly, until the mixture pulls away from the sides of the pot, about 20 minutes.

3. Fold the bean mixture into the cornmeal. Place the mixture into an 8-in loaf pan sprayed with oil. Refrigerate for 8 to 10 hours.

4. Unmold the loaf; it should come out easily, but if necessary, use a thin knife or spatula to help it out of the pan. Cut into 15 slices. Cut each slice on a diagonal to make 30 triangles. Lightly dust the triangles with the flour.

5. Heat the olive oil in a skillet over medium-high heat. Add the triangles and sauté, turning once, until golden brown, 3 to 4 minutes on each side. Serve at once.

CHAPTER FIVE

Vegetables

Almost all the advice we hear for healthy eating encourages us to consume a greater quantity and greater variety of vegetables. To make it easier to select a wide array of vibrant and flavorful vegetables, it helps to think about vegetables in color families: Dark green vegetables, orange or yellow vegetables, red vegetables, white vegetables, even a few purple vegetables all help you "paint" a vegetable rainbow in your meals.

Fresh Produce

Fruits, vegetables, and herbs have always been an important part of the human diet, but consumers today are more aware than ever that these foods are nutritional powerhouses. They provide impressive amounts of complex carbohydrates, fiber, water, vitamins, minerals, and phytochemicals, often with very little fat, modest amounts of protein, and no cholesterol. They come in a breathtaking array of flavors, colors, and textures as well.

Fresh, local, in-season produce is best. These foods have been minimally handled and shipped, the time between harvest and table is brief, and often the flavors are more pronounced, the colors brighter, and the nutrient levels higher. Sometimes, though, the dictates of common sense make this impractical: It would mean, for example, that many of us could never use lemons, or could use asparagus or tomatoes for only a few months of the year. When fresh versions are not in season, you have the option of choosing a frozen, dried, or canned vegetable.

When purchasing dried, frozen, or canned produce, choose brands of high quality. Be aware that many canned products contain added sodium and that dried foods tend to be concentrated in calories.

For the most part, fruits and vegetables do not require the same careful portion budgeting that meats, poultry, and fish do. For this reason, they play a key role in producing the necessary flavor boost and eye appeal that can help dispel the myth of bland and boring nutritious cuisine.

As a healthier alternative to fat- or cream-based sauces, fruits and vegetables can be used in the form of purées, coulis, salsas, chutneys, compotes, and relishes to add flavor and texture to a variety of dishes. Dried fruits in particular are a clever way to introduce an additional plant element to a recipe. They are wonderful in salads, sauces, stuffings, desserts, grain dishes, and breakfast cereals.

FRUIT

Although the Dietary Guidelines do not categorize fruits as they do vegetables, different groups of fruits provide different nutrients. Orange and red fruits like mango, cantaloupe, apricot, watermelon, and red or pink grapefruit are high in carotenoids. Citrus, berries, guava, papaya, kiwi, and cantaloupe are high in vitamin C, while oranges are rich in folate. Fruits like apples and pears aren't especially high in vitamins, but they contain phytochemicals as well as fiber.

Two cups of fruit should be consumed per day for a 2,000-calorie intake. Whole fruits, whether fresh, frozen, canned, or dried, are recommended over fruit juice for the majority of this amount to ensure adequate fiber intake.

Although unripe fruits can be stored at room temperature, most ripe fruit should be refrigerated. Berries in particular are extremely perishable and should be used within a day or two of purchase. Some fruits (including apples, bananas, and melons) emit ethylene gas; this can accelerate ripening in some unripe fruits, but it can also promote spoilage in produce that is already ripe. Store these fruits separately from other foods.

Fruits like lemons and melons emit odors that can permeate other foods; dairy products are prone to absorbing odors, as are fruits such as apples and cherries.

Vegetables by Color

The following amounts constitute a basic guideline for selecting a rainbow of vegetables and the amounts that you should enjoy over the course of a week:

COLOR	EXAMPLES	FREQUENCY
Green vegetables	broccoli, fennel, watercress, arugula, spinach and most leafy greens, artichokes, asparagus, green beans, garden peas, green peppers, avocados, green cabbage, bok choy, cucumbers, Brussels sprouts	3 to 4 cups/week
Orange or yellow vegetables	carrots, sweet potatoes, pumpkin, winter squash, sweet corn, yellow tomatoes, yellow squash, rutabagas	2 to 3 cups/week
Red vegetables	red tomatoes, rhubarb, red peppers, red beets, red cabbage, red potatoes	2 to 3 cups/week
White vegetables	white potatoes, kohlrabi, turnips, parsnips, onion, cauliflower, garlic	2 to 3 cups/week
Blue or purple vegetables	eggplant, purple potatoes	1 to 2 cups/week

DARK GREEN VEGETABLES

Dark green vegetables include most of the crucifers (cabbage family): broccoli, Brussels sprouts, boy choy, kale, and collards. They also include cooking greens such as Swiss chard and turnip greens, as well as salad greens such as arugula, leaf lettuce, and spinach.

These vegetables are extremely low in calories and fat (usually under 1 gram per serving) and contain generous amounts of fiber, vitamin C, beta carotene, iron, calcium, folate, and vitamin B_6. Crucifers, including cabbage and cauliflower, are also high in phytochemicals called glucosinolates, which are thought to protect against some types of cancer. It is best not to overcook these vegetables; doing so causes nutrient loss and releases the sulfur-containing phytochemicals that cause their unpleasant aromas.

ORANGE OR YELLOW VEGETABLES

Orange vegetables get their coloring from carotenoid pigments; your body converts beta carotene, the best-known carotenoid, into vitamin A. The flesh of vegetables in this family can range in color from deep yellow (such as yams) to dark orange (pumpkin), and their peels can be any color. These vegetables are typically very high in fiber and several of the B vitamins, as well as vitamin C and even vitamin E. Some supply iron and magnesium.

RED AND PURPLE VEGETABLES

Eggplant, tomatoes, beets, radishes, radicchio, even purple asparagus or beans, get their color from specific pigments. The presence of these pigments is also a signal that the produce has plenty of healthy antioxidants and phytochemicals. Lutein, for instance, is thought to benefit vision, while lycopene has benefits for the cardiovascular system.

WHITE, TAN, AND BROWN VEGETABLES

The health benefits of ingredients like onions and garlic have been well documented. They are loaded with antioxidants like vitamins C and E; this characteristic means that they can play a role in protecting cells from damage and even have some role to play in avoiding cancer. Potatoes, often maligned as fattening and lacking in nutrients, are actually an impressive source of vitamin C and a host of other vitamins and minerals.

Healthy Techniques for Vegetables

Vegetables are far more than simply a side dish meant to "fill up" a plate. They add flavor, color, and texture to any meal, and, more importantly, they provide significant amounts of nutrients, including complex carbohydrates, fiber, vitamins, minerals, antioxidants, and phytochemicals.

There is no single "perfect" vegetable cookery method. You must make a decision based on how the dish should taste and appear. The size and shape of the cut, if any, as well as whether moist heat or dry heat is applied, greatly influence the cooked vegetable's texture, color, appearance, and flavor.

Each vegetable cookery technique produces specific and characteristic results. For example, stir-frying, microwaving, and steaming are often preferred for cooking vegetables that should have a crisp texture and bright color. Boiled vegetables are generally more tender and moist. Baking a vegetable produces a texture that is fluffy, mealy, and dry, with a special "roasted" flavor.

WASHING AND TRIMMING VEGETABLES

All fresh produce, even if it will be peeled before cutting, must be washed well. Washing removes surface dirt, bacteria, and other contaminants that might otherwise come in contact with cut surfaces by way of your knife or peeler.

PEELING

Vegetables may be peeled in a variety of ways. Not all vegetables require peeling before cooking, but when it is necessary, you should use a tool that evenly and neatly removes the skin without removing too much of the valuable flesh. Rotary peelers are used for thin-skinned vegetables such as carrots, celery, and asparagus. Thick-skinned vegetables, such as rutabagas and winter squash, are peeled by cutting away the skin with a chef's knife. Fibrous or tough skins can be removed from broccoli, fennel, and similar vegetables by using a paring knife to trim away the skin; often the skin can then be pulled away after the initial cut by catching it between the flat side of the blade and your thumb and simply pulling it away.

BASIC VEGETABLE KNIFE CUTS

The way you cut vegetables determines not only how they will look, but also how they taste and how quickly or slowly they cook.

Chopping
Slice or cut through the vegetables at nearly regular intervals until the cuts are relatively uniform. You do not have to obtain perfectly neat cuts, but all of the pieces should be roughly the same size.

Mincing
Mincing is a very fine cut that is suitable for many vegetables (e.g., onions, garlic, and shallots) and herbs. You mince the same way you chop, except the cuts are smaller.

Shredding or Chiffonade
The chiffonade (French for "fine shreds") cut is mainly used for leafy vegetables and herbs, and items cut in this way often serve as a garnish or a bed for presenting other ingredients. When cutting firm heads of greens into shreds or chiffonade, first cut out the core. Then, to make it easier to handle the vegetable, you can cut the head into halves or quarters. Large leaves can be cut more easily if you roll the individual leaves into cylinders before cutting. Stack smaller leaves, such as basil, one on top of the other, and then roll them into cylinders and cut.

Julienne and Batonnet
The julienne and batonnet cuts are long and rectangular in nature and are seen most prominently in French fries or in a stir-fry as a matchstick cut. To julienne or batonnet a vegetable, rinse, trim, and peel it first. (To keep round vegetables from slipping as you work, cut a slice from one side; this cut is sometimes known as a footer.) Put the already peeled and trimmed vegetable on your work surface and make parallel cuts to produce slices of an even thickness. Stack the slices, align the edges, and make parallel cuts of the same thickness through the stack to produce stick shapes.

Dicing
The first step in making neat, even cubes or dice is to cut julienne or batonnet as described above. These sticks should be the same width as the cubes or dice you want to make. Gather the pieces together so that they are all arranged in a single direction, then cut through them crosswise at evenly spaced intervals to finish cubing or dicing. The recipes in this book call for variously sized dice. Cubes are usually 1 to 1½ inches wide. Large dice are about ¾ inch; medium dice, ½ inch; small dice are ¼ inch, and fine dice, ⅛ inch.

SPECIAL TECHNIQUES FOR SPECIFIC VEGETABLES

The cuts described on the previous page work well for any solid food, whether you are cutting potatoes or squash. Vegetables like peas, corn, tomatoes, onions, and leeks grow in specific ways that call for a special preparation and cutting technique.

Dicing Onions

Onions grow in layers, so you need a special approach to cut them into neat, relatively even dice. Cut onions just before you plan to cook them, since their flavor starts to escape once they are cut. First, trim away the roots, leaving the root end of the onion intact, then cut the onion in half from stem end to root end. Peel away the outer layers, discarding both the papery skin and the thin, tough layer just beneath it.

Place an onion half cut side down on the cutting board. Holding your knife with its blade parallel to the work surface, carefully make two or three horizontal cuts in the onion, spacing them from ½ inch apart (for coarse dice) to ¼ inch apart (for fine dice). Do not cut all the way through the root end. This will hold the onion layers together for easier, neater dicing.

Make parallel cuts lengthwise with the tip of the knife. Again, do not cut through the root end. Cut the strips crosswise to make dice of the desired size.

Cleaning Leeks

Leeks are especially prone to catching large amounts of grit and sand between their layers. First, trim the leaves to remove the very tough green portion, leaving just the white and light green or yellow portion. Next, trim the leek's roots, leaving enough of the root intact to hold the layers together—this will make it easier to cut the leek later. Then run water over the leek while pulling its layers back so that all of the grit can be flushed out.

Roasting and Peeling Peppers

When peppers and chiles are charred over a flame, grilled, roasted, or broiled, not only are the flavors brought out, but the skins are loosened as well. If you have gas burners, hold the peppers over the flame with tongs or a large kitchen fork, turning to char them evenly.

If your grill is hot, char the peppers over hot coals or high heat. To roast or broil peppers and chiles in a hot oven or under a broiler, halve them; remove their stems, seeds, and membranes; and place them cut side down on an oiled sheet pan. Broil or roast until their skin is black and blistered. Once the entire pepper is evenly charred, transfer it to a paper bag or bowl and close or cover tightly. By the time the pepper is cool enough to handle, about 10 minutes, steam will have loosened the skin enough that it peels away easily. Peel and rub it away with your fingertips or use a paring knife if the skin clings in some places.

Stringing Peas and Beans

Snow peas, sugar snap peas, and snap beans usually have a tough string that should be removed before they are cooked and served. This is an easy but time-consuming task, and there aren't any special tools to speed the process. To remove the string, snap the stem end of the pea or bean and pull downward toward the tail. The string should pull away easily. The fresher the pea or bean, the easier this process. This is a very important preparation technique, as it is quite possible for someone to choke on a tough string.

Preparing Artichokes

Artichokes require some special attention before cooking. The barbs at the tips of the leaves are simply snipped away with kitchen scissors. Spread the leaves apart to expose the feathery "choke" and scoop it out with a teaspoon. To make hearts, trim most of the leaves away from the base and the top of the artichoke. To make artichoke bottoms, pull away all the leaves and trim the stem away. Reserve cut artichokes in water mixed with a splash of lemon juice; otherwise, they may turn brown.

Working with Corn on the Cob

The traditional American way to serve corn is simply boiled, steamed, or roasted on the cob. To prepare other corn dishes, such as creamed corn or corncakes, you need to remove the kernels as well as the milk. First, score the kernels with a knife so that they to begin to release their juices (milk). Then, slice the kernels off the cob by cutting from the top of the ear to the bottom. Finally, scrape the cob to release any remaining milk.

Peeling and Seeding Tomatoes

Bring a large pot of water to a rolling boil. Cut a shallow X into the blossom (bottom) end of the tomato with the tip of a paring knife. The cut should be just deep enough to slice through the skin. Lower the tomatoes into the water with a slotted spoon, blanching no more than three or four at a time if they are small, or only two if large. After 10 to 15 seconds, depending on the tomatoes' size and ripeness, remove them from the water with the slotted spoon. Immediately plunge the tomatoes into ice water to stop the cooking. Peel away the tomato skins starting at the X, using your fingers or a paring knife.

To remove the seeds from tomatoes (including canned whole tomatoes), halve round tomatoes crosswise at their widest points. Cut plum (Roma) tomatoes lengthwise to seed them more easily. Gently squeeze each tomato half to extract the seeds, using your finger to help loosen and remove them.

Preparing Spinach and Leafy Greens

Spinach and other leafy greens can be very sandy and need careful washing. Fill a large bowl or a sink with cold water. Submerge the leaves in the water, turn them gently, then lift them out and transfer them to a colander. Change the water and repeat the washing as needed until the water remains clear. If the stems are thick and tough, trim them away. Fold a leaf in half lengthwise along its rib, veined side facing outward. With your other hand, grasp the stem firmly and strip it away from the leaf; the rib should also tear away cleanly.

Cleaning Mushrooms

Clean mushrooms with as little water as possible; they absorb water like sponges, which can interfere with cooking. If the mushrooms were relatively clean when you bought them, you may need only to rub them gently with a cloth or soft brush. If you have a number to clean or they are very dirty, put them in a colander and rinse in cool water just long enough to remove any dirt. Let the mushrooms drain well on layers of absorbent towels before you cut them. Some mushrooms, such as shiitake, must have their tough, woody stems removed. Even mushrooms with tender stems generally left intact should have the dried, discolored ends of their stems trimmed away.

SPECIAL CONCERNS

The goal for healthy vegetable cookery is to produce dishes that retain the greatest nutritive value, the best color, and the freshest, most appealing flavor. Outlined next are some of the factors that affect nutrient, color, and flavor retention in cooked vegetables.

Color Retention

A vegetable's color is determined by the pigments it contains. We know that the pigment of a vegetable gives us an idea of the nutritional makeup of the food. Strategies you can use to reduce or eliminate color loss during cooking also help to retain nutrients. Generally speaking, the best color is retained when vegetables are cooked for as short a time as possible.

Nutrient Retention

There is no way to retain all of a vegetable's nutrients during cooking. The major culprits in nutrient loss are heat, air, water, and enzymes. To keep vegetables as nutrient-rich as possible, keep the following in mind:

- Rinse, trim, peel, and cut vegetables as close as possible to cooking time.

- Avoid holding vegetables in liquid before or after cooking.

- Cook vegetables as quickly as possible, in as little liquid as possible.

- Cook vegetables as close to the time you plan to serve them as possible.

- When feasible, steam or bake vegetables whole, in their skins.

BOILING, BLANCHING, AND PARBOILING VEGETABLES

It is difficult to think of any vegetable that cannot be boiled. Even though many people tend to think of boiled vegetables as bland or boring, boiling is of great importance in vegetable cookery. Boiling also forms the basis for such fundamental operations as blanching and parboiling.

Blanching and parboiling are techniques used to make skins easy to remove, help eliminate or reduce strong odors or flavors, and "set" the color of vegetables to be served cold. They may also be the first step in other cooking techniques. In the case of parboiling, for example, the object is to partially cook the vegetable before adding it to another dish, such as a stew.

1. **BRING THE LIQUID TO A FULL BOIL.**
The amount of liquid required will vary, depending upon the vegetable and the length of cooking time. In general, there should be enough water to hold the vegetables comfortably, without excessive crowding. Add any seasonings, acids, and/or aromatic ingredients that are appropriate to the liquid at this point.

2. **ADD THE VEGETABLES TO THE BOILING LIQUID.**
Add them in small enough batches so that the liquid's temperature does not drop dramatically. Covering the pot allows for the best color (through retention of acids) in red cabbage, beets, and white vegetables (cauliflower, for example). You can also cover the pot while boiling orange and yellow vegetables (carrots and squash, for example). If preparing a green vegetable that will cook rapidly, such as peas or spinach, covering the pot helps shorten cooking time. Denser green vegetables, such as broccoli, should be boiled uncovered, at least for the first 2 to 3 minutes, to allow natural acids to escape. In their case, their natural acids could cause their color to turn a dull olive- or yellow-green.

3. **COOK THE VEGETABLES TO THE DESIRED DONENESS.**
The most reliable doneness tests for vegetables are taste and touch. Bite into a piece of the vegetable when it is raw, and then again at various points as it cooks. Notice the flavor and texture. If tasting the vegetable isn't practical, pierce it with a knife, fork, or skewer and gauge the resistance it gives.

4. **DRAIN THE VEGETABLES THOROUGHLY IN A COLANDER OR SIEVE.**
At this point the vegetable either may be served as is; combined with butter, fresh herbs, spices or other aromatics, or sauces; chilled with cold water to hold for later service; or used in other vegetable preparations, such as braises, gratins, grills, or purées.

STEAMING AND PAN STEAMING VEGETABLES

Steaming is an efficient and practical way to prepare vegetables, especially those that are naturally tender or thin or that have been cut into small, uniform pieces. This is one of the gentler cooking techniques for vegetables.

1. **BRING THE LIQUID IN THE BOTTOM OF A STEAMER TO A FULL BOIL WITH THE LID ON THE POT.**
Add any additional seasonings or aromatics to the liquid as it comes to a boil to help release their flavors.

2. **ADD THE VEGETABLES TO THE STEAMER IN A SINGLE LAYER SO THAT THE STEAM CAN CIRCULATE FREELY.**
This shortens cooking time and results in better flavor, color, and nutrient retention.

3. **RETURN THE LID TO THE STEAMER AND STEAM THE VEGETABLES TO THE DESIRED DONENESS.**
The appropriate degree of doneness is determined by how the particular vegetable will be handled once it is steamed. Vegetables may be blanched, parboiled, or fully cooked.

4. **REMOVE THE VEGETABLES FROM THE STEAMER.**
Once the appropriate doneness is reached, the vegetable may be served immediately. The vegetable may be handled in any of the same ways as boiled vegetables.

ROASTING AND BAKING VEGETABLES

This technique should not be confused with other techniques that cook vegetables in an oven, such as braised dishes and gratins. Roasting or baking is best suited to vegetables that have thick skins that will protect the interior from drying or scorching. Examples include various winter squashes and eggplant. Roasting also intensifies the flavor of a vegetable or dries it slightly.

1. PLACE THE PREPARED VEGETABLE IN A HOT OR MEDIUM OVEN.

    The oven's temperature depends upon the vegetable's size and density. The longer the roasting time required, the lower the temperature should be. Vegetables may be roasted on baking sheets or roasting pans, or, in some cases, directly on the oven rack, which allows the hot air to circulate readily.

2. ROAST THE VEGETABLE TO THE DESIRED DONENESS.

    Generally, vegetables are thoroughly roasted when they can be pierced easily with the tip of a knife or fork. Vegetables should be rotated as they roast to promote even cooking because most ovens have hot spots. The placement of other items in the oven also could cause uneven cooking.

3. SERVE THE VEGETABLE IMMEDIATELY ON HEATED PLATES.

    You may want to add some finishing ingredients or seasonings, a sauce, or a garnish. You can usually keep roasted or baked vegetables warm in the oven for up to an hour. Another common option for baked or roasted vegetables is to purée them in a food mill or food processor. If you plan to purée the vegetables, you will find that the texture and flavor is best if puréed while still hot.

SAUTÉING AND STIR-FRYING VEGETABLES

Some vegetables such as mushrooms, summer squashes, and onions are sautéed or stir-fried from their raw state. Denser vegetables, such as green beans, carrots, and Brussels sprouts, need to be fully cooked or parcooked by boiling, steaming, microwaving, or roasting before sautéing or stir-frying.

1. HEAT THE PAN, ADD THE OIL (OR COOKING MEDIUM), AND HEAT IT.

    Add the oil, and then swirl it around the edge so that it coats the pan well.

2. ADD THE AROMATICS, IF USING THEM.

    Both stir-fries and sautés may include aromatics like shallots, onion, or ginger. Adding those ingredients to the pan first infuses the oil with their flavors, which in turn flavor the entire dish.

3. ADD THE VEGETABLE(S).

    Unlike a sauté of meat or fish, vegetable sautés and stir-fries are usually stirred or tossed as they cook. Cook vegetables until very hot and tender to the bite. If more than one vegetable is being cooked, as in a stir-fry, add the vegetables in the proper sequence, beginning with those with the longest cooking times, to assure that all components complete cooking at the same point.

GRILLING AND BROILING VEGETABLES

Some vegetables can be grilled or broiled from the raw state; others require preliminary cooking or marinating to assure thorough cooking. Vegetables that hold up well when subjected to a grill's intense heat include eggplant, mushrooms, onions, summer squashes, and peppers.

1. THOROUGHLY HEAT THE GRILL OR BROILER.

2. PLACE THE PREPARED VEGETABLE DIRECTLY ON A RACK.

    If there is a danger that the vegetable might stick easily to the rack, it can be grilled in a handheld grill rack.

3. GRILL OR BROIL THE VEGETABLE UNTIL HEATED THROUGH AND TENDER.

Baste it with a marinade or oil during the cooking time, if appropriate. Turn grilled vegetables as necessary during cooking to cook them evenly and avoid scorching them. (Do not turn broiling vegetables.) Broiled vegetables should have a browned top; grilled vegetables should be lightly browned on both sides, with well-browned crosshatch marks.

STEWING AND BRAISING VEGETABLES

Vegetable stews and braises, such as ratatouille and peas *bonne femme*, are excellent ways to retain the vitamins and minerals lost from the vegetable into the cooking liquid, because the liquid is served as part of the dish. The distinction between a vegetable stew and a braise is the same as for meats (see page 159):

1. HEAT THE OIL OR A SMALL AMOUNT OF STOCK.

2. ADD APPROPRIATE SEASONINGS OR AROMATICS AND THE MAIN ITEM.

If using aromatics such as garlic, shallots, or onions, cook these ingredients over gentle heat with the lid on to encourage them to release their juices without developing additional color, or over more intense heat with the cover off for a more pronounced flavor and a darker color.

3. ADD A LIQUID, IF NEEDED, AND BRING IT TO A SIMMER.

Cook the vegetable over low heat or in a medium oven. Introduce additional vegetables and aromatics in the proper sequence so that all components complete their cooking times at the same point.

4. COOK THE STEW OR BRAISE UNTIL THE VEGETABLES ARE TENDER; THEN ADD A THICKENER AND/OR FINISHING INGREDIENTS AS APPROPRIATE.

Stews are typically cooked completely on the stovetop, whereas braises are more frequently cooked in a medium oven (325° to 375°F). It may be necessary to strain out the vegetables before adding the thickener to the liquid. If that is the case, return the vegetable to the sauce once it is properly thickened or finished.

STUFFING VEGETABLES

A plump mushroom cap or a shiny cherry tomato—both of these ingredients practically beg to be stuffed. You have cold options: salads made with vegetables and grains (such as the Curried Teff on page 102) or spreads like guacamole. Hot options include a spoonful of a robust bean stew or a vegetable ragoût, dusted with bread crumbs and cooked until crispy and hot. Or try a hearty rice pilaf, made from wild rice and garnished with chopped toasted pecans and dried cherries.

Stuffed vegetables can be small enough to eat in a single bite, like our Stuffed Cherry Tomatoes with Minted Barley-Cucumber Salad (page 55), to serve as hors d'oeuvres, or the perfect size for a first course or appetizer, or even made into satisfying main dishes. Mushrooms, celery, endive spears, lettuce cups, or cucumbers make perfect containers. Some of the most familiar vegetables for stuffing and baking include tomatoes, peppers, mushrooms, artichokes, eggplant, zucchini, and onions.

Stuffing Mushrooms

Break away the stem (save it to flavor a broth), and scrape away and discard the feathery gills. If your mushroom caps roll when you set them in the baking dish, cut a very thin slice away from the top of the cap to keep them steady.

Stuffing Cucumbers, Zucchini, and Eggplant

Slice away the stem end and then cut the vegetable in half lengthwise. Use a spoon to scoop out the seeds (and a bit of the flesh, if necessary). If you do have to remove some of the flesh, you can always dice it up to add to whatever filling you have planned or to some other dish.

Stuffing Peppers

To stuff peppers, you can use the tip of a paring knife to cut around the stem and then pull out the seeds and the ribs through the opening you've made, or, if the peppers are large enough, you can cut the pepper in half from top to bottom and clean out the halves.

Stuffing Onions

Onions are trimmed and prepared as follows: Cut away the stem end and remove the peel, but leave the root end intact (although you can and should "shave" it a little to help the onion sit flat in the baking dish). Then use the tip of a paring knife to pull out some of the innermost layers until you have enough room to hold the filling. Remember to save the removed layers to use in another dish!

Vegetable Main Dishes

STIR-FRIED GARDEN VEGETABLES with Marinated Tofu

Tofu absorbs marinade quickly and easily, so this dish can be made quickly with very little marinating time. You can use a variety of seasonal vegetables such as sugar snap peas, squashes, cauliflower, and bean sprouts. Other grains such as barley, quinoa, couscous, and basmati rice or noodles such as soba, lo mein, or cellophane may be used instead of brown rice.

MAKES 6 SERVINGS

MARINATED TOFU
One 14-oz block firm tofu

2 tbsp reduced-sodium soy sauce

2 tsp minced ginger

1 garlic clove, minced

GARDEN VEGETABLE STIR-FRY
1 tbsp peanut oil

All-purpose flour, as needed

3 tbsp thinly sliced green onion

2 tsp minced ginger

2 garlic cloves, minced

1 cup broccoli florets

1 cup julienned red pepper

1 cup shredded bok choy or napa cabbage

½ cup bean sprouts

⅔ cup Vegetable Broth (page 295), as needed

¼ cup reduced-sodium soy sauce

2 tsp hot red bean paste

½ tsp five-spice powder

¼ tsp dark sesame oil

2½ cups steamed brown rice (page 92) or cooked soba noodles

GARNISH
1 tbsp sesame seeds, toasted

1. For the marinated tofu, drain and press the tofu, then cut into cubes or slices, according to your preference.

2. Combine the soy sauce, ginger, and garlic in a small bowl. Add the tofu and toss to coat evenly. Marinate for 20 minutes.

3. Heat the oil in a wok or large sauté pan over medium heat. Blot the tofu dry with paper towels and dust with flour, shaking off any excess. Add the tofu to the pan and stir-fry until golden on all sides, about 4 minutes. Remove the tofu from the pan and reserve.

4. Add the green onion, ginger, and garlic to the pan and stir-fry until aromatic, about 1 minute. Add the broccoli and stir-fry for about 2 minutes. Push the broccoli up on the sides of the wok and let the center of the wok get hot again. Add the red pepper and stir-fry until bright and hot, about 2 minutes. Add the bok choy and stir-fry until just starting to wilt, 2 minutes more. Add the bean sprouts and stir into the other vegetables. If necessary, add a small amount of the broth to keep the vegetables from burning. Stir-fry until all of the vegetables are tender-crisp and very hot.

5. Add the stir-fried tofu, soy sauce, bean paste, five-spice powder, and sesame oil. Toss to heat through, 1 to 2 minutes.

6. Serve the stir-fry over rice, garnished with the sesame seeds.

PREPARING GINGER (284), **TOASTING SPICES, NUTS, AND SEEDS** (290), **JULIENNE AND BATONNET** (119), **SHREDDING OR CHIFFONADE** (119)

MU SHU VEGETABLES

This classic Chinese stir-fry dish is composed of thin, delicate pancakes that serve as wrapping for the tender vegetables. Try different combinations of vegetables for varied textures and flavors. To warm the pancakes before serving this dish, wrap them in a lightly dampened towel and place them in a 250°F oven for about five minutes.

MAKES 6 SERVINGS

½ oz dried wood ears (black fungus)

½ oz golden lily buds

2 tsp peanut oil

2 garlic cloves, minced

2 tsp minced ginger

1 cup julienned celery

1 cup julienned carrot

½ cup julienned fennel

2½ cups shredded napa cabbage

2 cups julienned red pepper

2 tbsp hoisin sauce, plus more as needed

1 tbsp rice wine or sherry vinegar

1 tbsp reduced-sodium soy sauce

12 Mandarin Pancakes (recipe follows), warmed

1. Place the wood ears and lily buds in a small bowl and add just enough hot water to cover them. Soak until soft and pliable, about 20 minutes. Drain and squeeze out any excess water. Remove and discard the stems from the wood ears and the hard ends of the lily buds. Cut the mushrooms and buds into shreds and reserve.

2. Heat the peanut oil in a wok or large sauté pan over high heat. Add the garlic and ginger and stir-fry until aromatic, about 1 minute. Add the wood ears and lily buds and continue to stir-fry until hot, about 1 minute.

3. Add the celery, carrot, fennel, cabbage, and red pepper and stir-fry until the vegetables are tender, 4 to 6 minutes. Stir in the hoisin, rice vinegar, and soy sauce and toss to combine completely.

4. Serve the mu shu vegetables immediately with the pancakes. To fill the pancakes, mound some of the vegetables onto the pancake and fold two sides of the pancakes in toward the center (this will keep the vegetables inside the pancake). Roll up, working from one of the unfolded sides, to make a cylinder. Serve with additional hoisin sauce.

PREPARING GINGER (284), **JULIENNE AND BATONNET** (119), **SHREDDING OR CHIFFONADE** (119)

MANDARIN PANCAKES

MAKES ABOUT 24 PANCAKES

¾ cup all-purpose flour

¾ cup boiling water, plus up to 1 tbsp more as needed

2 tsp sesame oil

1. Sift the flour into a large bowl. Add the boiling water and stir immediately, adding up to 1 tablespoon more of boiling water as needed to make a dough. Knead the warm dough until smooth. Wrap the dough and let it rest at room temperature for 30 minutes.

2. Turn the rested dough onto a floured surface. Cut the dough in half. Use a lightly floured rolling pin to roll each half out until it is about ¼ inch thick. Use a 4-inch cookie cutter to cut out 24 circles of dough.

3. Brush the sesame oil over the tops of half of the circles. Lay one pancake on top of another, so that the oiled sides are together. Roll out to form a 6-inch circle. Repeat with the remainder of the pancakes. Use a damp towel to cover the prepared pancakes.

4. Heat a skillet over low heat. Add one of the pancake pairs and cook until barely golden, dry, and blistered, about 1 minute. Turn and repeat on the second side. Remove from the pan and pull apart. Repeat with the remainder of the pancakes. Serve immediately or reserve them and reheat before serving.

VEGETABLES in Red Curry

This is a great main dish for a meatless meal. If you like, add some diced tofu to the curry while the sauce comes to a simmer in step 3.

MAKES 6 SERVINGS

2 tsp peanut oil

1 tsp minced ginger

1 garlic clove, minced

1 tbsp minced green onion, white part only

½ cup diced yellow pepper

½ cup diced red pepper

½ cup diced green pepper

½ cup snow peas

½ cup quartered shiitake mushrooms

½ cup cauliflower florets, cooked

½ cup broccoli florets, cooked

1½ cups Red Curry Sauce (recipe follows)

½ lb soba noodles, cooked

1. Heat the peanut oil in a wok or large sauté pan over high heat. Add the ginger, garlic, and green onion and stir-fry until aromatic but not brown, 2 minutes.

2. Add the peppers, snow peas, and mushrooms and continue to stir-fry until the vegetables are tender-crisp, 3 to 4 minutes.

3. Add the cauliflower and broccoli and stir-fry until heated completely, 2 to 3 minutes. Add the curry sauce and stir to combine. Bring the sauce to a simmer over medium heat and simmer for 2 minutes.

4. Serve the curry immediately over warm soba noodles.

PREPARING GINGER (284), **CLEANING MUSHROOMS** (122), **DICING** (119)

RED CURRY SAUCE

Prepared curry pastes can be found in jars in the Asian foods section of many supermarkets or in food shops that specialize in Asian products, if you don't wish to make your own.

MAKES 1½ CUPS

2 tbsp peanut oil	¼ cup minced lemongrass
1 tbsp minced ginger	2 tbsp Red Curry Paste (page 291)
3 garlic cloves, minced	1 cup coconut milk
2 Thai basil leaves, minced	½ tbsp soy sauce
1 single kaffir lime leaf	¼ tsp kosher salt
1 green onion, minced	¼ tsp freshly ground black pepper

1. Heat the oil in a wok or medium saucepan over medium heat. Add the ginger, garlic, basil, lime leaf, green onion, and lemongrass and cook, stirring frequently, over low heat until aromatic, about 2 minutes.

2. Add the curry paste and continue to cook, stirring frequently, until aromatic, about 1 minute more.

3. Add the coconut milk and soy sauce and bring to simmer. Remove from the heat and season with the salt and pepper. The sauce is ready to use, or it may be cooled and stored in a covered container in the refrigerator for up to 4 days.

RATATOUILLE

This classic Provençal dish hails from the south of France, where it makes the most of the Mediterranean bounty of late summer. On a hot day, it can be served cool for a light supper or lunch dish.

MAKES 6 SERVINGS

1 tsp extra-virgin olive oil

¼ cup diced red onion

1 garlic clove, minced

1 tbsp minced shallot

2 tbsp tomato paste

¾ cup chopped plum tomatoes (peeled and seeded)

½ cup diced zucchini

½ cup diced red or green pepper

½ cup diced yellow squash

⅔ cup Vegetable Broth (page 295)

2 tsp shredded basil

1 tsp chopped oregano

¼ tsp kosher salt

¼ tsp freshly ground black pepper

1. Heat the oil in a large pot over medium heat. Add the onion, garlic, and shallot and sauté until the onions are translucent, 3 to 4 minutes.

2. Add the tomato paste and sauté until rust colored, about 5 minutes more. Add the tomatoes, zucchini, pepper, squash, and broth and bring to a gentle simmer over medium-low heat. Cook, stirring occasionally, until the vegetables are tender, about 15 minutes. Season with the basil, oregano, salt, and pepper.

PEELING AND SEEDING TOMATOES (121), **SHREDDING OR CHIFFONADE** (119), **DICING** (119)

PUMPKIN, ZUCCHINI, AND CHICKPEA TAGINE

This is an incredibly flavorful stew, using a potent combination of ground spices to flavor an array of vegetables and legumes. Serve over a bed of Couscous (page 103).

MAKES 6 SERVINGS

2 tbsp olive oil

2 tsp minced ginger

1 cup diced onion

1½ cups diced leeks, white and light green parts only

3 garlic cloves, minced

2 tsp Curry Spice Blend (page 291)

2½ cups diced pumpkin (peeled)

½ cup diced zucchini

3½ cups Vegetable Broth (page 295)

1¾ cups diced eggplant (peeled)

½ cup small-dice carrot

½ cup diced celery

½ cup currants

¼ cup tomato purée

⅓ cup cooked chickpeas (drained and rinsed)

⅓ cup cooked fava beans (drained, rinsed, and peeled)

1 tbsp lemon juice

¼ tsp kosher salt

GARNISH

2 tsp grated lemon zest

1. Heat the oil in a large soup pot over medium heat. Add the ginger, onion, leeks, and garlic and cook, stirring frequently, over low heat until the onions are limp and translucent, 4 to 5 minutes. Add the spice blend and sauté until aromatic, about 1 minute.

2. Add the pumpkin, zucchini, and just enough of the broth to cover the vegetables, and cook over medium heat for about 10 minutes.

3. Add the eggplant, carrot, celery, currants, tomato purée, and the remaining broth and simmer until all the vegetables are tender, about 25 minutes.

4. Stir in the chickpeas and fava beans. Season with the lemon juice and salt. Cover and cook until heated completely. Garnish with the lemon zest.

PREPARING GINGER (284), **CLEANING LEEKS** (120), **STEWING AND BRAISING VEGETABLES** (125), **ZESTING AND JUICING CITRUS** (284), **COOKING DRIED LEGUMES** (95), **BOILING, BLANCHING, AND PARBOILING VEGETABLES** (123)

GRITS AND GREENS

The tofu gives this dish a smoky flavor. Carnivores can substitute bacon for a similar effect.

MAKES 6 SERVINGS

GRITS

1 tsp corn oil

1 tbsp minced onion

1 tbsp minced green onion

6 cups Chicken or Vegetable Broth (page 294) or as needed

1 cup coarse stone-ground grits

½ tsp kosher salt

¼ tsp freshly ground black pepper

GREENS

2 bunches collard greens, cut into strips

2 tbsp corn oil

⅔ cup minced onion

1 garlic clove, minced

2 cups Chicken or Vegetable Broth (page 294)

2 oz smoked tofu, diced

½ tsp kosher salt

¼ tsp freshly ground black pepper

1. For the grits, heat the oil in a large saucepan over medium-high heat. Add the onion and green onion and cook, stirring frequently, over low heat until they are tender and aromatic, 3 to 4 minutes.

2. Add the broth and bring to a boil. Slowly add the grits, stirring constantly. Return to a boil and immediately reduce the heat to medium-low.

3. Simmer gently until the grits are thick and soft, 20 to 30 minutes, adding more broth as needed. Season with the salt and pepper. Keep the grits very hot while you prepare the greens.

4. For the greens, bring a large pot of salted water to a boil. Add the greens, stirring a few times to submerge them, and cook until they are bright green and wilted, about 5 minutes. Drain and reserve.

5. Heat the oil in a large pot over medium heat. Add the onion and garlic and cook, stirring frequently, until soft, 3 to 4 minutes.

6. Add the greens and broth and reduce the heat to medium-low. Cover and simmer gently until the greens are tender, about 30 minutes. Add the tofu and continue to simmer until the tofu is very hot, 2 to 3 minutes. Season with the salt and pepper. Serve the greens immediately with the grits.

PREPARING SPINACH AND LEAFY GREENS [121], **SHREDDING OR CHIFFONADE** [119]

PAPADZULES with Roasted Tomato Salsa

This Mayan–inspired recipe is an enchilada-style dish known for its zesty sauce made from pumpkin seeds.

MAKES 6 SERVINGS

PUMPKIN SEED SAUCE

5 cups Vegetable Broth (page 295) or water

1 small onion, peeled and halved

2 serranos, cut in half

1 sprig epazote (or 6 sprigs cilantro)

1½ cups shelled raw pumpkin seeds

PAPADZULES

Twelve 6-in flour tortillas

4 cups chopped spinach (blanched and squeezed dry), loosely packed

3 hard-cooked eggs, chopped

¾ cup Tomato Salsa (page 304)

1. For the sauce, heat the broth in a large saucepan over medium heat. Add the onion, serranos, and epazote and bring to a simmer over medium-high heat. Simmer until flavorful, about 15 minutes. Strain and reserve, discarding the solids. Keep the broth warm.

2. Toast the pumpkin seeds in a dry skillet over medium heat until they "puff." Do not let them turn brown. Pour them onto a cool plate immediately to stop the cooking. Grind the pumpkin seeds in a mortar and pestle, spice grinder, or food processor, working in batches, until the seeds have a coarse, mealy texture. Transfer to a shallow bowl.

3. Sprinkle about ¼ cup of the reserved broth over the pumpkin seed meal and mix with your fingertips until a thick, heavy paste forms, adding a few more tablespoons of the broth as needed. Continue to work the paste with your fingertips; the oil from the pumpkin seeds will start to separate. Tilt the bowl so the oil collects on one side and pour it out into a small bowl; reserve until you are ready to serve the papadzules.

4. Transfer the pumpkin seed paste to a saucepan and add the remaining broth. Whisk well to combine, then bring to a simmer over medium heat. The sauce will be very thick and may appear curdled. Keep warm.

5. For the papadzules, preheat the oven 250°F. Wrap the tortillas in a clean cloth and heat them in the oven until they are soft and pliable, about 5 minutes. Meanwhile, thin the warm pumpkin seed sauce with a little water to a light, coating consistency. Top each tortilla with some spinach, egg (reserve some for garnish), and pumpkin seed sauce. Roll the tortilla around the filling.

6. Arrange the papadzules on a warmed plate and top lightly with pumpkin seed sauce. Ladle the salsa over the top and serve at once, garnished with the reserved egg.

TOASTING SPICES, NUTS, AND SEEDS (290), **PREPARING SPINACH AND LEAFY GREENS** (121)

STUFFED CABBAGE ROLLS

To enjoy these rolls as a main dish, serve them on a bed of Lentil Ragoût (page 109). Garnish with chopped tomatoes and chopped chives. Try preparing alternate stuffings for this roll: Add diced tofu, cooked ground turkey, or diced vegetables to the filling for a different effect.

MAKES 6 SERVINGS

1 large head savoy cabbage

2 tbsp vegetable oil

¼ cup minced onion

1¾ cups brown rice

3½ cups Vegetable Broth (page 295)

1 tbsp grated orange zest

1 tbsp chopped thyme

¼ tsp kosher salt

¼ tsp freshly ground black pepper

1½ cups Tomato Coulis (page 298); see Note

1. Preheat the oven to 325°F.

2. Carefully separate the cabbage leaves. Bring a large pot of salted water to a rolling boil over high heat. Add the cabbage leaves and cook until they tender and pliable, about 2 minutes. Drain the leaves in a colander, rinse with cold water until cool to the touch, and drain once more. Reserve 12 whole large leaves and julienne the remaining cabbage.

3. Heat the oil in a medium ovenproof saucepan over medium heat. Add the onion and sauté until translucent, 4 to 5 minutes. Add the rice and toss to coat with the oil. Add the broth, orange zest, thyme, salt, pepper, and julienned cabbage and bring to a simmer over medium-low heat.

4. Cover the pot tightly and cook in the oven until the rice is tender and has absorbed all the liquid, 35 to 40 minutes. Fluff with a fork.

5. Place about ½ cup of the rice mixture on each large cabbage leaf. Fold the sides of the leaf in toward the center and roll up into cylinders to completely enclose the rice. Place the filled cabbage leaves in a baking dish. Pour the tomato coulis over the top, cover the dish, and bake until the cabbage is very tender and the filling is very hot, about 20 minutes. Serve immediately.

NOTE: Add more vegetables to the Tomato Coulis for more texture and flavor. For the recipe in the photo, we added about 1 cup gently sautéed onions.

ZESTING CITRUS (284), **BOILING, BLANCHING, AND PARBOILING VEGETABLES** (123)

PORTOBELLOS with Tuscan Bean Salad and Celery Juice

Portobellos are a perfect vehicle for stuffing. Our Tuscan Bean Salad is delicious, but the mushrooms would be equally good stuffed with Ratatouille (page 131) or Roasted Corn and Black Beans (page 148).

MAKES 6 SERVINGS

6 portobello mushrooms

1 tbsp olive oil

Tuscan Bean Salad (recipe follows)

GARNISH

¼ cup celery juice

¾ cup shredded radicchio

1 tbsp chopped cilantro

1. Preheat the oven to 350°F and prepare a grill for a medium fire.

2. Place the mushrooms on a baking sheet and brush with the olive oil. Tent with foil (this traps some of the steam they release and helps to cook them evenly) and bake until tender, 15 to 20 minutes. Remove the mushrooms from the oven and finish on the grill, about 2 minutes on each side, or until the mushrooms are nicely browned.

3. Cut each mushroom on the diagonal. Serve with the bean salad, and garnish with a generous drizzle of celery juice, radicchio, and cilantro.

TUSCAN BEAN SALAD

MAKES 6 SERVINGS

⅓ cup cooked white beans (page 94)

⅔ cup small-dice carrot

½ cup small-dice celery

2 tbsp small-dice red pepper

2 tbsp small-dice yellow pepper

¼ cup small-dice green onion

⅔ cup Vinaigrette-Style Dressing (page 292; see Note)

1 tbsp chopped chives

1 tbsp chopped parsley

½ tsp kosher salt

¼ tsp freshly ground black pepper

Combine all the ingredients in a large bowl. Marinate at room temperature for 2 hours.

NOTE Substitute champagne vinegar for red wine vinegar in the Vinaigrette-Style Dressing recipe.

COOKING DRIED LEGUMES (95), **CLEANING MUSHROOMS** (122), **SHREDDING OR CHIFFONADE** (119), **DICING** (119)

Vegetable Side Dishes

HARICOTS VERTS with Walnuts

For additional flavor, try dressing the finished green beans with a little
bit of walnut oil, which has a rich, nutty aroma and flavor.

MAKES 6 SERVINGS

½ lb haricots verts, trimmed

1 tsp olive oil

1 tbsp minced shallot

1 garlic clove, minced

2 tbsp chopped toasted walnuts

¼ tsp kosher salt

Pinch freshly ground black pepper

1. Bring a large pot of water to a simmer. Add the haricots verts and cook until tender, about 4 minutes. Drain the beans, reserving about ⅓ cup of the cooking liquid.

2. Heat the oil in a small sauté pan over medium-low heat. Add the shallots and garlic and sauté until the shallots are translucent, 2 to 3 minutes.

3. Place the beans with the shallots, garlic, reserved cooking liquid, walnuts, salt, and pepper in a large bowl and toss to coat.

TOASTING SPICES, NUTS, AND SEEDS (290), **BOILING, BLANCHING, AND PARBOILING VEGETABLES** (123)

SAFFRON CAULIFLOWER AND ONIONS

Saffron, the collected stamens of crocus flowers, gives this dish incredible flavor and
a beautiful yellow color. It's a very expensive spice, but a little goes a long way.

MAKES 6 SERVINGS

1 tbsp olive oil

1⅔ cups pearl onions, peeled

1 garlic clove, minced

2¾ cups cauliflower florets

1 cup water

⅓ cup dry white wine

2 tbsp lemon juice

½ tsp saffron threads

½ tsp kosher salt

Pinch freshly ground black pepper

1 Spice Sachet (page 285), including 1 tsp coriander seeds and 2 extra bay leaves

1. Heat the oil in a medium saucepan over medium heat. Add the onions and cook until tender and deep gold, about 12 minutes. Add the garlic and sauté until aromatic, about 1 minute.

2. Stir in the remaining ingredients. Cover and continue to cook over low heat until the vegetables are tender, about 15 minutes. Remove the sachet before serving.

JUICING CITRUS (285), **SAUTÉING AND STIR-FRYING VEGETABLES** (124)

BRUSSELS SPROUTS with Mustard Glaze

Make sure to sort out any exceptionally large or small sprouts, as
they will not cook evenly or in the same amount of time.

MAKES 6 SERVINGS

6 cups Brussels sprouts, trimmed

½ cup Jus Lié (page 296)

2 tsp whole-grain mustard

1. Bring a large pot of water to a boil. Add the Brussels sprouts and boil until tender, 3 to 5 minutes. Drain.

2. Combine the jus lié with the mustard in a large sauté pan and heat over medium heat. Add the Brussels sprouts and toss to coat. Serve them very hot.

BOILING, BLANCHING, AND PARBOILING VEGETABLES (123)

STEAMED SPINACH with Garlic and Pernod

Pernod, a relative to the Greek ouzo, is an anise-flavored liquor. Its licorice flavor is the perfect complement to this garlicky spinach dish.

MAKES 6 SERVINGS

1 tsp extra-virgin olive oil

2 garlic cloves, minced

2 tsp minced shallot

2 bunches spinach leaves

2 tsp Pernod

¼ tsp freshly ground black pepper

¼ tsp kosher salt

1. Heat the oil in a large sauté pan over medium heat. Add the garlic and shallot and sauté until translucent, 2 to 3 minutes. Add the spinach, along with any water still clinging to the leaves from washing them. If the leaves are very dry, add a few spoonfuls of water to the pan. Cover tightly and steam until the leaves are barely wilted. Drain any excess water.

2. Drizzle the Pernod over the spinach and season with the salt and pepper. Toss and serve while very hot.

PREPARING SPINACH AND LEAFY GREENS (121)

OPPOSITE: Steamed Spinach with Garlic and Pernod (foreground), Braised Black-Eyed Peas (middle; page 108), and Herb-Breaded Chicken with Creamy Mustard Sauce (background; page 164)

ARTICHOKES AND MUSHROOMS in White Wine Sauce

Use a good dry white wine to best complement the buttery flavor of
the artichokes and the earthiness of the mushrooms.

MAKES 6 SERVINGS

1 tbsp olive oil

3⅓ cups halved white mushrooms

1 garlic clove, minced

1 tbsp tomato paste

6 artichoke hearts, halved

1 cup water

⅔ cup dry white wine

2 tbsp lemon juice

2 bay leaves

1 tsp coriander seeds

1 sprig thyme

1. Heat the oil in a medium saucepan over medium-high heat. Add the mushrooms and cook, stirring occasionally, over medium heat until tender, about 4 minutes. Add the garlic and cook until aromatic, about 1 minute. Stir in the tomato paste and continue to cook until the mixture has a sweet aroma, about 1 minute.

2. Add the artichokes, water, wine, lemon juice, bay leaves, coriander, and thyme, cover, and continue to cook over low heat until the artichokes are tender, 15 to 20 minutes. Lift the artichokes and mushrooms from the cooking liquid with a slotted spoon and set aside. Continue to simmer the cooking liquid until it thickens enough to lightly coat the back of a spoon and is very flavorful, about 5 minutes. Return the artichokes and mushrooms to the sauce and simmer until heated through. Serve immediately.

PREPARING ARTICHOKES (121), **CLEANING MUSHROOMS** (122), **JUICING CITRUS** (285)

MOROCCAN-STYLE ROASTED VEGETABLES

You can choose a number of vegetables to add to this dish: Chunks of fresh
tomato, zucchini, eggplant, or mushrooms would all be good choices.

MAKES 6 SERVINGS

1 large red onion, sliced about ¼ inch thick

2 red peppers, quartered

2 small zucchini, quartered lengthwise

3 leeks, quartered lengthwise

2 tsp extra-virgin olive oil

¼ tsp kosher salt

¼ tsp freshly ground black pepper

1 tsp Harissa (page 300)

1 medium sweet potato, quartered lengthwise

1. Preheat the oven to 400°F.

2. Place the onion, red peppers, zucchini, and leeks in a bowl, drizzle with the olive oil, and toss until the vegetables are lightly coated. Season with the salt and pepper. Transfer to a roasting pan or baking sheet.

3. Place the harissa in a small bowl. Add 1 teaspoon water and stir to combine. Pour the diluted harissa over the sweet potato and toss to coat evenly. Add the sweet potato to the roasting pan with the other vegetables.

4. Tent the vegetables with foil (this traps some of the steam they release and helps to cook them evenly) and place them in the oven. Roast the vegetables in the oven until they are tender, about 20 minutes. Remove the foil and roast uncovered until the vegetables are fully cooked and lightly browned, 10 to 12 minutes more. Serve warm.

CLEANING LEEKS (120)

CARAMELIZED PEARL ONIONS

Pearl onions are a classic addition to stews and braises. In this recipe, they are the starring ingredient, made both rich and savory by adding a touch of sugar and a bit of butter.

MAKES 4 SERVINGS

2 tsp butter

⅔ cup cooked and peeled white pearl onions

1 tsp sugar

¼ tsp kosher salt

Pinch freshly ground black pepper

Melt the butter in a large sauté pan over medium heat. Add the onions and caramelize slowly, turning often, 5 to 7 minutes. Add the sugar and allow the onions to glaze. Season with the salt and pepper.

BRAISED BELGIAN ENDIVE

Belgian endives are deliberately protected from light as they grow, eliminating production of chlorophyll to produce pale, satiny heads. Choose tight heads that show no scars or other blemishes. The leaves should be closed into a tight point and should have a pale ivory color, shading to a light yellow-green at the tips.

MAKES 6 SERVINGS

3 heads Belgian endive

1 tsp vegetable oil

1 tsp unsalted butter

3 tbsp diced onion

2 tbsp diced carrot

2 tbsp diced celery

⅓ cup dry white wine

2½ cups Vegetable Broth (page 295) or water

2 sprigs thyme

1 bay leaf

2 tsp lemon juice

¼ tsp kosher salt

¼ tsp freshly ground black pepper

1. Preheat the oven to 350°F (optional).

2. Cut the endive in half lengthwise and trim some of the core away (there should still be enough of the core to hold the leaves together). Trim away any browned edges or bruised outer leaves.

3. Heat the oil and butter in a large skillet over high heat. Add the endive, cut side down, and cook on the first side until golden, about 2 minutes. Turn and cook on the second side, 2 to 3 minutes more. Remove from the pan and reserve.

4. Add the onion, carrot, and celery to the pan and sauté over medium heat until the onions are translucent, 3 to 4 minutes. Add the wine, stir well, and let the wine cook almost completely away, about 2 minutes. Return the endive to the pan, add the broth (it will not completely cover the endive), and bring to a simmer. Add the thyme and bay leaf, cover, and finish cooking over low heat (or in the oven) until the endive is tender enough to pierce easily with the tip of a paring knife, 20 to 25 minutes. Add a little more broth or water if the dish starts to get dry.

5. Season with the lemon juice, salt, and pepper. Serve immediately.

JUICING CITRUS (285), **STEWING AND BRAISING VEGETABLES** (125), **DICIING** (119)

ROASTED CORN AND BLACK BEANS

Roasting corn in the husk brings out its inherent sweetness and is very simple to do. Pairing brilliant yellow corn kernels with black beans produces a stunning dish. Serve it as a side dish, or combine it with steamed grains like brown rice, quinoa, or barley for a hearty entrée.

MAKES 6 SERVINGS

1 tsp olive oil

¼ cup diced red onion

1 garlic clove, minced

1 tsp minced jalapeño

1¼ cups Roasted Corn Kernels (recipe follows)

⅔ cup cooked black beans (page 94)

¼ cup chopped tomato (peeled and seeded)

2 tsp lime juice

¼ tsp kosher salt

2 tsp chopped cilantro

1. Heat the oil in a large pot over medium heat. Add the onion, garlic, and jalapeño and sauté, stirring occasionally, until the onions are translucent, about 3 minutes.

2. Add the corn, beans, tomato, lime juice, and salt and sauté until the mixture is heated completely, about 5 minutes. Remove from the heat and stir in the cilantro. Serve at once.

ROASTING AND BAKING VEGETABLES (124), **PEELING AND SEEDING TOMATOES** (121)

ROASTED CORN KERNELS

MAKES 2 CUPS

8 ears corn, in their husks

1 tsp freshly ground black pepper

1 tbsp chopped parsley

1 tbsp chopped chervil

1. Preheat the oven to 400°F.

2. Pull the husks away from the ears of corn, loosening the husk but still leaving it attached. Pull off the silk. Sprinkle each ear with the pepper, parsley, and chervil. Pull the husks back into place to wrap up the corn and tie them closed with twine. Dampen the husks with water.

3. Place on a baking sheet and roast in the oven until tender, about 15 minutes. Cut the corn from the cob.

WORKING WITH CORN ON THE COB (121)

SPOON PUDDING

Baking this savory custard in a hot water bath helps the egg mixture retain its silky texture as it cooks.

MAKES 6 SERVINGS

⅓ cup diced onion

1 garlic clove, minced

⅓ cup diced red pepper

1 jalapeño, seeded and minced

⅔ cup Chicken Broth (page 294)

⅔ cup corn kernels

1 tsp chopped thyme

1 tsp chopped oregano

1 tsp chopped rosemary

1 tsp freshly ground black pepper

1 recipe Country Corn Bread (page 262), crumbled

3 large egg whites

Vegetable oil spray

1. Preheat the oven to 375°F.

2. Cook the onion, garlic, red pepper, and jalapeño in 2 tablespoons of the broth in a saucepan, stirring frequently, over low heat until the onions are translucent, 3 to 4 minutes. Add the remaining broth and reduce to half its original volume. Add the corn and bring to a boil.

3. Remove the pan from the heat and add the thyme, oregano, rosemary, and pepper. Cool slightly and stir in the corn bread and egg whites.

4. Lightly spray a 9-inch baking dish or six 6-oz ramekins with oil. Pour the pudding batter into the baking dish. (Fill individual ramekins two-thirds full.) Put the baking dish or ramekins inside a large baking dish or roasting pan and add enough boiling water to come halfway up the sides of the ramekins to make a hot water bath. Bake the pudding(s) until completely set, about 25 minutes for a large pudding, 18 minutes for individual puddings.

5. Let the pudding rest for 10 minutes before serving.

DICING (119), **WORKING WITH CORN ON THE COB** (121),

BOMBAY-STYLE POTATOES

Yukon gold potatoes are known for their creamy, buttery flesh. The addition of curry powder livens up this otherwise simple dish.

MAKES 6 SERVINGS

2½ cups quartered Yukon gold potatoes (peeled)

2 tsp vegetable oil

2 tsp minced onion

⅔ cup diced Granny Smith apple (peeled and cored)

1 tbsp Curry Spice Blend (page 291)

2 tsp all-purpose flour

2⅓ cups water

¼ tsp kosher salt

1. Place the potatoes in a pot with cold water to cover by 2 inches. Salt the water. Bring to a simmer over medium heat. Cover and continue to simmer until the potatoes are easily pierced with a fork, 10 to 12 minutes. Drain and transfer to a large bowl.

2. Heat the oil in a small saucepan over medium heat. Add the onions and apples and cook, stirring frequently, over low heat until the onions are translucent, 4 to 5 minutes.

3. Add the curry powder and flour and sauté until lightly toasted. Add the water and salt and simmer for 30 minutes.

4. Combine the curry mixture and the potatoes. Serve hot.

BOILING, BLANCHING, AND PARBOILING VEGETABLES (123)

CELERIAC AND POTATO PURÉE

Celeriac, also known as celery root, is less starchy than other root vegetables. It lightens up this purée without sacrificing flavor.

MAKES 6 SERVINGS

2²/₃ cups large-dice all-purpose potato (peeled)

1²/₃ cups diced celeriac

¼ cup nonfat milk

2 tbsp heavy cream

2 tbsp unsalted butter

2 roasted garlic cloves, mashed

½ tsp kosher salt

1. Preheat the oven to warm.

2. Bring two pots of water to a simmer. Add the potato and celeriac separately to each and boil until both are fork-tender, 10 to 12 minutes. Drain, and place the potatoes and celeriac on a baking sheet. Warm in the oven to steam dry, about 5 minutes.

3. Bring the milk, cream, and butter to a simmer in a small saucepan over low heat. Keep warm over very low heat.

4. Purée the hot potatoes and celeriac with a ricer or in a food mill. Place in a bowl and stir in the roasted garlic.

5. Whip the hot milk mixture into the potato mixture. Season with the salt. Serve at once.

ROASTING GARLIC (284), **DICING** (119)

SWEET POTATO CAKES

Sweet potatoes are richer in vitamins than any other potato. They are an excellent source of fiber, vitamin A, vitamin C, and vitamin B_6.

MAKES 6 SERVINGS

1 medium Idaho potato, peeled and quartered

1 medium sweet potato, peeled and quartered

$2/3$ cup bread crumbs

1 tbsp mayonnaise

$1/4$ cup nonfat milk

1 tbsp chopped chives

1 tbsp chopped dill

$1/2$ tsp freshly ground black pepper

1 tbsp chopped capers (drained and rinsed)

1. Preheat the oven to 475°F.

2. Place the potatoes in a pot with enough cold water to cover by 2 inches. Salt the water. Bring the water to a simmer over medium heat. Cover and continue to simmer until the potatoes are easily pierced with a fork, 10 to 12 minutes. Drain, and return them to the pan over low heat until no more steam rises from them.

3. Purée the hot potatoes with a ricer or in a food mill. Cool to room temperature.

4. Combine the remaining ingredients with the potatoes.

5. Form the mixture into small cakes. Arrange on a baking sheet lined with parchment paper.

6. Bake the cakes until heated completely and lightly browned, about 8 minutes.

CHAPTER SIX

Poultry and Meat

In the United States, meat has long been the centerpiece of a meal. Beef has traditionally been the most popular choice, but as Americans become aware of the effects of eating too much saturated fat, other options have made inroads. Pork, raised to be leaner than it once was, and chicken are the most common alternatives. Lamb, veal, turkey, game hens, and game have rich, robust flavors yet are still relatively lean.

Although red meat in particular can be high in fat, saturated fat, and cholesterol, some cuts are quite lean. By learning which cuts of meat are naturally lean, how to reduce the fat in cuts that aren't, and which sources of lean protein can be used in lieu of fattier ones, you can create menus that are healthy and delicious.

Purchasing and Storing Meats

Meats should be chosen based on the leanness of particular cuts and trimmed of as much surface fat as possible before cooking. In general, loin and round cuts from meats are the leanest choices.

The grade of meat can be an indication of fat content. The USDA standards for grading rely upon a number of factors. One is the amount of marbling—the streaks of fat found within the muscle. In the case of beef, Choice grade may be a better selection than Prime. The quality is still excellent in Choice, but there is generally less marbling throughout all the cuts.

Specialty breeds like Limousin, Belgian Blue, Chianina, and Chiangus are naturally leaner than beef from the more typical breeds. They can be substantially lower in fat and calories than standard USDA Choice beef, which must meet standards of quality but does not have to identify the specific breed of meat.

To find out if any of these specialty breeds are available in your area, check with your local meat purveyors. You may also be able to find grass-fed meats, raised in open pasture and free of antibiotics and hormones. Conventionally raised meats are grain-fed and held in

pens known as feedlots, rather than foraging for grass in a pasture. Grass-fed meat is usually organic and free of steroids and antibiotics, as well as lower in total fat and cholesterol. Some studies suggest that these meats have a significantly greater amount of omega-3s. On the negative side, however, grass-fed meats are often described as having strong or unpleasant flavors and aromas, perhaps because we have become accustomed to the relatively mild flavors of conventionally raised meats.

Keep in mind the option of using game instead of "traditional" meats. Many game meats have bolder, more interesting flavors and can be substantially lower in fat and cholesterol than their domestic counterparts. Several game breeds, such as ostrich, emu, venison, and bison, are farm raised and readily available.

All meats should be refrigerated as soon as you get home. Marinating should happen in the refrigerator. Discard marinades after use to prevent contamination.

LOW-FAT GAME MEAT

Animals in the wild rarely become fat. The limited fat stores they accumulate to protect them through a cold winter are usually deposited in layers just below the skin to act as both insulation and as an energy reservoir—the meat has little marbling. Traditional game recipes often call for braising or stewing to counteract any dryness in the meat, but you can cook some cuts of game by grilling, roasting, or broiling—the tenderloin and rib of deer, elk, bison, or antelope all respond beautifully to these dry heat techniques.

Poultry

Free-range birds are raised in ample outdoor space and given feed free of antibiotics and steroids. These birds are usually more expensive than commercially produced chickens that are fed a diet full of antibiotics, growth enhancers, and other ingredients to promote rapid weight gain and protect the chicken from disease. Many people prefer using free-range products whenever possible (see Free-Range Livestock and Poultry, page 156).

Most of the fat found in poultry is in the skin. Leaving the skin on during roasting, grilling, and sautéing does not increase the fat in the meat of the bird; rather it helps the meat retain its natural juices. Herbs and other aromatics may also be placed under the skin to flavor the meat during cooking. If the skin is left on while roasting the bird, thoroughly degrease the pan drippings before using the fond as a sauce (see page 159). When steaming, poaching, or simmering poultry, remove the skin to avoid incorporating the fat into the cooking liquids that are usually served as part of the dish.

PURCHASING AND STORING POULTRY

With its mild flavor, reputation for leanness, and versatility, poultry is one of the most popular entrée options. Chicken, duck, turkey, Cornish game hens, geese, and game birds like quail, squab, and pheasant all fall into this category. Like meat, poultry is an excellent source of high-quality protein, and it often contains minerals like iron, zinc, phosphorus, and selenium, as well as several B vitamins. Unlike meat, which often has fat marbling the flesh, most of the fat in poultry is in or near the skin. When the skin is removed and discarded before eating, most forms of poultry are exceptionally low in saturated fat.

Whole birds are labeled with a specific name—broiler, fryer, roaster—determined by the bird's breed, age, sex, and weight. These distinctions are helpful in choosing a cooking method, because the younger the bird, the more naturally tender it is. Mature birds, like well-exercised cuts of meat, need longer, gentler cooking techniques to turn out tender and flavorful.

Other marketing terms include *natural*, *free-range*, *organic*, and *fresh*. These terms often do not mean what you might think. "Fresh" poultry, for example, may have been stored at temperatures as low as 26°F—cold enough to freeze the meat. "Free-range" means that the bird was not penned, but it does not automatically mean that the bird is organic.

Healthy Techniques for Cooking Meats and Poultry

There is no need to ban beef or chicken from your table if you enjoy them. The key, as with most things to do with healthy cooking, is exercising control. Keep portion sizes small, or enjoy meats and poultry less often during the month to keep your meat consumption moderate, and choose a technique that takes full advantage of their flavors and textures.

MARINATING

You can marinate a wide variety of foods: vegetables, fish, meats, and poultry. There has been some concern in recent years that cooking high-protein foods at very high temperatures can lead to the development of harmful compounds on the surface of the meats. However, applying a marinade reduces the risk. Marinades include an acidic component, like vinegar or citrus, that gives fish a firmer texture as well as adding flavor.

FREE-RANGE LIVESTOCK AND POULTRY

At one time, cattle and sheep were allowed to graze in pastures and chickens meandered from coop to barnyard. Modern techniques in animal husbandry, however, make use of practices that are more concerned with high production and yield rather than flavor, safety, and humane treatment of animals.

Birds such as chickens and turkeys are carefully bred to produce a greater percentage of breast meat to meet consumer demand. Their diets include doses of antibiotics, growth enhancers, and ingredients intended to ward off the numerous diseases to which poultry are prone, as well as to promote rapid weight gain.

Cattle, pigs, chickens, and other animals may be kept in pens or feedlots that inhibit mobility. They may be fed doses of antibiotics, growth enhancers, steroids, and substances they are unable to digest, as well as ingredients intended to ward off the numerous diseases to which they are prone. Although there is no documented evidence that the residues from steroids and antibiotics in the animals' flesh actually cause cancer or other illnesses in humans, there is growing public concern about that potential. Also being raised are ethical objections to the crowded conditions in which the animals live. As a result, free-range birds have become increasingly popular with consumers. The term *free-range* conjures up images of birds roaming freely, but in fact this is often far from reality.

Although most people think of poultry when they hear the term *free-range*, it can apply to other meat animals as well. The only requirement that the USDA has for birds or livestock labeled free-range is that they are not kept in pens. There are no requirements pertaining to the size of the area, the number of birds per square foot, or the type of feed.

Farmers and ranchers who are willing to spend the money to give their animals space to move may also spend money to ensure that they are given appropriate feed and are not given hormones or steroids to speed up growth. Meat from these animals often costs considerably more than that of their conventionally raised counterparts. Some would argue that the improvement in nutritional value, flavor, and texture is worth the cost. Free-range birds appear to be lower in fat than their confined counterparts. As to whether or not allowing the birds and livestock access to the outdoors lowers their stress levels and results in better flavor, there is no definitive answer.

When you use a spice blend as a dry rub (also called a dry marinade) to coat food, typically you'll refrigerate the food after application to allow it to absorb the flavors. Very often these rubs contain some salt to help intensify all the flavors in the dish. Dry rubs may be left on the food during cooking or they may be scraped away first.

To use a marinade, combine the marinade and meat in a resealable plastic bag or shallow container. Turn the meat to coat it evenly, cover, and marinate it in the refrigerator for 30 minutes to overnight, depending on the size of the pieces and the level of acidity in the marinade. During longer marinating times, turn the meat once or twice. If a recipe calls for using part of the marinade in an accompanying sauce, reserve some of it before adding the meat or boil the marinade for several minutes after removing raw meat.

GRILLING

Grilling (and broiling, too), with its dry, direct heat and quick cooking times, is ideal for naturally tender portions of meat, poultry, or fish. Trim meat and poultry of excess fat and, if needed, pound the pieces lightly to an even thickness. Fish may be left whole, with the skin on. Meatier fish, like swordfish, may be cut into steaks. Marinate foods as your recipe suggests. Keep all foods cold until you are ready to grill them. Season with salt and pepper, or rub it with spices. For the best appearance and flavor, as well as to prevent sticking, lightly coat with oil before grilling or broiling.

1. **PREPARE THE GRILL.**
   Grills must be well cleaned and maintained. Scour the grill well with a stiff brush between uses to remove any charred particles. Preheat a gas grill, or use a chimney starter to start coals and let smolder until covered with white ash. If using skewers, oil metal ones to prevent sticking, or soak wooden ones to keep them from burning.

2. **PUT THE FOOD ON THE GRILL.**
   Place the better-looking side of the meat or poultry face down on the grill. When the food comes into contact with the heated rods, distinct marks are charred onto its surface. Let cook undisturbed on the first side until it is time to turn it. This develops better flavor and allows the meat or poultry to release naturally from the grill without sticking or tearing. Grill baskets ease turning of multiple items, large items, or delicate items such as fish.

3. **FINISH THE FOOD.**
   Because many grilling sauces and glazes contain sugar (which burns readily), cook the food partially before applying them so that they will caramelize lightly but not burn. Brush a single coat on each side, or build up a thick, crusty coating with several layers. Larger pieces of meat may need to be transferred to a cooler part of the grill to cook through more slowly and evenly. Remove meat, poultry, and fish when slightly underdone, as even thin pieces will retain some heat and continue to cook off the grill.

BROILING

Smaller or more delicate foods, such as cut vegetables or fish fillets, may be broiled more easily than grilled. The heat source for broiling is above, rather than below, the food. Preheat the broiler and the broiler pan completely first; a hot environment will prevent sticking and help to develop good texture and color. For more details about broiling, see page 186.

SAUTÉING AND DRY SAUTÉING

Sautéing is a natural choice for healthy cooking. Meat and poultry prepared in this manner are cooked quickly in a small amount of fat or oil over medium to high heat. Dry sautéing is the same basic procedure, except that no fat is added to the pan. Choose naturally tender cuts that are thin enough to cook quickly without toughening. Steaks and chops, poultry cuts, and fish fillets or steaks often come to mind when we think of sautéing (or "pan searing" rather than sautéing, especially if there is little or no fat added to the pan while the food cooks).

Sautéing presents a number of opportunities to add flavor. Season before cooking—this could be in form of a marinade, a dry spice rub, or a simple sprinkling of salt and freshly ground pepper. (Salt should be applied sparingly and just before cooking to prevent it from leaching out the food's natural juices.)

As meats and poultry are sautéed, their natural juices become concentrated in the drippings that cook down in the pan, forming what is referred to as the *fond*. Adding a flavorful liquid to the pan after the sautéed item has been removed dissolves the fond and allows the flavors to be recaptured in a sauce; this step is known as *deglazing the pan*. Pan sauces can be finished in an infinite number of ways. Sauces should be based on vegetables, vegetable or fruit purées, or reductions, but that does not mean you cannot use some high-fat ingredients like butter, cream, or cheese in small amounts to enrich the sauce, as long as those additions are kept moderate.

1. **SELECT THE INGREDIENTS.**
   Choose lean and tender rib, loin, or leg cuts, or poultry breasts. Thicker cuts should be sliced or pounded thin for quick cooking. Season with salt and pepper, spice blends, or rubs. Be sure to coat evenly and shake off any excess.

2. **PREHEAT A SAUTÉ PAN.**
   Get the pan hot before you add the food for dry sautés, or the oil for classic sautés. If the pan is already hot, the oil will heat up as soon as it hits the pan and then practically bond to the surface of the pan. You'll need less oil, foods will stick less, and you'll get

   a great color and flavor. A well-seasoned or nonstick pan also demands significantly less oil. Heat the oil until it shimmers for red meat; it may be less hot for other meats, poultry, or fish.

3. **ADD THE FOOD TO THE PAN.**
   If your meat or poultry has a "better-looking side," put that side down first. Make sure that each piece comes in direct contact with the hot fat and avoid overlapping pieces or overcrowding the pan; otherwise your meat or poultry will steam in its own moisture instead of sauté. Let it cook undisturbed until it is time to turn it; large pieces should be turned only once, but smaller

MORE THAN FLAVORING

Recent research indicates that marinades do more than just boost flavor. They can yield a significant health benefit.

All high-temperature cooking methods, including grilling, broiling, roasting, and frying, can result in potentially carcinogenic substances forming on foods. Grilling is particularly dangerous, because fat dripping on hot coals creates smoke that rises back to the foods. Scientists at the Lawrence Livermore National Laboratory in California found that marinating foods for as little as 5 minutes before grilling can dramatically reduce the presence of some carcinogens. The researchers tested commercial marinades as well as a homemade version; all produced the same positive results.

To lessen the potential for formation of carcinogens, partially cook foods using other methods. Poach, simmer, or steam foods, then finish them on the grill, or mark them briefly on the grill and finish them in the oven.

pieces, such as strips of meat or chicken breast, may be tossed or turned more often. If the sautéed meat takes more than 2 or 3 minutes on each side, you should lower the heat so that it cooks through without becoming charred on the outside.

4. MAKE A PAN SAUCE.
Remove the meat from the pan and set aside on a warm plate. Pour off all but a thin coating of fat or oil and return the pan to high heat. Add aromatic ingredients or garnishes and cook them briefly to release their flavor. Then deglaze the pan, pouring in liquid. Easy liquid options you may already have on hand include wine, cognac, broth, or water. Use a wooden spoon or spatula to scrape up the flavorful browned bits from the bottom of the pan. Let the liquid reduce to a saucelike consistency, or add a vegetable purée or a cornstarch slurry, if desired, to help thicken the sauce.

BRAISING AND STEWING

Gently cooking foods over low heat in a rich, flavorful liquid transforms tough cuts of meat into tender morsels while creating a thick, flavorful sauce. Braising is used for larger cuts, stewing for bite-sized pieces.

1. SELECT THE INGREDIENTS.
The cooking liquid in a braise or stew usually consists of a rich broth or a combination of a broth and a sauce suited to the main ingredients. If the vegetables will garnish the finished dish, cut them to an even size and shape. However, if they will be strained out of the sauce or puréed to thicken it, cutting them uniformly is less important. A recipe may use roux, reduction, or a starch slurry to thicken the cooking liquid into a sauce.

2. BROWN THE MEAT.
Choose a heavy-gauge pan with a lid that just is just large enough to hold all the ingredients. Season well. Depending on the dish, you may coat meat lightly with flour before searing to help it develop color and thicken the sauce later. Heat the pan, add oil, and sear the meat on all sides to give it an attractive color as well as good flavor. Add onions or leeks to the pan and cook them to the appropriate color—tender and translucent for pale braises and stews or deep golden for brown braises and stews.

3. BRAISE OR STEW THE FOOD.
After you return the main ingredient to the pot, add the liquid. For braises, add enough to come one-third to one-half of the way up the side of the food. The more tender the cut, the less liquid required, since the cooking time will be shorter. For stewing, the food is typically completely covered with liquid. Bring the liquid just to a simmer, not a full boil, to prevent toughening the meat. Adjust the heat as needed to maintain a slow simmer, cover the pan tightly, and finish cooking the braise or stew in a moderate oven or over low direct heat. Stir or baste the dish regularly to keep it evenly moist.

4. FINISH THE SAUCE.
Transfer the meat to a warm plate. Skim off any surface fat on the braising liquid and return it to a simmer. Add any thickeners, such as puréed vegetables or a cornstarch slurry at this point. To thicken the sauce by reduction, simmer it, uncovered, over medium heat until it reaches the desired consistency.

STIR-FRYING

Stir-fried dishes can be great choices for healthy meals because they are often based predominantly on vegetables and grains; high-protein foods like fish or meats are typically added in very small amounts. Sauces included with stir-fried foods are traditionally combinations of intensely flavored liquids thickened with a small amount of cornstarch. As long as soy sauce and sesame oil are used judiciously, these sauces are generally healthy.

Asian stir-frying shares many characteristics with sautéing. Traditionally, Chinese chefs cut ingredients into strips, dice, or shreds and use a wok or bowl-shaped pan that distributes high heat evenly and allows rapid yet gentle stirring. When stir-frying, add food in sequence: Start with foods that require the longest cooking times and finish with those that cook in only a few moments at the end.

SPICY CHICKEN with Apples and Pecans on a Bed of Greens

Apples in various forms combine in this dish for a savory main-course salad. Apple cider is reduced to give it a bit of kick, cider vinegar adds tartness, and fresh apples add texture and coolness to the dish.

MAKES 6 SERVINGS

1½ lb skinless, boneless chicken breast

APPLE CIDER VINAIGRETTE

¾ cup apple cider

2 tbsp cider vinegar

2 tsp Worcestershire sauce

2 tsp Tabasco sauce

2 tsp chopped thyme

2 tbsp canola oil

APPLE-PECAN SALAD

1½ cups mixed greens (mesclun, spring greens, baby spinach), loosely packed

½ cup julienned endive

½ cup arugula, loosely packed

1½ cups diced Granny Smith apples (cored)

½ cup pecan halves, toasted

1. Trim any visible fat from the chicken and cut away any cartilage or sinew in the breast. Pound the chicken lightly to even out the thickness. Set aside.

2. For the vinaigrette, simmer the apple cider in a small saucepan over medium heat until reduced to one-third its original volume. Pour the cider into a small bowl. Add the vinegar, Worcestershire, Tabasco, and thyme. Slowly whisk in the canola oil. Pour 2 tablespoons of the vinaigrette over the chicken breasts, turning to coat them evenly, and reserve the rest to dress the salad.

3. Prepare a grill for a medium-high fire. If using coals, they should be glowing red with a moderate coating of white ash.

4. Place the chicken breasts on the grill. Grill undisturbed on the first side until browned, about 3 minutes. Turn the chicken over and continue grilling until cooked through, 3 to 4 minutes more. Remove from the grill to a pan and let it rest while you prepare the salad.

5. For the salad, place the mixed greens, endive, and arugula in a large bowl and toss with half of the reserved vinaigrette. Transfer to a serving platter or individual plates. Slice the chicken breast into cubes or strips. Top the salad with the chicken, apples, and pecans. Spoon the remaining vinaigrette over the salad and serve.

TOASTING SPICES, NUTS, AND SEEDS (290), **GRILLING** (157), **PREPARING SPINACH AND LEAFY GREENS** (121)

CHICKEN BREAST with Peaches in Zinfandel Wine Sauce

Using fruits in a savory dish is a time-honored custom. Here, we pair the brilliant flavors of ripe peaches with a fruity Zinfandel in the sauce. Try other fruits, including plums or cherries.

MAKES 6 SERVINGS

1½ lb skinless, boneless chicken breast

MARINADE
½ cup apple cider
1 tbsp cider vinegar
2 tsp diced shallot
1 garlic clove, minced

2 tsp canola oil
1 tsp unsalted butter
2 tsp minced shallot
¼ cup Zinfandel
1 cup sliced peaches (peeled and pitted)
1¼ cups Jus Lié (page 296)
1 tsp minced tarragon
⅛ tsp kosher salt, or as needed
⅛ tsp ground black pepper, or as needed

1. Trim any visible fat from the chicken and cut away any cartilage or sinew in the breast. Pound the chicken lightly to even out the thickness. Set aside.

2. For the marinade, combine the cider, vinegar, shallot, and garlic in a bowl. Add the chicken, turning once or twice to coat evenly with the marinade. Cover and marinate in the refrigerator for at least 30 minutes and up to 3 hours.

3. Remove the chicken from the marinade. Drag the pieces along the edge of the bowl to scrape away any excess marinade.

4. Heat a sauté pan over medium-high heat. Add the oil and swirl to coat the pan bottom evenly. Add the chicken smooth side down and sauté undisturbed on the first side until browned, about 2 minutes. (The pieces should not touch or overlap; work in batches or use two pans if needed.) Turn the chicken over and continue sautéing until cooked through, 3 to 4 minutes more. Reduce the heat slightly as you sauté if needed. Transfer the chicken to a dish as it finishes cooking.

5. Return the sauté pan to medium heat and melt the butter. Add the shallots and sauté, stirring occasionally, until they are tender, about 2 minutes. Add the wine and stir well. Simmer until the wine is almost completely cooked away, about 2 minutes. Add the peaches and cook, stirring occasionally, until they are hot and have a developed a bit of color, about 2 minutes. Add the jus lié and any of the juices released by the chicken on the dish. Simmer until the sauce is very hot, about 1 minute. Add the tarragon and taste the sauce. Adjust the seasoning with the salt and pepper.

6. Return the chicken to the pan and turn to coat lightly with the sauce and heat completely. Serve the chicken immediately on a heated platter or individual plates with the sauce.

PREPARING GARLIC (284), **SAUTÉING** (158)

*Jerk Chicken with Mango Salsa
(page 87) and Faro (page 99)*

JERK CHICKEN

You can substitute other meats, such as lean pork or beef, for the chicken thighs we suggest here, but we believe that the texture of thighs is a good match to the intense heat of the grill. Try the chicken with Mango Salsa (page 87), with cilantro instead of chipotle and pine nuts.

MAKES 6 SERVINGS

12 skinless, boneless chicken thighs

½ cup Jerk Rub (page 292)

1. Trim any visible fat from the chicken thighs and cut away any gristle or cartilage. Transfer to a baking dish. Set aside.

2. Spread the jerk rub over all surfaces of the chicken thighs with your fingers. Cover and marinate in the refrigerator for at least 4 and up to 12 hours.

3. Prepare a grill for a medium-high fire. If using coals, they should be glowing red with a moderate coating of white ash.

4. Place the chicken thighs on the grill. Grill undisturbed on the first side until browned, about 4 minutes. Turn the chicken over and continue grilling until cooked through (165°F), 4 to 5 minutes more.

GRILLING (157)

To coat the chicken evenly, toss with the jerk rub in a large plastic bag.

HERB-BREADED CHICKEN with Creamy Mustard Sauce

This dish takes some of its elements from a classic Southern-style fried chicken. A buttermilk-and-herb marinade adds a lot of flavor, and the cornflake-cornmeal crust adds a crunch. Instead of a cream-based country gravy, we've opted for a pungent mustard sauce with just a touch of cream to mellow the flavor. Country Corn Bread (page 262) and sugar snap peas and morels pan-steamed in chicken broth are excellent accompaniments to the chicken.

MAKES 6 SERVINGS

1½ lb skinless, boneless chicken breast

BUTTERMILK-HERB MARINADE

1 cup buttermilk

1 tbsp chopped parsley

2 tbsp chopped tarragon

1 tsp ground black pepper

CORNFLAKE-CORNMEAL CRUST

⅔ cup cornflakes

½ cup cornmeal

1 tbsp chopped parsley

1 tbsp chopped tarragon

1 tbsp chopped chives

¼ tsp kosher salt

1½ cups Creamy Mustard Gravy (page 296)

1. Trim any visible fat from the chicken and cut away any cartilage or sinew in the breast. Set aside.

2. For the marinade, combine the buttermilk, parsley, tarragon, and pepper in a bowl. Add the chicken, turning once or twice to coat evenly with the marinade. Cover and marinate in the refrigerator for at least 30 minutes and up to 3 hours.

3. For the crust, use your hands to crush together and mix the cornflakes, cornmeal, parsley, tarragon, chives, and salt in a shallow bowl or baking dish; the cornflakes should be broken up into small crumbs.

4. Preheat the oven to 375°F. Place a rack in a baking dish to hold the chicken as it bakes.

5. Remove the chicken pieces from the marinade. Drag the pieces along the edge of the bowl to scrape away any excess marinade. Coat the chicken pieces evenly with the cornmeal mixture on all sides and transfer to the baking dish.

6. Bake the chicken until it is cooked through (165°F and firm to the touch) with a golden, crisp exterior, about 20 minutes.

7. Gently heat the mustard gravy in a small saucepan over medium-low heat, and serve with the chicken.

MARINATING (156)

TENDERLOIN OF TURKEY with Mild Ancho Chile Sauce

The combination of flavors in this robust sauce is reminiscent of a Mexican mole sauce. Roasted peppers, garlic, and ancho chiles (or dried poblano peppers) give the sauce a sweet, mildly spicy flavor. You may be able to purchase turkey tenderloins, or simply replace that cut with cutlets of turkey breast. The turkey should be cooked over gentle heat; as the medallions or cutlets cook, their natural juices will reduce on the surface, creating a flavorful glaze.

MAKES 6 SERVINGS

MILD ANCHO CHILE SAUCE

5 dried ancho chiles

¼ cup boiling water

2 tbsp olive oil

¾ cup diced onion

⅓ cup tomato paste

1½ cups diced roasted red peppers

¼ large bulb roasted garlic

1 tbsp brown sugar

1 tbsp white wine vinegar

½ cup Chicken Broth (page 294)

1 cup Jus Lié (page 296)

½ tsp ground cumin

1 tsp dried oregano

¼ tsp ground cinnamon

Pinch cayenne

1½ lb turkey tenderloin, trimmed

1. For the chile sauce, steep the dried chiles in the boiling water until soft, about 30 minutes. Drain the chiles, discarding the water. Remove the stems and seeds and dice the flesh.

2. Heat the olive oil in a medium saucepan over medium heat. Add the onion and sauté until translucent, 4 to 5 minutes. Add the tomato paste and cook until rust colored, about 3 minutes more. Add the chiles, red peppers, garlic, sugar, vinegar, and broth and reduce the heat to a simmer. Add the jus lié, cumin, oregano, cinnamon, and cayenne and simmer for 30 minutes.

3. Remove the sauce from the heat and let it cool slightly before puréeing it in a food processor or blender until smooth. Reserve.

4. Cut the turkey into 6 medallions. Tie butcher's twine around the circumference of each medallion to maintain an even shape and thickness, if necessary.

5. Dry-sauté the turkey medallions in a large skillet over medium-low heat, turning as necessary so that the pieces are an even golden color on all sides and fully cooked (165°F), about 12 minutes total.

6. Remove the turkey from the skillet and keep warm. Add the ancho chile sauce to the skillet and stir well to release any drippings. Simmer over low heat. Return the turkey to the sauce and turn to coat evenly. Serve on a heated platter or individual plates with the sauce.

DRY SAUTÉING (158), **ROASTING AND PEELING PEPPERS** (120), **ROASTING GARLIC** (284)

SPICED TURKEY MEDALLIONS with Tomato-Basil Jus

Turkey is a great option for healthy meals. This dish combines a lean source of protein with two pungent and powerful flavors—tomato and basil. The sauce recipe (page 297) makes more than you will need for this dish, but you can serve it with other meats, such as beef, pork, or game, as well as with chicken. Serve this dish with sautéed mushrooms, steamed broccoli rabe, and fresh pasta (page 64).

MAKES 6 SERVINGS

1½ lb skinless, boneless turkey breast

DRY SPICE MIX

1 tbsp dry mustard

2 tsp dried oregano

1 tsp dried thyme

1 tsp ground celery seed

½ tsp ground coriander

½ tsp kosher salt

½ tsp ground black pepper

¾ cup all-purpose flour (for dredging)

2 tsp peanut oil

1 cup Tomato-Basil Jus (page 297)

¾ cup chopped tomatoes (peeled and seeded)

2 tbsp basil chiffonade

Freshly ground black pepper, as needed

1. To make turkey cutlets from a single piece of breast meat, slice the turkey evenly into 6 pieces about ½ inch thick. Pound each cutlet between sheets of plastic wrap to a thickness of ¼ inch. Transfer to a baking sheet as each piece is pounded.

2. Combine all the ingredients for the spice mix in a medium bowl. Sprinkle the turkey cutlets generously with the spice mix. Place the flour in a shallow bowl and dredge the cutlets in the flour, shaking off the excess. Return them to the baking sheet.

3. Heat a sauté pan over medium heat. Add the oil and swirl to coat the pan evenly. Add the turkey cutlets and sauté until golden brown on the first side, 2 to 3 minutes. (The pieces should not touch or overlap; work in batches or use two pans, if needed.) Turn the cutlets once and finish cooking on the second side, 2 to 3 minutes more. Remove the cutlets from the pan as they finish cooking and keep warm while sautéing the remaining pieces.

4. Return the sauté pan to medium-high heat. Add the jus to the pan and stir well to release any drippings. Simmer the sauce until it is very hot and flavorful. Add the tomatoes and basil and continue to simmer until the tomatoes are heated completely, 2 minutes more. Adjust the seasoning with a little pepper, if needed.

5. Serve the cutlets on heated plates with the sauce.

SAUTÉING (158), **PEELING AND SEEDING TOMATOES** (121), **SHREDDING OR CHIFFONADE** (119)

GRILLED QUAIL Wrapped in Prosciutto with Figs and Wild Mushrooms

Prosciutto is an Italian ham, generally aged and dry-cured. It often is served uncooked, but it provides great flavor and texture to the quail in this grilled dish. This recipe works well with other small game birds, like pheasant or Cornish game hen, as well as with rabbit or chicken pieces.

MAKES 6 SERVINGS

12 very thin slices prosciutto

12 skinless quail, halved

¼ cup dry sherry

2 garlic cloves, minced

½ tsp ground black pepper

2 tbsp diced shallot

1¼ cups Jus Lié (page 296)

¾ cup sliced wild mushrooms

⅓ cup sun-dried figs

1. Cut the prosciutto slices in half; wrap a piece of prosciutto around each quail half and thread on a skewer.

2. Combine the sherry, garlic, pepper, and 1 tablespoon of the shallot in a large shallow pan. Add the skewered wrapped quail and marinate in the refrigerator for 30 minutes.

3. Meanwhile, prepare a grill for a medium-high fire. If using coals, they should be glowing red with a moderate coating of white ash.

4. Remove the quail from the marinade and place on the grill. Grill undisturbed on the first side until browned, about 2 minutes. Turn the quail over and continue grilling until cooked through, 2 minutes more. Remove from the grill and brush with the jus lié.

5. Dry-sauté the remaining 1 tablespoon shallot and the wild mushrooms in a large nonstick skillet over medium heat. When the mushrooms begin to release their juices, add the figs and any remaining jus lié and heat gently.

6. Serve the grilled quail with the hot sauce.

GRILLING (157), **CLEANING MUSHROOMS** (122)

INDIAN GRILLED BUFFALO

Buffalo, or bison, has great flavor and has less fat and cholesterol than beef. It is available in specialty and gourmet markets and in the meat sections of some grocery stores. Beef or pork may be substituted for the buffalo. The buffalo skewers may be served with grilled zucchini slices and basmati rice.

MAKES 6 SERVINGS

INDIAN MARINADE

1 cup yogurt

¼ cup diced onion

2 tbsp minced ginger

3 garlic cloves, minced

½ tsp cumin seeds, toasted and ground

½ tsp freshly ground black pepper

¼ tsp grated nutmeg

1½ lb buffalo round, cut into 1½-in cubes

1. Combine the yogurt, onion, ginger, garlic, cumin, pepper, and nutmeg in a shallow bowl or baking dish. Add the buffalo, turning once or twice to coat evenly with the marinade. Cover and marinate in the refrigerator for at least 12 and up to 24 hours.

2. Prepare a grill for a medium-high fire. If using coals, they should be glowing red with a moderate coating of white ash.

3. Thread the buffalo onto skewers and grill until medium rare, about 6 minutes. Serve.

TOASTING SPICES, NUTS, AND SEEDS (290), **GRILLING** (157), **PREPARING GINGER** (284)

LOIN OF PORK with Honey-Mustard Pan Sauce

Whole-grain mustard is made by combining the whole mustard seed with other ingredients, rather than using ground seeds. It has a pungent mustard flavor.

MAKES 6 SERVINGS

1½ lb pork loin, trimmed

2 tsp canola oil

1 tsp butter

1 tbsp minced shallot

1 garlic clove, minced

1 tbsp tomato paste

2½ tsp whole-grain mustard

2 tbsp honey

3 tbsp red wine vinegar

1½ cups Jus Lié (page 296)

2 tsp chopped thyme

⅛ tsp kosher salt, or as needed

⅛ tsp ground black pepper, or as needed

1. Trim any visible fat from the loin and cut it into 3-inch-long pieces.

2. Heat a sauté pan over medium-high heat. Add the oil and swirl to coat the pan evenly. Add the pork and sauté undisturbed on the first side until browned, about 2 minutes. (The pieces should not touch or overlap; work in batches or use two pans if necessary.) Turn each piece and continue to sauté until the pork is evenly browned on all sides and ends, about 10 minutes total. The pork should be cooked through at this point (155°F). Transfer the pork to a dish as it finishes cooking and reserve.

3. Return the sauté pan to medium heat. Add the butter and melt. Add the shallot and garlic and sauté, stirring occasionally, until they are tender, about 2 minutes. Add the tomato paste to the pan and continue to stir until it is rust colored and has a sweet aroma, about 1 minute. Stir in the mustard, honey, and vinegar until blended. Add the jus lié and any of the juices released by the pork on the dish. Simmer until the sauce is very hot, about 1 minute. Add the thyme and taste. Adjust the seasoning with the salt and pepper.

4. Return the pork pieces to the pan and turn to coat lightly with the sauce to reheat them. Serve at once on a heated platter or individual plates with the sauce.

Variation

ROASTED PORK LOIN WITH SOUTHWESTERN-STYLE PAN SAUCE: *To make a Southwestern-style sauce, use cilantro in place of the thyme (add just before serving), spicy Creole mustard in place of whole-grain mustard, maple syrup or molasses instead of honey, and habanero or other chile-flavored vinegar instead of red wine vinegar. Garnish the sauce with a fine dice of jalapeños.*

COCOA-RUBBED PORK TENDERLOIN

Use a good-quality cocoa powder for this rub. Cocoa nibs are pieces of roasted cocoa beans removed from their husks, and they have a delicious, nutty flavor. They can be found in gourmet and specialty grocery stores. Plantain chips make a great garnish; instructions are in the note following this recipe.

MAKES 6 SERVINGS

COCOA-SPICE RUB

1 tbsp white peppercorns

1 tbsp coriander seed

4½ tbsp ground cinnamon

2 tsp grated nutmeg

1 tsp ground cloves

¼ cup cocoa powder

2 tbsp ground chipotle

2 tbsp cocoa nibs

1 tbsp kosher salt

2¼ lb pork tenderloin

2 tbsp corn oil

⅓ cup **Mango Salsa** (page 87)

1. Preheat the oven to 325°F.

2. For the spice rub, combine all the ingredients in a coffee or spice grinder and pulse to a slightly coarse powder.

3. Coat the tenderloin lightly with the corn oil and rub generously with the spice mix.

4. Place the tenderloin on a rack in a large roasting pan and roast until the meat is nicely browned and has reached an internal temperature of 155°F, 30 to 45 minutes.

5. Let rest for 10 minutes before carving. Serve with the salsa.

NOTE To make plantain chips, choose yellow plantains. Peel them, and slice the plantains on an angle to make long chips. Place the slices on a lightly oiled baking sheet. Spray the slices with a little cooking oil and season them with a few drops of lime juice. Bake at 350°F until they are crisp and golden, about 20 minutes.

MARINATING (156)

SAUTÉED MEDALLIONS OF PORK with Warm Cabbage Salad

Use a good-quality sherry vinegar for this sauce. Sherry vinegar is made from sherry, a Spanish fortified wine, and the resulting vinegar is sweet and wonderfully acidic. While delicious in this sauce, it also is excellent in vinaigrettes.

MAKES 6 SERVINGS

1½ lb pork loin, trimmed

SHERRY VINEGAR SAUCE

1 tsp butter

2 tbsp brown sugar

2 tbsp sherry vinegar

1¼ cups Jus Lié (page 296)

2 tsp canola oil, or as needed

1 recipe Warm Cabbage Salad (page 47)

1. Cut the pork into 12 medallions. Pound the medallions slightly to even their thickness and shape.

2. For the sauce, heat a saucepan over medium heat. Add the butter and melt. Add the brown sugar and stir until blended and the sugar melts. Add the vinegar and stir to combine. Add the jus lié and reduce the heat to low. Simmer until the sauce is very flavorful and lightly thickened, about 6 minutes. Set aside.

3. Heat a large skillet over medium-high heat. Add enough oil to lightly film the pan evenly. Add the pork and sauté undisturbed on the first side until browned, about 2 minutes. (The pieces should not touch or overlap; work in batches or use two pans if necessary.) Turn each piece and continue to sauté until the pork is evenly browned on all sides and ends, about 10 minutes total. The pork should be cooked through at this point (155°F). Transfer the pork to a dish as it finishes cooking and reserve.

4. Return the skillet to medium heat. Add the sauce and stir well to release any drippings. Return the pork pieces to the pan and turn to coat lightly with the sauce to reheat them. Serve at once on a heated platter or individual plates with the sauce on a bed of the cabbage salad.

SAUTÉING (158)

GRILLED KIBBE KEBABS

Kibbe, or *kibbeh*, is a Middle Eastern mixture of bulgur, meat, and spices.
It is delicious, full of flavor, and very simple to prepare.

MAKES 6 SERVINGS

KIBBE

½ cup fine-grind bulgur

9½ oz ground turkey

⅔ cup diced onion

2 jalapeños, minced

1¾ tsp yogurt

1 tbsp olive oil

1 tbsp chopped parsley

1 tbsp chopped cilantro

2 tsp chopped mint

1 tbsp ground cumin

⅔ tsp ground allspice

Pinch ground cinnamon

¼ tsp ground black pepper

Pinch cayenne

MOLASSES GLAZE

2 tsp molasses

2 tsp reduced-sodium soy sauce

2 tsp olive oil

1. Thoroughly rinse the bulgur and soak in warm water for 10 minutes. Drain in a sieve for 20 minutes. Squeeze any excess moisture from the bulgur.

2. Pulse the bulgur with the remaining ingredients in a food processor and mix completely.

3. Mold the meat mixture onto 8-inch wooden skewers that have been soaked in water for 1 hour; they should look like hot dogs that have been skewered the long way.

4. For the glaze, whisk all the glaze ingredients together in a small bowl. Brush the meat mixture with the glaze just before grilling.

5. Prepare a grill for a medium-high fire. If using coals, they should be glowing red with a moderate coating of white ash.

6. Grill the skewers, turning to cook on all sides, until marked on the exterior and very hot all the way through, 6 to 8 minutes total. Serve at once.

GRILLING (157)

LOIN OF LAMB with Blood Orange Sauce

The sauce for this dish is intensely flavored and piquant, making a great counterpoint to the rich flavor of the meat. It is based on a *gastrique*, the culinary term for a sweet-and-sour flavor base in a sauce.

MAKES 6 SERVINGS

3 lb bone-in lamb loin or 12 loin chops

ORANGE GLAZE

¼ cup Vegetable Broth (page 295)

1 tbsp cornstarch

2 tbsp orange juice concentrate

1 tsp freshly ground black pepper

BLOOD ORANGE SAUCE

⅔ cup blood orange juice

½ cup orange juice

1 tsp cornstarch

⅓ cup Jus Lié (page 296)

2 tsp chopped tarragon

1. Cut the lamb loin into 12 chops by slicing between the bones. Trim away most of the fat, but leave a very thin layer to protect the lamb as it cooks. Reserve in the refrigerator.

2. For the glaze, combine 2 tablespoons of the broth with the cornstarch to form a paste. Bring the remaining broth to a boil in a small pot over medium-high heat. Remove the broth from the heat.

3. Gradually add the cornstarch slurry to the broth and bring the mixture back to a boil over medium heat, whisking constantly, until it has thickened, about 2 minutes. Add the orange juice concentrate and pepper. Remove from the heat.

4. For the sauce, combine the orange juices. Combine 2 tablespoons of the orange juice with the cornstarch to form a paste. Heat the remaining juice in a small pot over medium heat and bring it to a simmer. Gradually add the cornstarch slurry to the juices and simmer until thickened, about 2 minutes. Add the jus lié and continue to simmer gently for 2 minutes more.

5. Prepare a grill for a medium-high fire. If using coals, they should be glowing red with a moderate coating of white ash.

6. Dip the lamb in the orange glaze and grill, turning once, until medium rare, about 4 minutes on each side. Add the tarragon to the sauce and serve the grilled lamb with the sauce.

JUICING CITRUS (285), **GRILLING** (157)

LAMB SHANKS Braised with Lentils

Braising is a gentle, slow cooking technique that transforms tough cuts of meat into tender morsels in a rich, flavorful sauce.

MAKES 6 SERVINGS

6 lamb shanks, trimmed (about ½ lb)

2½ cups Jus Lié (page 296)

1¼ cups dry white wine

1 cup dried lentils

1 Bouquet Garni (page 285)

1 cup diced celery

1 cup diced carrot

1 tbsp chopped parsley

2 tsp chopped thyme

Pinch freshly ground black pepper

1 tbsp orange juice

¼ tsp kosher salt

1. Preheat the oven to 325°F.

2. Pan sear the shanks in a large ovenproof skillet over medium-high heat, turning to get a good brown color on all sides, about 8 minutes total.

3. Add the jus lié, wine, lentils, and bouquet garni and bring to a simmer over medium-low heat.

4. Cover and braise in the oven until the lamb and lentils are tender, about 90 minutes.

5. Remove from the oven, transfer the shanks to a platter, and cover loosely to keep warm. Degrease the sauce by skimming the surface.

6. Add the celery and carrot to the sauce and simmer until the vegetables are tender and the sauce has reduced slightly, 4 to 5 minutes.

7. Season the sauce with the parsley, thyme, pepper, orange juice, and salt. Serve each shank with spoonfuls of lentils and sauce.

JUICING CITRUS (285), **BRAISING AND STEWING** (159), **DICING** (119)

SHABU-SHABU with Beef

Shabu-shabu is a Japanese version of the Chinese hot pot concept. An extremely hot broth infused with vegetables and herbs is prepared as the base. Thinly sliced meat and other garnishes are dipped into the broth, cooking the components, and completing the finished soup.

MAKES 6 SERVINGS

BROTH

6 cups Vegetable Broth (page 295)

2⅓ cups sliced mushroom stems

3 garlic cloves, peeled

1½-inch piece peeled ginger, sliced

1½ stalks lemongrass, chopped

3 tbsp chopped cilantro roots

1 tbsp reduced-sodium soy sauce

1¾ cups chopped daikon

2¼ cups sliced shiitake mushrooms

¾ lb udon noodles, cooked

⅓ cup sliced green onion

6 oz tofu, diced

12 oz beef strip loin, sliced very thin

Soy sauce, as needed

1. For the broth, combine the vegetable broth, mushroom stems, garlic, ginger, lemongrass, and cilantro roots in a large soup pot. Bring to a boil over high heat and reduce to a simmer over medium-low heat. Simmer gently until the broth is flavorful, 30 to 45 minutes. Season with the soy sauce. Strain through a fine-mesh sieve, discarding all solids, and use immediately or cool completely before storing in the refrigerator.

2. For the soup, bring the strained broth to a boil in a large soup pot over medium-high heat and reduce to a simmer over low heat.

3. Add the daikon and simmer until about halfway cooked, about 5 minutes. Add the mushrooms and udon noodles and continue to simmer until noodles are tender, another 5 minutes.

4. Add the green onion, tofu, and steak slices. Adjust seasoning with soy sauce as needed.

5. Serve immediately. The meat should be just barely cooked.

PREPARING GINGER (284), **CLEANING MUSHROOMS** (122)

Vegetable broth is made even more flavorful by simmering it with mushrooms, garlic, ginger, lemongrass, cilantro, and soy sauce.

GRILLED FLANK STEAK with Roasted Shallot Sauce

Roasting shallots gives them a sweet flavor, which is an excellent complement to any kind of grilled meat or poultry.

MAKES 6 SERVINGS

1¾ lb flank steak

MARINADE

1¾ cups pineapple juice

¾ cup chopped fresh pineapple

⅓ cup thinly sliced red onion

1 tbsp low-sodium soy sauce

2 tsp red wine vinegar

2 tsp olive oil

2 limes, sliced

½ bunch cilantro, chopped (including leaves, stems, and roots)

2 garlic cloves, minced

1 tsp minced jalapeño

2 tsp chili powder

2 drops Tabasco sauce

Roasted Shallot Sauce (page 297)

1. Trim the steak, removing any visible fat from the surface. Most of it will pull away easily, but you may need to use a boning or paring knife to remove it completely.

2. Combine all of the ingredients for the marinade in a shallow bowl or baking pan. Add the flank steak, turning once or twice to coat evenly with the marinade. Cover and place in the refrigerator to marinate for at least 1 and up to 3 hours.

3. Prepare a grill for a medium-high fire. If using coals, they should be glowing red with a moderate coating of white ash.

4. Remove the flank steak from the marinade. Drag it along the edge of the bowl to scrape away any excess marinade. Place the flank steak on the grill. Grill undisturbed on the first side until browned, about 2 minutes. Turn the steak over and continue grilling until cooked through, 3 to 4 minutes more.

5. Let the steak rest for about 5 minutes before slicing on an angle. Serve on heated plates with the shallot sauce.

GRILLING (157), **JUICING CITRUS** (285)

TENDERLOIN OF BEEF with Wild Mushrooms

Many wild mushrooms sold in supermarkets are in fact cultivated and as a result are available year-round instead of only in their natural season. Wavy-capped, apricot-colored chanterelle mushrooms are an exception, since they are still usually foraged rather than cultivated. Look for them at farmers' markets in the autumn and spring.

MAKES 6 SERVINGS

1½ lb beef tenderloin, trimmed

⅔ cup finely shredded leeks, white and green parts only

⅓ cup Chicken Broth (page 294)

⅔ cup Jus Lié (page 296)

5 cups sliced wild mushrooms

¼ cup Madeira

½ tsp chopped sage

1 tsp chopped thyme

¼ tsp freshly ground black pepper

1. Cut the beef into 6 medallions. To maintain an even shape and thickness, tie butcher's twine around the circumference of each medallion. Reserve in the refrigerator.

2. Cook the leeks in the broth in a medium skillet over low heat, stirring frequently, until limp and translucent, 2 to 3 minutes. Drain and set aside.

3. Heat the skillet over medium-high heat. Dry-sauté the beef medallions, turning once, about 6 minutes for medium rare, 8 minutes for medium. Remove the meat from the skillet and keep warm in a low-heat oven.

4. Add the jus lié to the skillet and stir well to release any drippings. Simmer over medium heat until reduced by one-fourth, about 3 minutes. Add the mushrooms and cook until almost done, about 5 minutes.

5. Add the wine, sage, thyme, and pepper and simmer over medium-low heat until reduced enough to lightly coat a spoon, about 3 minutes. Add the stewed leeks.

6. Serve the beef medallions coated with mushroom sauce.

CLEANING LEEKS (120), **SAUTÉING** (158), **CLEANING MUSHROOMS** (122)

CHAPTER SEVEN

Fish and Shellfish

Great seafood dishes are a mainstay in cuisines in virtually every corner of the globe. Many recipes are often deceptively simple, relying as they do upon the seafood's absolute freshness. Your fish and seafood dishes deserve extra attention and care; fish is a great choice for a healthy dish, but as rising demand is changing how many different types of fish you can find, it is also influencing their cost. If you have a local fish market or fish counter that stocks wild salmon, catfish, haddock, trout, and other fish, take full advantage of the fishmonger's knowledge about the fish offered in the shop and the best ways to enjoy them.

Fish and Shellfish

Fish consumption has doubled in the last few decades as people have become more aware of the health benefits it confers. As fish has become increasingly popular, demand has begun to outstrip supply. Many longtime favorites are increasingly unavailable. Because fish is typically low in the saturated fats that can cause health problems and may be high in beneficial fats, the American Heart Association recommends eating at least two servings of fish per week, especially fatty fish like mackerel, lake trout, herring, sardines, albacore tuna, and salmon. However, there are serious concerns about toxins in fish. The discussion about how much and what type of fish to eat, as well as how fish are raised and harvested, can be confusing. The Monterey Bay Aquarium has created purchasing guides and substitution lists. They are readily available on their Web site (www.seafoodwatch.org).

PURCHASING AND STORING FISH

All fish are extremely perishable. It is important to select absolutely fresh fish of the best quality. The most important test of freshness is smell. No matter how clear the eyes are or how firm the flesh, a fish that smells bad should always be rejected.

Do not allow freshwater to come into contact with lobsters or crabs, as it will kill them. Bivalves should be tightly closed; they start to open as they age. Tap any that are slightly ajar and reject or discard any that do not snap shut; those shellfish are dead.

You should be able to choose fish that are pan-dressed, filleted, or cut into steaks; live lobsters in tanks; shrimp in a range of sizes, either cooked and peeled or in the shell; a variety of clams and oysters in the shell; and squid or octopus.

When you start with a great fresh ingredient, pair it with a cooking technique that makes the most of it. Certain cooking techniques are a perfect fit, while others may be adapted slightly to marry with a specific fish's unique flavor and texture, depending on whether it is naturally lean or oily, meaty or delicate.

The way fish swim, the water they swim in, and their diets all influence the flavor and texture of their flesh. Being familiar with these distinctions is useful when you want to substitute one type of fish for another in a recipe or want to find a recipe for a type of fish that is new to you. A fish can have a firm, meaty texture or a delicate one that tends toward flakiness. Its flavor can be mild or robust; often, the fattier the fish, the more pronounced its flavor. Round fish varieties include trout, bass, cod, haddock, snapper, tuna, and salmon. The most popular flatfish varieties include flounder, sole, halibut, and turbot. Shellfish falls into four basic groups: bivalves with hinged shells, including mussels, clams, oysters, and scallops; univalves, with one shell, like escargot and conch; crustaceans, including lobster, shrimp, and crab; and cephalopods, such as cuttlefish, squid, and octopus.

Cooking Fish and Shellfish

Fish and shellfish are naturally low in calories and saturated fat. If you've taken the time to select your fish from a reputable source, the next decision is the cooking method.

MATCHING FISH AND SHELLFISH WITH COOKING METHODS

FISH OR SHELLFISH	CHARACTERISTICS	BEST COOKING METHODS
Anchovy, fresh	Moderately fatty, strong flavor	Broiling, baking, grilling
Bass	Moderately fatty, fairly firm, smooth	Steaming, poaching, sautéing, roasting, grilling
Bluefish	Oily, flaky, soft, strong taste	Roasting, baking, grilling, broiling
Catfish	Moderately fatty, firm, sweet	Pan frying, baking, grilling, broiling, shallow-poaching
Cobia	Lean, firm, mild taste	Poaching, shallow-poaching, sautéing, steaming, roasting, baking, grilling, broiling
Cod	Lean, firm, mild taste	Poaching, shallow-poaching, sautéing, steaming, roasting, baking, grilling, broiling
Escolar	Lean, firm, mild taste	Sautéing, grilling, broiling, roasting, baking, steaming, shallow-poaching
Flounder	Lean, flaky, mild taste	Sautéing, shallow-poaching, baking
Grouper	Lean, firm, mild taste	Sautéing, grilling, broiling, roasting, baking, steaming, shallow-poaching
Halibut	Lean, fine texture, flaky, mild taste	Poaching, sautéing, steaming, shallow-poaching, roasting, baking, grilling, broiling
Herring, fresh	Moderately fatty, firm, full flavor	Sautéing, grilling, broiling, roasting, baking
Mahi mahi	Lean, firm, mild taste	Sautéing, grilling, broiling, roasting, baking, steaming, shallow-poaching
Perch	Lean, delicate, sweet flavor	Sautéing, baking
Pompano	Moderately fatty, firm, full flavor	Sautéing, grilling, broiling, roasting, baking, steaming, shallow-poaching
Salmon	Moderately fatty, firm, rich flavor	Sautéing, grilling, broiling, roasting, baking, shallow-poaching, poaching
Shad	Lean, flaky, sweet	Poaching, steaming, shallow-poaching, roasting, baking
Snapper	Lean, firm	Sautéing, grilling, broiling, roasting, baking, steaming, shallow-poaching
Sole	Lean, flaky, delicate flavor	Sautéing, pan frying, shallow-poaching, baking

FISH OR SHELLFISH	CHARACTERISTICS	BEST COOKING METHODS
Swordfish	Lean, very firm	Sautéing, grilling, broiling, roasting, baking, stewing
Trout	Moderately oily, flaky	Sautéing, pan frying, baking, poaching
Tuna	Moderately oily, firm	Sautéing, grilling, broiling, roasting, baking, stewing
Clams	Lean, tender, briny	Steaming, poaching, simmering, stewing, sautéing, baking, grilling
Crab, blue or Dungeness	Texture varies from firm and resilient to fibrous; tender, sweet	Steaming, poaching, simmering
Crab, soft-shell	Texture varies from firm and resilient to fibrous; tender, sweet	Pan searing, sautéing, grilling
Lobster	Texture varies from firm and resilient to fibrous; tender, sweet	Steaming, boiling, poaching, simmering, stewing, sautéing, baking, grilling, broiling
Mussels	Tender with a chewy "band," salty or briny, savory	Steaming, poaching, simmering, stewing, sautéing, baking, grilling
Oysters	Tender and very moist, salty or briny flavor	Steaming, poaching, simmering, stewing, sautéing, baking, grilling
Scallops	Tender and very moist, firm flesh, sweet	Sautéing, stir-frying, deep-frying, grilling, broiling, poaching, steaming
Shrimp	Tender with a resilient "bite," salty or briny, savory	Sautéing, stir-frying, deep-frying, grilling, broiling, poaching, steaming

PAN SEARING AND PAN GRIDDLING

Fish and shellfish have less of the tougher connective tissues found in meats, which means that you can employ high-heat, quick-cooking methods very effectively. Fish don't demand long, gentle cooking to be tender and tasty.

Pan searing and pan griddling give you the option of developing a rich, dark, flavorful crust. The best pan for pan searing or griddling is one with a perfectly flat surface made of a metal that transfers heat easily. Cast iron is a good choice, since it holds heat and can get quite hot.

Adding a coating of an herb mixture, a spice blend or rub, or powdered mushrooms adds more flavor to the dish. These coatings also help the fish release from the pan without sticking, which means you don't have to use a lot of cooking oil. Some pan-seared dishes call for searing on one side only, then finishing the fish in a moderate oven. Others may call for the fish to be turned over and finished in the pan on the top of the stove.

BROILING

Broiling is a great technique for fish. Like pan searing or griddling, you get the flavor boost of a deeply colored exterior and a bit of texture contrast with the moist, tender interior.

While some classic recipes for broiled fish call for liberal amounts of butter, we've opted instead for aromatic vinaigrettes, wines, and similar ingredients. You can create a bed of sautéed greens or julienned vegetables for serving. You'll get a nutrient and flavor boost, of course, and the added benefit of one less pan to wash up later.

Setting up your oven for broiling successfully is simple: Position a rack so that it is at least 3 and up to 5 inches away from the heat source for most broiled fish dishes. Choose a baking dish or pan with relatively low sides; the higher the sides, the more likely the dish is to steam than to actually broil. One last word of advice: Give the broiler enough time to properly preheat, 10 to 15 minutes for most ovens.

STEAMING

If you think of steaming as a boring cooking technique, you will likely change your mind after trying our mussel recipe (page 210) or the Cobia and Scallops en Papillote (page 212). What steaming lacks in the way of deeply browned and roasted flavors, it more than makes up for by virtue of its unmatched ability to produce the most tender, juicy fish and seafood dishes.

To steam mussels and other shellfish, create a little flavorful broth in a deep pan that has a tight-fitting lid. Start with some aromatics—ginger, garlic, lemongrass, onions, shallots, or green onions, for instance—and add some flavorful liquids like wine, broth, beer, tea, fruit, or vegetable juices. When the broth is simmering, add the seafood, cover the pot, and cook. The broth is now enriched with the juices from the shellfish, so remember to get all the goodness from the dish by serving the broth either directly with the shellfish or on the side as a soup.

Wrapping fish up in a parchment bag (en papillote) is another steaming technique. In this case, the paper traps the steam released by the ingredients to cook them. This classic method of preparing fish is perfect for the home cook because you can assemble individual portions a few hours ahead of time. Cooking your dinner in paper means there is practically nothing left to clean up after dinner is over.

Working with Fish and Shellfish

Small fish like trout, anchovies, herring, and sardines are sometimes sold as either "whole" or "pan-dressed" fish. Whole fish usually indicates that the fish has been gutted and scaled. Pan-dressed generally means that the fish has been gutted and scaled; the head, tail, and fins may also be removed. Other fish may already be cut into fillets or steaks. When you get your fish home, you can cut larger fillets (sometimes known as "sides") into portion-size pieces.

WHOLE OR PAN-DRESSED FISH

Rinse the fish to make sure that any scales that might be clinging to the fish, inside or out, are flushed away. Let the water run into the fish, and rub away any bits of blood that might remain. Use a knife or kitchen scissors to cut away the tail and fins, if you wish, or a chef's knife to cut away the head. Blot the fish dry inside and out with paper towels.

FILLETS

Many fillets are sold both boneless and skinless, but in some cases, the skin is left intact. If you prefer to remove the skin, use a flexible filleting knife or a chef's knife. Lay the fillet skin side down and nearly parallel to the edge of the cutting surface. Make a small cut at the tail end between the skin and flesh to create a small flap. Hold the flap at the tail end taut, using a cloth if needed for a surer grip. Insert the blade into the flap so that it is nearly parallel to the work surface and the cutting edge is pointing away from the hand holding the skin. Use short, back-and-forth sawing motions to push the knife down the length of the fillet.

Removing Pin Bones

Some fish have a row of narrow pin bones running the length of their fillets. Most fishmongers will remove the pin bones, either before selling the fish or on request, but it is always good to check for any stray ones before cooking the fillet. Run your finger down the middle of the fillet against the grain (from the thicker head end to the thinner tail end) to locate the pin bones. Grasp a pin bone firmly with clean tweezers or needle-nose pliers and pull it out with the grain toward the direction of the fish's head. Repeat, removing the bones methodically from one end to the other to make sure none are overlooked.

Slicing the Fillets

Once the skin and pin bones are removed, a large fish fillet may be sliced into serving portions. You can make straight cross cut to produce individual portions, usually 1 or 2 inches wide depending on the thickness of your fillet (the thicker the fillet, the narrower the slice). To give the cuts a more generous appearance, make your slices on an angle to expose more surface area; the fish will look attractive and cook more quickly. Smaller fillets may be left as is, or you may wish to fold or roll them. To create strips to stir-fry or thread on skewers to grill, make cuts that are about ½ inch wide.

SCALLOPS, MUSSELS, CLAMS, AND OYSTERS

These shellfish belong to a group known as bivalves, because they have two hinged shells. You'll find mussels, clams, and oysters sold in the shell as well as shucked. Scallops are less often sold in the shell, although you may occasionally find them in the market, with the red roe still attached.

Scallops

Scallops are commonly cut away from the shell and sold shucked, along with some of the scallop liquor. To get them ready for a dish, you'll want to pull away the muscle tab that held the scallop to its shell; otherwise, the tougher muscle tab will shrink and toughen before the rest of the scallop finishes cooking.

The tab is on the side of the scallop and is usually easy to spot since it is more opaque than the rest of the scallop. Sometimes it is easy to pull the tab away, but if necessary, you can use a sharp paring knife to trim it off.

Mussels

The first thing to do with mussels is check them over. When you buy fresh mussels, they are still alive and their shells should be tightly shut. Any that aren't closed should snap shut quickly when tapped against the countertop. If they don't close, discard them. Sometimes, a mussel shell may feel unusually heavy for its size. Those shells may be full of mud or silt; discard those too.

To clean mussels, hold them one at a time under cold running water. Use a brush with stiff bristles to thoroughly scrub the mussel, removing grit, sand, and mud from the shell's exterior.

Mussels attach themselves to rocks and other surfaces by means of a fibrous, shaggy beard (which is sometimes absent in farmed mussels). Since removing the beard kills the mussel, plan on debearding them just before cooking. Pull the beard away from the shell until taut, and yank it sharply down toward the pointed hinge until it snaps away.

Clams and Oysters

Check clams and oysters to be sure they are still alive as described above for mussels. Scrub thoroughly with a brush under running cold water to remove mud and other debris. Be meticulous about this, especially if you are adding clams and oysters still in the shell to a dish. Otherwise, you may have grit in your sauce or broth.

Take care when cooking clams and oysters. Overcooking them can turn them into rubber bands. When they are properly cooked, they are plump and juicy and loaded with a wide array of nutrients, including a number of minerals that are important to your health.

SHRIMP, LOBSTER, AND CRAB

If you are going to simply boil or steam these crustaceans, you don't need to remove their shells. For other techniques, like grilling or sautéing, you may need to do a bit more preparation. If you have a good fish market or counter, they will clean and prepare your shellfish to save you a few steps in the kitchen.

Peeling and Deveining Shrimp

To peel shrimp, start from the belly side and peel away the legs along with the shell. Pull off the tail if desired. To devein shrimp, lay the peeled shrimp on a work surface, with the curved outer edge of the shrimp facing your cutting hand. Make a shallow cut into the shrimp's back with a paring knife. Use the tip of the knife to scrape out the gray or black vein, which is actually the shrimp's intestinal tract. To remove the vein without cutting into the shrimp (a nice touch for boiled or steamed shrimp), use the tip of your paring knife, a skewer, or a toothpick to pierce the shrimp just below the center point of the vein and slowly pull the vein out.

Butterflying Shrimp

If you would like to butterfly shrimp for grilling or broiling, cut more deeply into the curve of the back as you are deveining the shrimp. Hold the knife blade parallel to the work surface and place the fingertips of your guiding hand (the hand not holding the knife) flat on top of the shrimp to hold it steady. Make a horizontal cut along the outer curve of the shrimp toward the inner curve. Don't cut all the way through the shrimp, however; leave about ¼ inch of shrimp uncut and leave the tail end of the shrimp intact.

Boiling Whole Lobster and Hard-Shell Crab

To boil live lobsters or hard-shell crabs, choose a large pot to allow plenty of room. You will need 1 gallon of water for 1 lobster or 3 or 4 crabs. You may wish to add some seasonings to the water: salt, bay leaf, whole peppercorns, strips of citrus zest, or Old Bay Seasoning (especially for crab). Bring the water to a rolling boil, and then lower the crustacean into the pot. Once the water returns to a boil, reduce the heat to maintain a simmer. Cook for about 8 minutes for a 1½-pound lobster and add 2 minutes for every additional pound. A Maryland blue crab takes about 6 minutes and a Dungeness crab about 8.

Removing the Meat

If a recipe calls for only the meat of a cooked lobster or crab, let the shellfish cool completely. Twist the tail away from the body and cut through the underside of the tail to get at the meat. To get the meat from the claws and legs, use the heel of the knife to cut into the shell, without cutting too deeply into the meat, and then twist the knife sharply to the side to crack apart the shell. Use a large knife or kitchen shears to cut through the leg knuckles, and then pull out the knuckle meat. Pull out any bits of meat from the body as well. Once you've taken the meat from the shell, check it carefully to find and remove any bits of shell or cartilage (this is known as "picking" the meat).

PAN-GRILLED TUNA NIÇOISE-STYLE

A traditional Niçoise salad is made from oil-packed tuna, but this version, prepared with a pan-griddled piece of fresh tuna, is a great one-dish meal. If you are concerned about the safety of tuna in your diet, look for fish harvested by pole-and-line or trolling methods: albacore from the Pacific; bigeye, skipjack, or yellowfin tuna.

MAKES 6 SERVINGS

¾ lb tuna fillet, trimmed

1¼ cups Vinaigrette-Style Dressing (page 292)

¾ tsp kosher salt

2½ cups romano beans (about ¾ lb)

1¾ lb small red potatoes

7 cups mixed salad greens, loosely packed

Oil

2 tbsp Salsa Verde (page 304)

2 cups cherry tomatoes, halved

18 Niçoise olives

2 hard-boiled eggs, quartered

1. Brush the tuna lightly with ¼ cup of the vinaigrette, and set aside (keep refrigerated if you plan to wait longer than 20 minutes before cooking the tuna).

2. Bring a large pot of water to a rolling boil and add ½ teaspoon of the salt. Add the beans and cook, uncovered, until they are cooked through but still have a bit of snap, about 5 minutes. Drain the beans in a colander, rinse with cold water until cool to the touch, and let them continue to drain while preparing the rest of the ingredients.

3. Place the potatoes in a pot and add enough cold water to cover them. Add the remaining ¼ teaspoon salt and bring to a boil over medium heat. Cook the potatoes at a slow boil until they are easy to pierce with the tip of a paring knife, about 15 minutes. Drain the potatoes and let them cool for a few minutes. Combine the potatoes and the beans with ½ cup of the vinaigrette in a small bowl while the potatoes are still quite hot. Toss to coat evenly and set aside.

4. Toss the mixed greens with the remaining ½ cup vinaigrette. Mound on a serving platter or individual plates.

5. Heat a grill pan over medium-high heat until very hot. Brush or rub lightly with a little oil. Place the tuna on the griddle and cook on the first side until the fish releases easily and is nicely marked, about 3 minutes. Turn the tuna once and finish cooking on the second side, 3 to 4 minutes more (the total time will vary depending upon how thick your tuna pieces are and how well-done you like them).

6. Serve the tuna on a bed of the dressed greens topped with the salsa and accompanied with the potatoes, green beans, tomatoes, olives, and eggs.

PAN SEARING AND PAN GRIDDLING (185), **BOILING, BLANCHING, AND PARBOILING VEGETALBES** (123), **PREPARING SPINACH AND LEAFY GREENS** (121)

GRILLED MAHI MAHI with Roasted Red Pepper Salad

Mahi mahi is usually sold as skin-on fillets. The skin actually helps keep this moist and flaky fish from falling apart as it cooks. If mahi mahi is not available, try this dish with mullet, amberjack, or grouper.

MAKES 6 SERVINGS

MARINADE

Juice of 1 lime

2 tbsp minced onion

2 tsp white wine vinegar

1 tsp honey

Pinch ground white pepper

1½ lb mahi mahi fillets

2 cups julienned roasted red peppers

¼ cup Balsamic Vinaigrette (page 293)

3 tbsp dried currants

2 tbsp pine nuts, toasted

1 tbsp chopped parsley

1. Combine the marinade ingredients in a small bowl and add to the mahi mahi in a resealable bag. Turn the fish to coat evenly with the marinade. Cover and marinate in the refrigerator for at least 30 minutes and up to 2 hours.

2. Combine the ingredients for the red pepper salad. Let the salad marinate for at least 30 minutes. (It can be made up to 2 days in advance; keep refrigerated.)

3. Prepare a grill for a medium fire. If using coals, they should have a moderate coating of white ash.

4. Remove the mahi mahi from the marinade. Drag the pieces along the edge of the bag to scrape away any excess marinade. Place the mahi mahi on the grill skin side down. Grill undisturbed on the first side until browned, about 3 minutes. Turn the fish over and continue grilling until cooked through, 3 to 4 minutes more.

5. Serve the mahi mahi on a heated platter or individual plates with the red pepper salad.

GRILLING (157), **MARINATING** (156), **JUICING CITRUS** (285)

THYME-SCENTED TROUT Baked with Marinated Tomatoes

Trout is an excellent choice, since these small fish accumulate lesser quantities of toxins than larger fish. Trout are often sold pan-dressed, and one trout equals one satisfying serving of fish.

MAKES 6 SERVINGS

6 brook trout, about ¾ lb each

18 to 24 sprigs thyme (about 1 bunch)

1 lemon, thinly sliced

¼ tsp kosher salt

Pinch freshly ground black pepper

MARINATED TOMATOES

⅔ cup chopped tomatoes (peeled and seeded)

3 tbsp Balsamic Vinaigrette (page 293)

2 tbsp chopped parsley

⅛ tsp kosher salt

Pinch freshly ground black pepper

1. Preheat the oven to 350°F. Place a rack in a baking dish.

2. Rinse the trout inside and out and blot dry with paper towels. (If you wish, cut away the head, tail, and fins.) Open each trout, spreading it flat, and fill with a few sprigs of thyme and 2 or 3 slices of lemon. Season the fish lightly with the salt and pepper and place in a baking dish.

3. Combine all the ingredients for the marinated tomatoes in a bowl. Pour the mixture into the baking dish around the trout.

4. Bake the trout until cooked through and the tomatoes are nicely browned, about 20 minutes. Serve the trout on a heated platter or individual plates topped with the tomatoes. Spoon any baking juices over the fish.

PEELING AND SEEDING TOMATOES (121)

GRILLED HERBED SALMON with Southwest White Bean Stew

Marinating the salmon in herbs gives this dish an incredibly fresh flavor that's perfect for grilling. We've paired slightly steamed green beans and a julienne of crunchy jicama for texture as well as flavor.

MAKES 6 SERVINGS

1½ lb salmon fillet, skin on

SALMON MARINADE

¼ cup lime juice

¼ cup canola oil

1 tbsp chopped parsley

2 tsp chopped thyme

2 tsp chopped cilantro

2 tsp chopped Mexican oregano

½ tsp freshly ground black pepper

2 cups Southwest White Bean Stew (page 113)

1½ cups julienned green beans, blanched

¾ cup julienned jicama

1. Trim the salmon, removing any pin bones, and cut into 6 pieces, about ¼ pound each. Blot dry with paper towels. Place the fish in a baking dish.

2. For the marinade, combine all the ingredients in a small bowl. Pour half of the mixture evenly over the salmon, reserving the rest to use as a sauce. Turn the fish to coat evenly with the marinade. Cover and marinate in the refrigerator for at least 30 minutes and up to 2 hours.

3. Prepare a grill for a medium-high fire. If using coals, they should be glowing red with a moderate coating of white ash.

4. Remove the salmon from the marinade. Drag the pieces along the edge of the dish to scrape away any excess marinade. Place the salmon on the grill skin side down. Grill undisturbed on the first side until browned, about 3 minutes. Turn the fish over and continue grilling until cooked through, 3 to 4 minutes more.

5. Meanwhile, bring the bean stew to a simmer over low heat and heat completely. Toss the green beans and jicama together with a little of the marinade reserved to use as a sauce.

6. Serve the salmon on a heated platter or individual plates with the bean stew. Drizzle the fish and the stew with the reserved marinade and serve with the green bean salad, if desired.

GRILLING (157), **FILLETS** (187), **JUICING CITRUS** (285), **MARINATING** (156)

BROILED FRESH SARDINES with Shaved Fennel and Orange Salad

Orange and fennel are two signature Mediterranean flavors, found throughout the region. If you come across fennel pollen or dried fennel, you can add them to this aromatic, highly perfumed dish. Fresh sardines are a seasonal delicacy, so if you want to try this when they are out of season, substitute fresh herring, anchovy, or smelt.

MAKES 6 SERVINGS

1½ lb fresh sardines, cleaned

CRUMB TOPPING

¾ cup plain fresh bread crumbs

2 tbsp chopped parsley

1 tbsp grated Parmesan

2 tsp olive oil

1 tsp minced garlic

SHAVED FENNEL AND ORANGE SALAD

1½ cups very thinly shaved fennel

1 navel orange, peeled, sectioned, and diced

½ cup thinly sliced red onion

¼ cup pitted black olives

⅛ tsp kosher salt

⅛ tsp ground black pepper

1. Preheat the broiler to high and position the rack 3 to 4 inches from the heat source.

2. Rinse the sardines inside and out and blot dry with paper towels. (If you wish, cut away the head, tail, and fins.) Open each sardine, spreading it flat, and place in a baking dish. (The fish should not be touching or overlapped; use a second dish if needed.)

3. For the crumb topping, combine all the ingredients in a small bowl, working them together with your fingertips until blended. Top each sardine with some of the bread mixture.

4. For the salad, combine the ingredients in a large bowl and set aside to marinate while broiling the sardines.

5. Broil the sardines until the crumb topping is golden and crisp and the fish is cooked through, 12 to 15 minutes. If necessary, lower the rack to prevent the crust from scorching.

6. Serve the sardines on a heated platter or individual plates with the salad.

BROILING (186)

GRILLED PEPPERED SWORDFISH with Mango Salsa

The sweet-hot flavors in this dish are the perfect match for the rich flavor and texture of swordfish. Do make sure, though, that the swordfish you purchase is from a domestic source. If you prefer, try this dish with tuna or wild salmon.

MAKES 6 SERVINGS

1½ lb swordfish

PEPPERCORN MARINADE

⅓ cup balsamic vinegar

2 tbsp olive oil

1 tsp cracked or coarsely ground black pepper

1 tsp shredded basil

2 garlic cloves, minced

¼ tsp kosher salt

¾ cup Mango Salsa (page 87)

1. Trim the swordfish; remove the skin if desired. Place the fish in a shallow baking dish.

2. Combine all the ingredients for the marinade in a small bowl and pour evenly over the swordfish. Turn the fish to coat evenly with the marinade. Cover and marinate in the refrigerator for at least 30 minutes and up to 2 hours.

3. Prepare a grill for a medium-high fire. If using a charcoal grill, the coals should be glowing red with a moderate covering of white ash.

4. Remove the swordfish from the marinade. Drag it along the edge of the dish to scrape away any excess marinade. Place the swordfish on the grill. Grill undisturbed on the first side until browned, about 3 minutes. Turn the fish over and continue grilling until cooked through, 3 to 4 minutes more.

5. Serve the swordfish on a heated platter or individual plates topped with the salsa.

GRILLING (157), **SHREDDING OR CHIFFONADE** (119)

SPICY ASIAN GRILLED SHRIMP

Butterflying the shrimp allows the marinade to penetrate more of the shrimp's surface, making for a more flavorful result.

MAKES 6 SERVINGS

1½ lb shrimp, peeled and butterflied

SPICY ASIAN MARINADE

1 tsp five-spice powder

½ tsp Tabasco sauce

1 tsp minced ginger

2 garlic cloves, minced

1 tbsp rice wine vinegar

½ tsp fish sauce

½ tsp sesame oil

1. Place the shrimp in a shallow baking dish. Combine all the ingredients for the marinade in a reseable plastic bag. Pour the mixture over the shrimp, turning once or twice to coat evenly. Cover and place in the refrigerator to marinate for at least 30 minutes and up to 3 hours.

2. Prepare a grill for a medium-high fire. If using coals, they should be glowing red with a moderate coating of white ash.

3. Place the shrimp on the grill. Grill undisturbed on the first side until the shrimp has a bright color, about 2 minutes. Turn the shrimp over and continue grilling until cooked through, 2 to 3 minutes more.

4. Serve the shrimp at once on a heated platter or individual plates.

PEELING AND DEVEINING SHRIMP (188), **BUTTERFLYING SHRIMP** (189), **GRILLING** (157)

GRILLED SOFT-SHELL CRABS

Soft-shell crabs are crabs in the process of molting, making it possible to eat them whole. The citrus marinade amplifies their fresh flavor.

MAKES 6 SERVINGS

1½ lb soft-shell crabs

CITRUS MARINADE

⅓ cup lemon juice

¼ cup minced red pepper

1 cup red wine vinegar

1 cup dry white wine

¼ cup extra-virgin olive oil

⅓ cup minced green onion

1 roasted jalapeño, minced

2 tsp chopped basil

2 tsp chopped fennel sprigs

2 tsp chopped tarragon

2 tsp chopped thyme

2 garlic cloves, minced

1. Clean the crabs by pulling off the flap on the belly (known as the apron) and cutting away the head. Blot dry with paper towels. Place the crabs in a shallow bowl or baking dish.

2. For the marinade, combine all the ingredients in a shallow dish. Add the crabs, turning once or twice to coat evenly with the marinade. Cover and marinate in the refrigerator for at least 2 and up to 8 hours. Remove the crabs from the marinade and drag them along the edge of the bowl to scrape away any excess marinade.

3. Prepare a grill for medium-high fire. If using coals, they should be glowing red with a moderate coating of white ash.

4. Place the crabs on the grill. Grill undisturbed on the first side until the shells turn bright red, about 2 minutes. Turn the crabs over and continue grilling until cooked through, 4 to 5 minutes more.

5. Serve the crabs at once on a heated platter or individual plates.

JUICING CITRUS (285), **ROASTING AND PEELING PEPPERS** (120), **GRILLING** (157)

Grilled Soft-Shell Crabs with Barley and Wheat Berry Pilaf (page 98)

SEARED SCALLOPS with Beet Vinaigrette

Add the juice of a lemon to the water used for boiling the beets to keep their colors bright.
For an even more intense color and flavor, juice the beets raw using a juicer.

MAKES 6 SERVINGS

BEET VINAIGRETTE

1 lb beets, greens trimmed

3 tbsp cider vinegar

2 tbsp extra-virgin olive oil

1 tsp chopped dill

¼ tsp kosher salt

¼ tsp freshly ground black pepper

1½ lb sea scallops, muscle tabs removed

1½ cups mixed greens, loosely packed

½ cup julienned carrot

½ cup julienned cooked beets

½ cup julienned daikon

6 sprigs dill, for garnish

18 slices cooked red beets

1. Bring a medium pot of water to a boil. Add the beets and boil until tender, 12 to 15 minutes. When the beets are cool enough to handle, peel them. Cut the beets into slices. Cut some into julienne for the salad. Use a small round cutter to make 1 round for each scallop; reserve. Chop enough of the trim and remaining slices to make 1 cup.

2. Purée the chopped beets with the vinegar in a food processor or blender until smooth. Transfer the mixture to a medium bowl. Whisk in the oil and season with the dill, salt, and pepper.

3. Blot excess moisture from the scallops with a paper towel. Heat a large sauté pan over medium-high heat; the pan needs to be very hot for a successful pan-seared dish. Sear the scallops until brown on both sides and cooked through, 5 to 7 minutes. Serve the scallops on a beet circle with a salad of mixed greens and julienned beets, carrot, and daikon; drizzle with 2 tablespoons of the beet vinaigrette. Garnish with a dill sprig.

SCALLOPS [188], **PAN SEARING AND PAN GRIDDLING** [185], **JULIENNE AND BATONNET** [119]

PAN-SEARED ARCTIC CHAR with Moroccan Spices and Lentil Ragoût

In addition to using the infused curry oil in the dish, drizzle it over the finished fish or toss it with the greens served on the side.

MAKES 6 SERVINGS

1¼ lb Arctic char fillets

MOROCCAN-STYLE SPICE PASTE

1 tsp coriander seeds

1 tsp cumin seeds

1 tsp caraway seeds

1 tsp cardamom seeds

1 tsp anise seeds

1 tsp black peppercorns

3 tbsp light sesame oil

1½ cups Lentil Ragoût (page 109)

⅔ cup Caramelized Pearl Onions (page 147)

1. Trim the char to remove the belly flap. Place the fish in a shallow dish skin side down.

2. For the spice paste, grind the coriander, cumin, caraway, cardamom, anise seeds and black peppercorns in a spice grinder until a coarse texture forms. Pour the spice mixture into a small bowl and stir in the sesame oil. Pour the spiced oil over the char and turn the fish once or twice to coat evenly.

3. Heat a large sauté pan over medium-high heat; the pan needs to be very hot for a successful pan-seared dish. Remove the char from the marinade, dragging it across the edge of the dish to scrape away any excess marinade. Sear on the skin side until the fish is a deep golden color, about 2 minutes. Do not disturb the fish. Turn the fish once and continue to cook on the second side until the char is cooked through, 4 to 5 minutes more.

4. Serve the char at once on a heated platter or individual plates, accompanied by the lentil ragoût and caramelized pearl onions.

PAN SEARING AND PAN GRIDDLING (185), **FILLETS** (187)

SEARED WILD ATLANTIC SALMON with Corn, Potato, and Arugula Salad

This dish has traces of spice in each component. Try adding additional Tabasco or cayenne for even more heat.

MAKES 6 SERVINGS

YELLOW TOMATO COULIS

1 tsp olive oil

1 cup minced onion

1 tsp minced garlic

1¼ cups quartered yellow tomatoes (seeded)

¼ tsp kosher salt

1 tsp sugar

2 bay leaves

½ tsp Tabasco sauce

1½ lb wild Atlantic salmon fillet, cut into six ¼-lb pieces

¼ tsp kosher salt

¼ tsp freshly ground black pepper

Corn, Potato, and Arugula Salad (recipe follows)

GARNISHES

2 tbsp chopped chives

2 tbsp chopped parsley

2 tbsp chopped chervil

½ cup cherry tomatoes, halved

1. For the tomato coulis, heat the oil in a large skillet over medium heat until smoky. Add the onions and garlic and cook until the onions are translucent, 4 to 5 minutes. Add the tomato and the remainder of the coulis ingredients and simmer until the mixture is dry, about 30 minutes. Remove and discard the bay leaves. Purée the mixture in a food processor or blender until smooth. Strain through a fine-mesh sieve to remove the fibers, if desired.

2. Season the salmon with the salt and pepper. Heat a large sauté pan over high heat; the pan needs to be very hot for a successful pan-seared dish. Sear on the skin side until the fish is a deep golden brown, 2 to 3 minutes. Do not disturb the fish. Turn the fish once and continue to cook on the second side until the salmon is cooked through, 3 to 4 minutes more.

3. Mound the salad on a platter or individual plates. Sprinkle the chives, parsley, and chervil over the salad and place the salmon on top. Pour the coulis around the salmon and garnish with cherry tomatoes.

JUICING CITRUS (285), **PREPARING SPINACH AND LEAFY GREENS** (121), **FILLETS** (187)

CORN, POTATO, AND ARUGULA SALAD

MAKES 6 SERVINGS

1 tsp Dijon mustard	2½ cups cooked, sliced red potatoes
2 tbsp lemon juice	3 cups arugula, loosely packed
1 tbsp lime juice	1 tbsp chopped cilantro
3 tsp sugar	¼ tsp kosher salt
2½ tsp peanut oil	Pinch freshly ground black pepper
1 tbsp extra-virgin olive oil	Dash Tabasco sauce
1 cup corn kernels	

Combine the mustard, lemon juice, lime juice, and sugar in a small bowl. Slowly whisk in the oils. Place the corn, potatoes, arugula, cilantro, and dressing in a small bowl and toss. Season with the salt, pepper, and Tabasco.

FISH CAKES with Cucumber-Tomato Relish

Serve this dish with a refreshing and simple salad of mixed greens
tossed with the reserved liquid from the cucumber relish.

MAKES 6 SERVINGS

2½ cups peeled and cubed Idaho potatoes

¾ lb cod or pollock, poached, cooled, and flaked

1 cup plain dry bread crumbs

⅔ cup nonfat milk

3 tbsp whole-grain mustard

3 tbsp mayonnaise

2 tbsp minced smoked salmon (optional)

1½ tsp chopped capers

2 tbsp chopped chives

2 tbsp chopped dill

¼ tsp kosher salt

1 tsp freshly ground black pepper

Cucumber-Tomato Relish (recipe follows)

1. Place the potatoes in a pot and add cold water to cover by 2 inches. Salt the water. Gradually bring the water to a simmer over medium heat. Cover and simmer until the potatoes are easily pierced with a fork, 10 to 12 minutes. Drain the potatoes. Purée the potatoes while they are still hot with a ricer or food mill. Let the potatoes to cool to room temperature.

2. When the potatoes are cool, combine with the cod, bread crumbs, milk, mustard, mayonnaise, salmon, if desired, capers, chives, dill, salt, and pepper. Form into 12 cakes, pressing them firmly so they will hold together.

3. Heat a cast-iron skillet over medium heat. Add enough oil to barely cover the pan bottom, swirling to coat evenly. Add the fish cakes (do not crowd the pan; work in batches if needed) and cook on the first side until golden brown, about 3 minutes. Turn them once and continue to cook on the second side until golden, crisp, and very hot, about 3 more minutes.

4. Serve the cakes on a heated platter or individual plates with the cucumber relish.

CUCUMBER-TOMATO RELISH

MAKES 3 CUPS

1½ cups diced seedless cucumber, skin on

¾ cup diced tomato (peeled and seeded)

½ cup diced red onion

1 tsp minced jalapeño

4 tsp balsamic vinegar

1 tbsp chopped cilantro

2 tsp olive oil

Combine all the ingredients in a large bowl. Marinate in the refrigerator for at least 30 minutes and up to 12 hours before serving.

DICING (119), **PEELING AND PEELING AND SEEDING TOMATOES** (121)

STIR-FRIED SHRIMP with Lo Mein and Ginger-Sesame Vinaigrette

Add more variety to this dish by expanding the number of vegetables. Try adding daikon julienne, sugar snap peas or snow peas, and colorful bell peppers.

MAKES 6 SERVINGS

1½ lb shrimp, peeled and deveined

½ cup Ginger-Sesame Vinaigrette (page 293)

¼ tsp kosher salt

1¼ lb lo mein noodles

2 tsp peanut oil

2½ cup julienned green cabbage

¾ cup julienned carrot

2½ cups thickly sliced shiitake mushrooms

GARNISHES

⅓ cup thinly sliced green onion

2 tsp white sesame seeds, toasted

2 tsp black sesame seeds, toasted

1. Toss the shrimp with ¼ cup of the vinaigrette in a small bowl. Marinate in the refrigerator for at least 2 and up to 12 hours.

2. Bring a large pot of water to a rolling boil over high heat. Add the salt. Add the noodles all at once, stirring once or twice to separate them. Cook until the noodles are tender, about 5 minutes. Drain the noodles in a colander and rinse under running cold water until they are cool. Drain well and transfer to a bowl. Add the remaining ¼ cup of the vinaigrette and toss until evenly coated.

3. Heat a wok or large sauté pan over high heat. Add the oil, swirling the pan to coat evenly. When the oil is very hot, remove the shrimp from the marinade and add to the pan. Stir-fry until the shrimp is bright in color and cooked through, 3 to 4 minutes. Transfer the shrimp to a bowl and reserve.

4. Add the cabbage, carrots, and mushrooms to the hot pan and stir-fry until the vegetables are tender, 3 to 5 minutes. Return the shrimp along with any juices to the wok and stir-fry until all of the ingredients are very hot, 2 to 3 minutes more.

5. Mound the lo mein nodles on a platter or individual plates. Top with the shrimp stir-fry and garnish with the green onion and sesame seeds.

PEELING AND DEVEINING SHRIMP (188), **CLEANING MUSHROOMS** (122), **SAUTÉING AND STIR-FRYING VEGETABLES** (124)

STIR-FRIED SCALLOPS

Bean pastes have concentrated flavors. Hot bean paste is spicy and flavored with chiles, while red bean paste is sweet. They can be found in gourmet markets and Asian groceries.

MAKES 6 SERVINGS

1½ lb bay scallops or sea scallops, quartered

2 tbsp peanut oil

2 tsp minced ginger

1 garlic clove, minced

⅓ cup julienned celery

¼ cup julienned red pepper

¼ cup julienned yellow pepper

¼ cup julienned green pepper

¼ lb snow peas

½ cup quartered mushrooms

½ cup julienned zucchini

1 cup Fish Broth (page 295)

1 tsp hot bean paste

½ tsp red bean paste

1 tbsp cornstarch

1 tbsp oyster sauce

3 cups cooked brown rice

GARNISH

2 tbsp black sesame seeds, toasted

1. Blot excess moisture from the scallops with a paper towel. Heat 1 tablespoon of the oil in a wok or large sauté pan over medium-high heat until smoky. Add the scallops and sear until browned on both sides and cooked through, 2 to 3 minutes. Remove from the pan and set aside.

2. Heat the remaining oil in the pan over medium heat until smoky. Add the ginger and garlic and stir-fry until aromatic, about 1 minute.

3. Add the celery, peppers, snow peas, mushrooms, and zucchini and stir-fry until the zucchini is cooked almost completely, 3 to 5 minutes.

4. Combine the broth, bean pastes, cornstarch, and oyster sauce in a small bowl. Add to the vegetables and bring to a boil over high heat, whisking constantly, until the liquid has thickened.

5. Return the scallops to the pan and toss to evenly distribute. Serve the stir-fry on a bed of rice and garnish with sesame seeds.

SCALLOPS (188), **PREPARING GINGER** (284), **SAUTÉING AND STIR-FRYING VEGETABLES** (124), **STRINGING PEAS AND BEANS** (120)

Ginger, garlic, and green onion serve as the base aromatics flavoring the stir-fry.

CIOPPINO

Cioppino is a fish stew whose origin is attributed to Italian immigrants—mostly fishermen from Genoa—who settled in San Francisco and brought their taste for boldly flavored, easily made fish stews with them. In San Francisco, you'll find cioppino made from large, sweet-fleshed Dungeness crabs and a mixture of local Pacific rockfish, but the more readily available blue crabs and swordfish are suggested here.

MAKES 6 SERVINGS

1 tbsp olive oil

½ cup diced onion

1 bunch green onions, diced

1 green pepper, diced

1 cup diced fennel

2 garlic cloves, minced

6 cups chopped tomatoes (peeled and seeded)

½ cup tomato purée

⅔ cup dry white wine

1 bay leaf

1 tsp freshly ground black pepper

12 cherrystone clams, scrubbed

1 blue crab, disjointed

12 shrimp, peeled and deveined

¾ lb swordfish, cubed

2 tbsp shredded basil

Garlic Croutons (recipe follows)

1. Heat the oil in a large soup pot over medium heat until smoky. Add the onion, green onions, pepper, fennel, and garlic and cook, stirring frequently, until tender and translucent, 4 to 5 minutes.

2. Stir in the tomatoes, purée, wine, and bay leaf. Cover the pot and simmer over medium-low heat for about 45 minutes. Add the pepper. Remove and discard the bay leaf.

3. Add the clams and crab and simmer, covered, until the clams begin to open, about 10 minutes.

4. Add the shrimp and swordfish and continue to simmer until cooked, about 5 minutes more.

5. Just before serving, stir in the basil. Serve with a garlic crouton.

PEELING AND SEEDING TOMATOES (121), **PEELING AND DEVEINING SHRIMP** (188), **DICING** (119)

GARLIC CROUTONS

SERVES 6

6 slices whole wheat baguette

Vegetable oil spray, as needed

1 tbsp minced garlic

1. Preheat the oven to 400°F.

2. Lightly spray each slice of bread with vegetable oil and top with minced garlic. Toast in the oven until golden brown, 5 to 6 minutes. The croutons are ready to serve now, or they may be stored in a tightly covered container at room temperature for up to 4 days.

SALMON Baked with Spinach in Sparkling Wine Sauce

You don't have to use the highest quality sparkling wine, but make sure to use one with a good flavor that you would like to drink. Since this recipe calls for very little, you can pair the remaining wine with the finished meal.

MAKES 6 SERVINGS

1½ lb salmon fillet, cut into six ¼-lb pieces

¼ tsp kosher salt

⅛ tsp freshly ground black pepper, or as needed

2 tsp butter or canola oil

2 tsp minced shallot

6 cups spinach leaves, lightly packed

½ cup sparkling wine

1 tbsp tarragon vinegar

½ cup Fish Broth (page 295)

1 tsp Dijon mustard

Dash Tabasco sauce

3 tbsp chopped chives

1. Trim the salmon, removing the skin if desired. Pull out any pin bones. Season with ⅛ tsp of the salt and the pepper.

2. Heat a sauté pan or cast-iron skillet over medium-high heat. Add 1 tsp of the butter and melt. Add the shallot and cook, stirring occasionally, until the shallot is tender and translucent, about 2 minutes. Add the spinach and sauté, stirring and turning the spinach, until it turns a dark green and wilts, 3 to 4 minutes. Transfer the spinach to a baking dish.

3. Preheat the oven to 350°F.

4. Return the sauté pan to high heat. When the pan is very hot, melt the remaining 1 teaspoon butter. When you see a haze, add the salmon pieces. (The fish should not be touching or overlap; work in batches if needed.) Sear on the flesh side until the fish is deep golden, about 3 minutes. Transfer the salmon to the baking dish (seared side facing up) on top of the spinach.

5. Return the pan to medium heat. Add the sparkling wine and vinegar to the pan and stir to release any drippings. Simmer over low heat until reduced by about half, about 4 minutes. Add the fish broth, mustard, Tabasco, and the remaining ⅛ teaspoon of salt and a pinch of pepper and bring to a boil. Immediately pour the sauce into the baking dish around the salmon. Sprinkle the dish with the chives.

6. Bake until the salmon is cooked through, 10 to 12 minutes. Serve the salmon at once with the spinach and sauce on a heated platter or individual plates.

PREPARING SPINACH AND LEAFY GREENS [121], **FILLETS** [187]

ESCOLAR in Tomato, Fennel, and Saffron Broth

This broth is strongly flavored with citrus zest, saffron, and the aromatic juices released by the mussels, which complement the fish broth used as the base for the sauce.

MAKES 6 SERVINGS

2 tsp olive oil

1 garlic clove, minced

¾ cup julienned leeks, white and green parts only

¾ cup diced fennel

2 tbsp tomato paste

2½ cups Fish Broth (page 295)

2 tbsp dry white wine

2 tsp lemon juice

¼ tsp saffron threads

1 bay leaf

¼ tsp grated orange zest

¼ tsp kosher salt

Pinch ground white pepper

¾ lb escolar fillets, cut into 6 portions

12 wedges fennel, parcooked

24 mussels, scrubbed and debearded (about 1 lb)

3 cups coarsely chopped Swiss chard

1½ cups chopped tomato (peeled and seeded)

1 tsp chopped tarragon

1. Heat the oil in a large soup pot over medium heat. Add the garlic and cook, stirring frequently, until tender and translucent, about 1 minute.

2. Add the leeks and fennel, cover, and cook for 3 to 4 minutes. Add the tomato paste and sauté until rust colored, 5 minutes more.

3. Add the fish broth, wine, and lemon juice to the pan and stir well to release any bits stuck to the bottom of the pan. Simmer over low heat until reduced by half, about 5 minutes. Add the saffron, bay leaf, orange zest, salt, and pepper. Reduce the heat to medium low and simmer until the vegetables are tender, about 30 minutes.

4. Add the escolar and fennel wedges to the broth and poach until the fish begins to change color around the edges, 3 to 4 minutes.

5. Add the mussels, Swiss chard, tomatoes, and tarragon and simmer over very low heat, covered, until the mussels begin to open, about 10 minutes. Remove the bay leaf before serving.

CLEANING LEEKS (120), **ZESTING AND JUICING CITRUS** (284), **PEELING AND SEEDING TOMATOES** (121), **MUSSELS** (188)

MUSSELS in Saffron and White Wine Broth

As the mussels cook, they release their own aromatic juices into the simmering white wine, creating a flavorful broth.

MAKES 6 SERVINGS

3 lb mussels

SAFFRON BROTH

1 tsp butter

2 garlic cloves, minced

⅔ cup dry white wine

2 tbsp heavy cream

¼ tsp saffron threads

½ cup thinly sliced green onion

⅔ cup chopped tomato (peeled and seeded)

2 tbsp lemon juice

1¼ cups Fish Broth (page 295)

1 tbsp chopped chives, for garnish

1. Scrub the mussels under cold running water. Discard any mussels that remain open or that are filled with sand. Pull away the beards. (Note that you should cook the mussels within a short period of time once you've removed their beards.)

2. For the saffron broth, melt the butter in a large soup pot over medium heat. Add the garlic and cook, stirring constantly, until tender and translucent, about 1 minute. Add the wine, cream, and saffron and simmer over medium-low heat for about 5 minutes more. Add the green onion, tomato, lemon juice, and broth and continue to simmer until flavorful and slightly reduced, about 5 minutes.

3. Add the mussels and cover the pot tightly. Steam the mussels until their shells open, about 6 minutes. (Discard any mussels that do not open.) Serve the mussels in a heated serving bowl or individual bowls with the broth and garnish with the chives.

PEELING AND SEEDING TOMATOES [121], **JUICING CITRUS** [285], **MUSSELS** [188]

COBIA AND SCALLOPS en Papillote

Cobia is considered a great game fish. It has become more widely available in markets as some fish farmers in the United States have begun producing this delicious fish in a sustainable fashion. If cobia (sometimes know as lemonfish) is not available, you can use sablefish instead, or cod harvested from the cold northern waters of the Atlantic.

MAKES 6 SERVINGS

½ cup Vegetable Broth (page 295)

¼ cup dry vermouth

3 cups julienned celeriac

1½ cups julienned carrot

3½ cups thinly sliced red bliss potatoes

3 cups julienned cucumber

12 oz cobia fillet, cut into 6 portions

10 oz scallops

6 tbsp Gremolata (page 300)

1. Preheat the oven to 375°F.

2. Heat the broth and vermouth in a large sauce pot over medium heat and bring to a simmer, 2 to 3 minutes. Cook the celeriac, carrot, and potatoes in the broth mixture until tender, 8 to 10 minutes. Drain the vegetables and transfer to a bowl. Add the cucumber and toss.

3. Cut 6 sheets parchment paper about 10 by 13 inches. Place a bed of the vegetable mixture in the center of each piece of paper. Top the vegetables with the cobia and scallops. Spoon the gremolata over the fish.

4. Bring the long edges of the paper together and make a 1-inch-wide fold. Make 2 or 3 more folds to seal the packet. Twist the open ends to seal them; fold the ends underneath the packet.

5. Place the parchment packages on a baking sheet and bake in the oven until the fish is cooked and the vegetables are tender, 7 minutes. Serve immediately and open the packets at the table.

STEAMING (186), **SCALLOPS** (188), **JULIENNE AND BATONNET** (119)

SEARED COD in a Rich Broth with Fall Vegetables and Chive Pasta

Dusting cod with powdered mushrooms gives the fish a wonderful
color and a earthy, savory aroma as it cooks.

MAKES 6 SERVINGS

1¼ cups dried shiitake mushrooms

1½ lb cod fillet, skin removed

¼ tsp kosher salt

1 tsp ground white pepper

3 cups Vegetable Broth (page 295)

⅔ cup julienned carrot

⅔ cup julienned yellow turnip

⅔ cup julienned white turnip

2½ cups haricots verts, cut into 1-inch lengths

¾ lb Chive Pasta (see Note)

1 tsp olive oil

¾ cup enoki mushrooms, stems trimmed

2 tbsp chives, sliced into ½-inch lengths

1. Preheat the oven to 450°F.

2. Grind the dried shiitakes in a blender or spice grinder until a powder forms. Transfer to a shallow bowl or plate.

3. Trim the cod if necessary and cut into 6 equal pieces. Season the cod with the salt and pepper. Dredge the cod in the mushroom powder.

4. Heat the broth to a gentle boil in a large sauce pot over medium heat. Add the carrot, turnips, haricots verts, and pasta and simmer until all are tender and cooked through, 3 to 4 minutes.

5. Heat a sauté pan or cast-iron skillet over high heat. When the pan is very hot, add the oil. When you see a haze or shimmer, add the cod pieces. (The fish should not be touching or overlap; work in batches if needed.) Sear on the flesh side until the fish is deep golden, about 3 minutes. Transfer the cod to a baking dish (seared side facing up) and finish cooking the fish in the oven, 4 to 6 minutes more. (If your pan or skillet has an ovenproof handle, you can simply put the skillet in the oven instead of using a baking dish.)

6. Serve the cod in large soup bowls with the broth and vegetables around the cod. Top with the enoki and chives.

NOTE To make chive pasta, follow the recipe for Basic Pasta Dough (64) and add 2 tablespoons minced chives with the eggs.

LOBSTER Wrapped in Rice Paper with Asian Salad

Rice paper is an extremely thin, paperlike sheet made from rice products. It makes the perfect crust for this lobster dish and can be found in specialty grocery stores or Asian markets.

MAKES 6 SERVINGS

LOBSTER ROULADES

3 live lobsters (1 lb each)

2 tsp butter

¾ cup julienned leek (white part only)

2 tbsp brandy

½ tsp kosher salt

¼ tsp freshly ground black pepper

ASIAN SALAD

1 tsp peanut oil

¾ cup julienned shiitake mushrooms

1 tbsp reduced-sodium soy sauce

½ cup julienned carrot

1 cup bean sprouts

1 cup julienned snow peas

¾ cup julienned daikon

¼ cup pickled ginger

⅓ cup thinly sliced green onion

2 cups mixed greens, loosely packed

½ cup Citrus Vinaigrette (page 293)

12 rice paper sheets

2 tbsp peanut oil

1. Bring 1½ gallons of water to a boil in a large stockpot over high heat. Add the live lobsters and boil for 3 minutes, just long enough to release the meat from the shell. Drain the lobster in a colander, rinse with cold water until cool to the touch, and drain once more. Remove all the meat from the tail, claws, and knuckles and cut into medium dice.

2. Melt the butter in a large sauté pan over medium heat. Add the leeks and cook until tender, 2 to 3 minutes. Add the lobster meat, brandy, salt, and pepper and continue to cook until the lobster is cooked completely, 5 minutes more. Remove the solids from the pan and reduce any excess liquid to a syrup. Add the reduced liquid to the lobster meat and chill thoroughly.

3. For the Asian salad, heat the oil in a large sauté pan over medium heat until smoky. Add the mushrooms and cook until tender, 3 to 4 minutes. Add the soy sauce and reduce until no liquid remains, 5 to 6 minutes. Cool completely. Combine the mushrooms with the remaining ingredients, tossing with the citrus vinaigrette.

4. Soften the rice paper sheets in a bowl with enough warm water to cover for a few minutes. Drain. Place a small amount of the lobster mixture in each rice paper. Fold the sides in and roll to completely enclose the mixture. Set aside.

5. Heat the oil in a large skillet over medium heat until smoky. Add the lobster roulades and sauté, turning as necessary, until golden brown on all sides, about 6 minutes.

6. Mound some of the salad in the middle of each plate. Arrange 2 roulades over the greens and serve.

BOILING WHOLE LOBSTER AND HARD-SHELL CRAB (189), **CLEANING LEEKS** (120), **JULIENNE AND BATONNET** (119), **STRINGING PEAS AND BEANS** (120), **CLEANING MUSHROOMS** (122)

CHAPTER EIGHT

Breakfast and Beverages

Breakfast and brunch are perhaps the most intensely "personal" of meals. Breakfast is a hard habit to change, but if you are in the habit of stumbling out the door with just a mug of coffee or tea, you owe it to yourself to try and get into the breakfast habit.

Coffee

Good-quality coffee is more widely available today than ever before. You have the choice of a wide variety of coffees, both whole bean and ground. There are two types of coffee beans, arabica and robusta. Arabica is widely considered far superior to robusta; if you buy your coffee from bulk dispensers, robusta is usually the type of bean you are getting. So, if possible, sample a variety of beans. Blends incorporate a number of different varieties, and even different roasts, to give the coffee a specific aroma and flavor.

The roasting process is an important element in a coffee's flavor. The darker the roast, the more pronounced and complex the flavor will be. Lighter roasts have a more delicate flavor. Espresso, French, and Italian roasts are the darkest. These roasted beans have a very dark color with a pronounced sheen from the oils in the beans that are driven to the surface as they roast. American roasts are lighter in color and tend to look matte rather than shiny.

Whole beans maintain their quality longer than ground coffee. You can store whole beans in a dark, covered container at room temperature for several days. For longer storage, keep the beans in the freezer.

Grind coffee yourself, right before brewing the coffee, using a coffee grinder or a coffee mill. Each type of coffee maker calls for a specific degree of grind. Drip-style coffee makers use a fine grind. Express or plunger-style pots call for a slightly coarser grind. If you aren't sure, be sure to look at the instructions that come with your coffeepot.

The standard ratio for coffee calls for one *measure* of coffee, which translates as 1½ to 2 tablespoons of ground coffee for every 6 ounces of water you use. The more coffee you use in relationship to the water, the stronger the brewed coffee will be.

THE POT OR COFFEE MAKER

Most dedicated coffee drinkers have a favorite pot they use. Drip-style coffee makers hold the coffee in a basket lined with a disposable paper filter or a reusable gold mesh or nylon filter. Some baskets are cone-shaped and others have a flat bottom.

Clean your pot and the basket well after each use. If you use an electric coffee maker that holds the water in a reservoir, be sure to clean it periodically with a vinegar-and-water mixture to remove any mineral deposits that the water can leave behind. This will keep your coffeepot functioning properly. It also improves the flavor of your coffee. Follow the instructions that came with your coffee maker for cleaning.

THE WATER

Most coffee makers call for cold water. Use bottled or filtered water if your tap water has an unpleasant odor or taste. Your coffee maker should bring the water to around 190°F for the best extraction. If the water is colder than that, the coffee may taste weak. If it is too hot, the volatile oils that give coffee its rich aroma may be lost.

If you use a manual coffee maker, fill your kettle with fresh cold water and bring it to a boil. Turn off the heat and let the water rest for a minute or two so that it can cool from 212°F (the boiling point of water) down to 190°F. Clean your kettle with vinegar and water periodically to remove any buildup left behind by the water.

Tea

Dedicated tea drinkers know that your water should be at the boil, your pot preheated, and your tea selected carefully.

There are three categories of teas: black, green, and oolong. Black tea comes from leaves that have fermented; the brew is crimson color with an aroma that has been described as sweet and fruity. Green tea is made from unfermented tea leaves and is milder in flavor, with a pale yellow-green color. Oolong's leaves are rolled into long quills or into small balls to produce gunpowder tea, then roasted to soften their natural astringency. Some teas are flavored with herbs, spices, or citrus. Herbal teas are made using herbs such as mint, chamomile, or ginger.

While some tea drinkers prefer loose teas, others find the convenience of tea bags appealing. Whether you use bags or loose tea, be sure to observe some basic guidelines.

THE WATER

Fill your kettle with fresh cold water. Use bottled or filtered water if your tap water has an unpleasant odor or if you have a water softener.

Bring the water to a full boil and then pour some into your pot to preheat it.

THE BREWING

Once the pot is hot, pour out the water and add the tea. Loose tea is added directly to the pot, but if you prefer, use either tea bags or a tea ball. A tea cozy keeps the pot hot while the tea brews.

Most teas require at least two or three minutes for a proper infusion. Remove tea bags or tea balls once the tea is the strength you like. If you like loose tea, then the leaves will stay in the pot. In that case, you should have a second pot filled with hot water so you can adjust the intensity of your own cup.

Health Benefits of Tea and Coffee

Tea leaves contain catechins, phytochemicals that can reduce the risk of some cancers and that are thought to boost the immune system. Green tea has become popular recently because it contains higher concentrations of these compounds than black tea. Although green tea was the first tea studied for its cancer-fighting benefits, research shows that any tea derived from the leaf of a warm-weather evergreen (*Camellia sinensis*) contains chemicals called polyphenols that give tea its antioxidant properties.

Iced teas can provide as much antioxidant power as hot teas. Bottled, prepared iced teas often have a lower antioxidant level, however, because they contain mostly water and sugar.

Coffee may have health benefits as well. Studies report that coffee drinkers are less likely to develop conditions ranging from Parkinson's to diabetes. The caffeine in coffee appears to play a role in these reductions, as well as giving a mental boost. On the other hand, excessive caffeine can have a negative effective on your health, and some people cannot tolerate any amount of caffeine. If you drink coffee, drink it in moderation and enjoy it.

Formal tea service includes the following setup: two heated tea pots, one for brewing the tea and one to hold hot water, so the you can adjust the potency of teas brewed with loose tea. Accompaniments for black tea typically include milk and sugar (or honey). Some tea drinkers add lemon to their brewed black teas, although typically not when they add milk to the tea.

Iced teas can be left unsweetened, of course, or they may be sweetened with a bit of syrup (plain or flavored with herbs, citrus zest, or spices). Long-handled spoons—iced-tea spoons—are critical, especially if you are sweetening one glass at a time with a bit of sugar or honey, since iced-tea glasses are typically tall and narrow.

Herbal teas, more properly referred to as *tisanes*, are not derived from the same plant as tea and so do not have the same health-promoting polyphenols. What they do provide, however, is a caffeine-free beverage that may offer other benefits. Herbs like chamomile or mint, flowers like hibiscus, or spices such as clove or cinnamon are brewed and served in the same manner that you would a traditional brewed tea.

Blender Drinks

Blender drinks, often referred to as smoothies, are increasingly popular breakfast options. They are a quick and easy way to include a serving of dairy and some fresh fruit in your day. You can use any fresh fruits you like, including berries, tropical fruits like mangos and papaya, peaches, pineapple, and melons. If fresh fruits aren't at their peak, frozen fruits or fruit juices are another option.

Most smoothies include yogurt as their base. Choose a good-quality unflavored yogurt. It is up to you whether you prefer to use whole-milk, reduced-fat, or soy yogurts. Experiment with goat's or sheep's milk yogurt if they are available in your market.

Eggs

Keep eggs in the refrigerator to keep them wholesome and delicious. If you have access to farm-fresh eggs in your area, by all means try them. The fresher the egg, the better the flavor. You can also find cage-free eggs, eggs enriched with omega-3, eggs from hens fed a vegetarian diet, and certified organic eggs.

SEPARATING EGGS

Eggs separate most easily when they are cold, so keep them in the refrigerator until you are ready. You'll need a clean bowl to break each egg into, as well as bowls to hold the whites and yolks separately, and also a container to hold any eggs that don't separate cleanly.

Crack each egg's shell and carefully pull apart the halves. Gently pour the egg yolk back and forth from one half to the other, allowing the egg white to fall into the empty bowl. Drop the egg yolk into another bowl.

Examine the white in the first bowl to be sure that it contains no bits of yolk. If it is clean, transfer it to the egg white bowl. If you see drops of yolk in the egg white, however, the fat in the yolk will prevent the whites from whipping to their fullest volume. Save it for another dish such as scrambled eggs or to use as egg wash for baked goods, and wash and dry the bowl before separating the next egg.

Fruits for Breakfast

Keep fresh fruit on hand for breakfast and brunch. You can slice bananas into a bowl of cereal or dish of yogurt, cut wedges of melon or scoop them into balls, or cook fresh or dried fruits into sauces and compotes. Fruit salads are a simple make-ahead dish for breakfast on busy mornings. You can even pack some in a container to take on the road.

When berries, peaches, and cherries are in season locally, buy plenty to freeze. Blueberries and cranberries freeze beautifully; simply put them in freezer bags, seal, and store. More delicate berries (raspberries, strawberries, and blackberries) should be spread in a single layer on a sheet pan and frozen (uncovered) until solid. Then transfer the berries to freezer containers or bags. Usually there is no need to thaw frozen berries before adding them to pancakes or muffins.

A wide variety of dried fruits can be found in most markets. Stock up on breakfast favorites like raisins, currants, prunes (dried plums), cranberries, and cherries to give a sweet-tart punch to baked goods like muffins.

Mixing Methods for Waffles, Crêpes, and Pancakes

The straight mixing method (page 255) is the most common way to blend a batter, whether you are making pancakes, waffles, or crêpes. For the best results, have all of your ingredients at the correct temperature and mix the batter quickly and gently by hand. Consult your recipe to see if the batter should rest or if it is ready to use directly after mixing.

MAKING WAFFLES

Waffles, made on a special griddle, are no more difficult to make than any other pancake as long as you take a few minutes to get familiar with your waffle iron. We've included several tips for making and enjoying waffles.

1. PREHEAT THE WAFFLE IRON.
Clean the waffle iron before you start to remove any debris that might make your waffles stick. Very lightly rub the iron with a little oil or shortening, even if your waffle iron is nonstick.

Position the waffle iron so that it is stable and well away from the usual traffic flow. The outside of a waffle iron will be extremely hot once it is fully preheated. Allow the waffle iron plenty of time to heat up. Some models may take 10 minutes or longer.

2. ADD THE BATTER.
Make a sample waffle or two, until you determine how much batter you need to completely fill the iron and make a good-size waffle. Adjust the temperature on your waffle iron and, again, make a note about what setting made the best waffle.

3. FINISH COOKING THE WAFFLE.
The time it takes to cook a waffle will vary according to the thickness or thinness of your waffles. Make a note of the time it takes on your machine for future reference.

Let the waffle iron cool completely before cleaning it and putting it away.

MAKING CRÊPES

The thinner the crêpe, the better, but don't be discouraged if the first crêpe or two is a little uneven. With each crêpe you make, you'll get better at gauging the right amount of batter and level of heat for your pan.

1. MIX THE BATTER.
Crêpe batters have a more liquid consistency than other pancake batters. Whisk well to remove any lumps, and then let the batter rest for 30 to 60 minutes to ensure tender crêpes.

2. PREPARE THE PAN.
Crêpes are typically prepared in a small, flat, round pan with short, sloped sides. Small nonstick skillets also work well. Heat

the pan over medium heat and grease lightly with butter or oil to prevent sticking or, in the case of nonstick pans, to add flavor.

3. **COOK THE CRÊPES.**
With a ladle or small measuring cup, quickly pour a small amount of batter into the pan. Immediately tilt and swirl the pan to spread the batter in a thin, even layer that just covers the bottom of the pan. Cook for a few minutes, and then check the doneness of a crêpe by carefully lifting one edge and looking underneath it for a golden color with specks of light brown. With a metal spatula, loosen the edge of the crêpe from the pan, flip, and cook on the other side until golden.

Crêpes are easily made in advance. Cool them completely on baking sheets lined with parchment or waxed paper, then stack the crêpes with parchment or waxed paper between them. They can be wrapped well and refrigerated or frozen for later use.

GRIDDLES, SKILLETS, AND CRÊPE PANS

A gentle touch for mixing pancake batters is one important factor in success. The other is selecting and preparing your pan properly.

Medium- or heavy-gauge pans can hold heat evenly and tend to develop few hot spots. If one part of the pan is significantly hotter than other parts, your pancakes will not cook evenly. The pan or griddle must have a very flat, smooth surface as well. To keep your pans from becoming warped or buckled, use the following guidelines:

- Preheat pans and griddles completely before adding oil or butter.

- Adjust the heat whenever your senses (smell, touch, sight) tell you that the pan is getting too hot or too cold.

- Use a thin layer of oil or butter to lubricate the pan.

- If your pan or griddle has a nonstick surface, use tools designed to prevent scratches when you turn the cakes.

If you like to use cast-iron griddles or skillets, condition them before using them the first time: Get the pan hot, add a liberal amount of oil, and let the oil heat up. Pour out the oil and rub the pan or griddle with paper toweling. (This is the same method you should use to condition unlined crêpe pans.)

Once cast-iron pans are conditioned, maintain their surfaces by wiping out the pan with paper toweling. You can use a little salt as an abrasive if necessary. Do not wash cast-iron pans with soap and water if you can avoid it. Be sure cast-iron pans, skillets, and griddles are completely dry before you put them away, otherwise they can rust.

Soapstone griddles are another classic choice for making griddle cakes. Like cast iron, soapstone has the advantage of being heavy enough to hold and release heat very evenly. Also like cast iron, soapstone griddles require some special maintenance to keep them properly seasoned: Oil the griddle before using it and whenever the surface starts to stick; clean the griddle with a sponge and hot water; avoid abrasives and detergents. (Both cast iron and soapstone can be scrubbed and washed when necessary; you simply need to repeat the seasoning process.)

GRANOLA

Since nuts, seeds, and coconut are high in fat, granola is recommended as a topping rather than a cereal, since one serving would barely cover the bottom of a small bowl.

MAKES 12 SERVINGS

¼ cup sesame seeds, toasted

¼ cup sunflower seeds, toasted

¼ cup slivered almonds, toasted

¼ cup cashews, toasted

½ cup unsweetened shredded coconut, toasted

1 cup rolled oats, toasted

3 tbsp honey

⅓ cup dried currants

1. Preheat the oven to 350°F.

2. Mix the toasted seeds, nuts, coconut, oats, and honey in a large skillet over medium heat, tossing until all ingredients are coated with honey.

3. Remove the pan from the heat and stir in the currants. Spread the mixture on a baking sheet lined with parchment paper.

4. Bake the granola in the oven until the granola has a rich golden brown color, about 15 minutes.

5. Line another baking sheet with several layers of paper towels. Spread the granola onto the towels and cover with additional towels. Let the granola cool completely. Break the granola into small chunks and store in an airtight container.

TOASTING SPICES, NUTS, AND SEEDS (290)

STEEL-CUT OATS with Cinnamon and Dried Fruits

Steel-cut oats take longer than rolled oats to cook and have a chewy texture.

MAKES 6 SERVINGS

6 cups nonfat milk or water

1 cup steel-cut oats

¼ tsp kosher salt

2 cups dried fruits, chopped if necessary

½ tsp ground cinnamon

2½ tsp honey

1. Bring the milk to a boil in a medium saucepan over medium heat. Gradually add the oats, stirring constantly.

2. Simmer the oats, stirring frequently, for about 20 minutes.

3. Stir in the salt, dried fruits, and cinnamon and simmer until the oatmeal has absorbed all the liquid, 10 minutes more.

4. Serve in heated bowls and drizzle honey over each portion.

OATMEAL WAFFLES

Add a spoonful of fresh berries or sliced bananas and a touch of honey or syrup for a nourishing breakfast full of flavor, as well as fiber, vitamins, and minerals.

MAKES 4 SERVINGS

1 cup whole wheat flour

1 cup quick-cooking or rolled oats

1 tbsp molasses or honey

1 tsp baking powder

½ tsp baking soda

¼ tsp kosher salt

½ tsp ground cinnamon

Pinch grated nutmeg

Pinch ground cloves

2 large eggs

2 cups buttermilk

2 tbsp unsalted butter, melted

1. Mix the flour, oats, molasses, baking powder, baking soda, salt, cinnamon, nutmeg, and cloves in a large bowl and make a well in the center.

2. Combine the eggs with the buttermilk in a separate bowl and mix well. Pour the wet ingredients into the center of the dry ingredients and stir until the dry ingredients are moistened. Add the butter and stir in just until blended. Do not overmix. The batter is ready to use, or it may be covered and refrigerated for up to 12 hours.

3. Preheat the waffle iron to medium-high. Lightly spray it with vegetable oil. Pour about ¾ cup batter onto the waffle iron and cook the waffles until they are crisp, golden, and cooked through, 3 to 6 minutes per waffle. Serve at once.

THE STRAIGHT MIXING METHOD (255)

FOUR-GRAIN WAFFLES

Buttermilk gives these waffles a unique flavor, as well as their light texture. If you don't have buttermilk, you can sour regular milk by adding 1 tablespoon of either lemon juice or white vinegar to 1 cup of warmed milk. Let it rest for 10 to 15 minutes before using.

MAKES 6 SERVINGS

1 cup nonfat buttermilk

1 large whole egg

1 large egg white

3 tbsp vegetable oil

⅔ cup all-purpose flour

½ cup whole wheat flour

¼ cup cornmeal

⅓ cup rolled oats

2¼ tsp baking powder

2 tbsp sugar

1. Combine the buttermilk, whole egg, egg white, and oil in a large bowl.

2. Combine the flours, cornmeal, rolled oats, baking powder, and sugar in a separate bowl.

3. Add the dry ingredients to the wet ingredients and stir just until moistened.

4. Preheat the waffle iron to medium-high. Lightly spray it with vegetable oil. Pour about ¾ cup of the batter onto the waffle iron and cook until the waffles are crisp, golden, and cooked through, 3 to 6 minutes per waffle.

MAKING WAFFLES (220), **SEPARATING EGGS** (219)

MAPLE AND APPLE BUTTER SYRUP

MAKES 1 CUP

½ cup apple butter

¼ cup apple cider

⅓ cup maple syrup

Gently heat the apple butter and cider in a small saucepan. Add the syrup and return to a simmer. The sauce can be stored in a covered container in the refrigerator for up to 10 days. Serve warm.

PUMPKIN PANCAKES

An equal amount of mashed bananas can be added in place of the pumpkin to make banana pancakes.

MAKES 6 SERVINGS

1⅓ cups oat bran

1 cup all-purpose flour

1 tbsp baking powder

1 tbsp sugar

1 cup nonfat yogurt

⅔ cup canned pumpkin

1 tsp vanilla extract

1 tbsp vegetable oil

4 large egg whites, beaten to medium peaks

1. Combine the oat bran, flour, baking powder, and sugar in a large bowl.

2. Combine the yogurt, mashed pumpkin, vanilla, and oil in a separate bowl. Add the wet ingredients to the dry ingredients and stir just until moistened. Fold the egg whites into the batter.

3. Heat a large skillet or griddle over medium-high heat. Oil it lightly by brushing or spraying with oil. Drop the pancake batter into the hot pan by large spoonfuls (about ¼ cup). Leave about 2 inches between the pancakes to allow them to spread and to make turning easier.

4. Cook on the first side until small bubbles appear on the upper surface of the pancake and the edges are set, about 2 minutes. Use an offset spatula or a palette knife to turn the pancakes and finish cooking on the second side, another 2 to 3 minutes. Adjust the temperature beneath the skillet or griddle to produce a good brown color. Serve at once.

THE STRAIGHT MIXING METHOD (255), **SEPARATING EGGS** (219)

CHOCOLATE CHIP–PECAN PANCAKES

Nuts and chocolate are delicious, healthy additions to pancakes. If you have some leftover pancakes, freeze them and reheat in your toaster on your next busy morning.

MAKES 8 SERVINGS

1 cup whole wheat flour

1 cup all-purpose flour

2 tbsp sugar

1 tsp baking powder

½ tsp baking soda

¼ tsp kosher salt

2¼ cups buttermilk

2 large eggs

2 tbsp unsalted butter, melted

¾ cup chocolate chips

⅓ cup chopped toasted pecans

1. Sift together the flours, sugar, baking powder, baking soda, and salt into a large bowl and make a well in the center.

2. Combine the buttermilk, eggs, and butter in a separate bowl and mix well. Pour the wet ingredients into the center of the dry ingredients and stir just until the dry ingredients are evenly moistened.

3. Heat a large skillet or griddle over medium-high heat. Oil it lightly by brushing or spraying with cooking oil. Just before making the pancakes, fold the chocolate chips and pecans into the batter. Drop the pancake batter into the hot pan by large spoonfuls (about ¼ cup), leaving 2 inches between the pancakes to allow them to spread and to make turning easier.

4. Cook on the first side until small bubbles appear on the upper surface of the pancake and the edges are set, about 2 minutes. Use an offset spatula or a palette knife to turn the pancakes and finish cooking on the second side, another 2 to 3 minutes. Adjust the temperature beneath the skillet or griddle to produce a good brown color. Serve at once.

THE STRAIGHT MIXING METHOD (255), **TOASTING SPICES, NUTS, AND SEEDS** (290)

CORN AND GREEN ONION PANCAKES

Cut the kernels away from the cob and then scrape the cob with a table knife to remove some of the milk. Add the corn milk with the buttermilk mixture for a great fresh flavor.

MAKES 8 SERVINGS

¾ cup whole wheat flour

¾ cup all-purpose flour

½ cup cornmeal

1 tsp baking powder

½ tsp baking soda

¼ tsp kosher salt

1 tbsp sugar

2¼ cups buttermilk

3 large eggs

2 tbsp unsalted butter, melted

½ cup corn kernels, fresh or frozen

2 green onions, thinly sliced

1. Sift together the flours, cornmeal, baking powder, baking soda, salt, and sugar into a large bowl and make a well in the center.

2. Combine the buttermilk, eggs, and butter in a separate bowl and mix well. Pour the wet ingredients into the center of the dry ingredients and stir just until the dry ingredients are evenly moistened. The batter is ready to use or may be stored covered and refrigerated for up to 12 hours.

3. Heat a large skillet or griddle over medium-high heat. Oil it lightly by brushing or spraying with cooking oil. Just before making the pancakes, fold the corn and green onions into the batter. Drop the pancake batter into the hot pan by large spoonfuls (about ¼ cup), leaving 2 inches between the pancakes to allow them to spread and to make turning easier.

4. Cook on the first side until small bubbles appear on the upper surface of the pancake and the edges are set, about 2 minutes. Use an offset spatula or a palette knife to turn the pancakes and finish cooking on the second side, another 2 to 3 minutes. Adjust the temperature beneath the skillet or griddle to produce a good brown color. Serve immediately.

WORKING WITH CORN ON THE COB (121), **THE STRAIGHT MIXING METHOD** (255)

SPICY MUSHROOM AND QUESO FRESCO CRÊPES

You may want to make a double batch of these crêpes so you can freeze
some to have on hand for a quick breakfast, brunch, or lunch dish.

MAKES 12 CRÊPES

1 cup whole wheat flour

1 cup all-purpose flour

¼ tsp kosher salt

2 cups nonfat milk

2 large eggs

1 tbsp butter, melted, plus extra for the pan

Spicy Mushroom and Queso Fresco Filling (recipe follows)

1. Sift the flours and salt together into a large bowl and make a well in the center.

2. Combine the milk, eggs, and butter in a separate bowl and mix well. Pour the wet ingredients into the center of the dry ingredients and stir just until the batter is smooth. Let the batter rest in the refrigerator for at least 1 and up to 12 hours before preparing the crêpes. Strain the batter if necessary to remove lumps before preparing the crêpes.

3. Heat a crêpe pan or small skillet over medium-high heat. Brush with melted butter. Pour about ¼ cup of batter into the crêpe pan, swirling and tilting the pan to coat the bottom with batter. Cook until the first side is set and has a little color, about 2 minutes. Adjust the temperature under the pan if needed. Use a thin metal or heatproof rubber spatula to lift the crêpe and turn it over. Cook on the other side until the crêpe is cooked through, about 1 minute more. Stack the crêpes to fill now, or refrigerate or freeze them and assemble later.

4. Spoon about ¼ cup of the mushroom-cheese filling onto each crepe and roll them up. Place the filled crêpes seam side down in a baking dish. Cover the dish loosely with foil and warm the crêpes in a 325°F oven, if needed. Serve very hot.

THE STRAIGHT MIXING METHOD (255), **MAKING CRÊPES** (220), **CLEANING MUSHROOMS** (122), **JUICING CITRUS** (285)

SPICY MUSHROOM AND QUESO FRESCO FILLING

The mushrooms need to be added to the pan in a single layer
to brown properly, so sauté them in two batches.

MAKES 2 CUPS

2 tsp olive oil

½ cup minced onion

1½ tsp minced garlic

4 cups sliced mushrooms

2 tsp minced serrano

1 tbsp lime juice

¾ tsp minced epazote

¼ tsp kosher salt

¼ tsp freshly ground black pepper

¾ cup crumbled queso fresco

1. Heat the oil in a sauté pan over medium-high heat. Add the onion and garlic and sauté, stirring frequently, until the onion is tender and translucent, 2 to 3 minutes.

2. Increase the heat to high. Add the mushrooms and serrano. Sauté the mushrooms without stirring until they are browned on one side, 3 to 4 minutes. Stir the mixture and continue to cook over medium heat until the mushroom liquid cooks away. Add the lime juice, epazote, salt, and pepper.

3. The mushroom mixture is ready to use as a topping or filling, or it may be refrigerated for up to 3 days and then reheated when you are ready to assemble the crêpes. When filling, the queso fresco can be placed on the crêpe and the mushroom filling spooned over it, or you can mix it into the mushroom filling.

BUCKWHEAT BLINIS with Apple Butter

This blini recipe makes breakfast-size pancakes. You can make smaller blinis to top with sour cream and caviar for a classic Russian hors d'oeuvre. Or try them with apple butter for a hearty breakfast on a cold winter morning.

MAKES 4 SERVINGS

1 package (2¼ tsp) active dry yeast

2½ cups nonfat milk, warmed to 110°F

1 cup all-purpose flour

½ cup buckwheat flour

1 tbsp sugar

½ tsp kosher salt

3 large eggs, separated

Melted butter, as needed

2 cups Apple Butter (page 302)

1. Dissolve the yeast in the warmed milk and set aside for 5 to 10 minutes or until yeast blooms.

2. Sift together the flours, sugar, and salt into a large bowl and make a well in the center.

3. Add the egg yolks and yeast mixture into the center of the dry ingredients and stir until smooth. Cover with plastic and let rise until doubled, 2 to 3 hours.

4. Beat the egg whites to soft peaks in a mixer and fold into the batter.

5. Heat a griddle on medium heat. Oil it lightly by brushing it with melted butter. For each blini, ladle ⅓ cup batter onto the griddle. Flip the blini when bubbles appear on the upper surface and burst and the bottom is golden brown, about 2 minutes. Cook on the second side, about 1 minute. Repeat until the batter is finished. Serve warm with the apple butter.

USING YEAST (259), **MAKING CRÊPES** (220)

OAT BRAN AND DRIED FRUIT MUFFINS

Any type of dried fruit would work well for this recipe, including apricots, cranberries, cherries, raisins, and so on. Try plumping them for about 10 minutes in fruit juice for more flavor.

MAKES 12 MUFFINS

2²/₃ cups dried fruits, coarsely chopped

1 cup oat bran

⅓ cup rolled oats

⅓ cup all-purpose flour

3 tbsp brown sugar

1 tbsp baking powder

¾ tsp ground cinnamon

½ cup mashed banana

1½ tsp grated orange zest

3 tbsp orange juice

2 tbsp vegetable oil

1 large egg white

¾ cup nonfat milk

1. Preheat the oven to 400°F.

2. Process the dried fruit, oat bran, rolled oats, flour, sugar, baking powder, cinnamon, and banana in a food processor just until evenly mixed. Transfer to a large bowl.

3. Combine the orange zest, orange juice, oil, egg white, and milk in another bowl.

4. Add the orange juice mixture to the dried fruit mixture and fold just until combined.

5. Spoon the batter into lightly oiled muffin tins and bake until the surface of the muffins is golden and springs back when lightly pressed, about 20 minutes.

6. Turn the muffins out onto a cooling rack and allow to cool for 10 minutes before serving.

ZESTING AND JUICING CITRUS (284), **DETERMINING DONENESS** (256), **SEPARATING EGGS** (219)

SPICED GRAHAM MUFFINS

Graham flour is a whole wheat flour that is slightly coarser than regular grind. It can be found in gourmet markets and natural food stores.

MAKES 12 MUFFINS

½ cup warm water

½ cup raisins

1 cup all-purpose flour

¾ cup graham flour (see headnote)

2 tsp baking powder

1 tsp ground cinnamon

¼ tsp ground cloves

1 large egg

¼ cup nonfat yogurt

2 tbsp vegetable oil

⅓ cup sugar

1. Preheat the oven to 375°F.

2. Pour the water into a small bowl, add the raisins, and plump for 20 minutes. Drain, reserving the liquid.

3. Combine the flours, baking powder, cinnamon, and cloves in a small bowl.

4. Whisk together the egg, yogurt, oil, sugar, and reserved raisin liquid in a large bowl.

5. Add the dry ingredients to the wet ingredients and mix just until combined. Fold the plumped raisins into the batter.

6. Spoon the batter into lightly oiled muffin tins and bake until the surface of the muffins is golden brown and springs back when lightly pressed, about 15 minutes.

7. Turn the muffins out onto a cooling rack and allow to cool for 10 minutes before serving.

THE STRAIGHT MIXING METHOD (255), **DETERMINING DONENESS** (256)

EGGS EN COCOTTE

Add garnishes to the bottom of the ramekin (about 2 tablespoons per ramekin) before putting in the eggs. Ratatouille (page 131) is a good choice, as is Spicy Mushroom and Queso Fresco Filling (page 228). Be sure the garnish is hot before you add it. Other options include stewed or braised beans or lentils.

MAKES 4 SERVINGS

4 large eggs

¼ tsp kosher salt, or as needed

¼ tsp freshly ground black pepper, or as needed

2 tsp unsalted butter

1. Preheat the oven to 350°F.

2. Bring a kettle or pot of water to a boil.

3. Butter the inside of four 4-ounce ceramic soufflé dishes or ramekins and set in a large baking dish. Break an egg into each ramekin, season with the salt and pepper, and top with ½ teaspoon butter.

4. Place the pan in the oven and add about ½ inch of boiling water to the pan. Cover loosely with aluminum foil. Cook until the egg whites are opaque and firm and the yolks are set, about 20 minutes. Serve in the ramekins.

DUTCH BABY with Spiced Fruit

Substitute other fruits, or combinations of fruits such as bananas, raspberries, apples, and/or strawberries, in the spiced fruit to take advantage of whatever is in season.

MAKES 6 TO 8 SERVINGS

½ cup all-purpose flour

½ tsp unsalted salt

2 large eggs

½ cup nonfat milk

2 tbsp unsalted butter, melted

SPICED FRUIT

2 tbsp butter, melted

2¾ cups sliced peaches (peeled)

1 tsp ground cinnamon

2 tbsp packed brown sugar

1 tbsp lemon juice

Powdered sugar, as needed

¼ cup plain Greek-style yogurt

1 tsp lemon zest

1. Preheat the oven to 450°F.

2. Sift together the flour and salt into a small bowl.

3. Beat the eggs in a blender at low speed. Add the flour mixture and the milk to the blender alternately, in thirds. Scrape down the sides of the blender and continue to blend until smooth. Add the butter and blend in.

4. Pour the batter into a lightly oiled 10-inch cast-iron skillet or ovenproof sauté pan and bake for 20 minutes without opening the oven door. Reduce the heat to 350°F and bake 10 minutes longer.

5. Meanwhile, prepare the spiced fruit. Heat the butter in a medium sauté pan over high heat. Add the peaches, cinnamon, and brown sugar and cook until the peaches are browned, 5 to 6 minutes.

6. Remove the Dutch baby from the oven. Drizzle with the lemon juice and sprinkle with powdered sugar. Fill the Dutch baby with the hot fruit mixture. Top with the yogurt and lemon zest. Serve at once.

ZESTING AND JUICING CITRUS FRUITS (284)

TORTILLA DE PAPAS

This flat Spanish-style omelet makes a great brunch or supper dish, or you can cut it into cubes to enjoy at room temperature as part of a tapas spread. Ideally, the tortilla should be about an inch thick after it cooks, so choose your pan accordingly.

MAKES 6 SERVINGS

2 cups quartered cooked artichoke hearts

2 roasted red peppers, sliced

2 roasted yellow peppers, sliced

2 tbsp Vinaigrette-Style Dressing (page 292; see Note)

1 tbsp chopped parsley

1 tbsp chopped thyme

Freshly ground black pepper, as needed

4 tsp unsalted butter

8 Yukon gold potatoes, peeled and thinly sliced

½ tsp kosher salt

2 Spanish onions, sliced

4 large eggs

⅓ cup crumbled goat cheese

1. Combine the artichokes, peppers, vinaigrette, parsley, thyme, and a pinch of pepper in a large bowl and toss to coat evenly. Set aside.

2. Melt 1 teaspoon of the butter in a large sauté pan over medium heat. Add the potatoes, season with the salt and a pinch of pepper, and cook, turning them occasionally to cook evenly, about 8 minutes. Add the onions and cook until the potatoes are tender but not browned, 4 to 7 minutes more.

3. Break the eggs into a large bowl and blend with a fork. Do not whip them to a foam. Add the potato mixture to the eggs and toss gently to coat with the eggs.

4. Return the pan to medium heat and melt 2 teaspoons of the remaining butter. Pour the egg-vegetable mixture into the pan and cook without stirring until the bottom is set and golden brown, about 5 minutes. Tip the tortilla out of the pan onto a platter. Return the pan to the heat and melt the remaining teaspoon of butter. Slide the tortilla back into the pan, browned side facing up, and cook until the second side is browned, 3 to 4 minutes more.

5. Serve the tortilla sliced into wedges, topped with the artichoke and peppers and sprinkled with the goat cheese.

NOTE Use sherry vinegar in the Vinaigrette-Style Dressing.

ROASTING AND PEELING PEPPERS (120), **PREPARING ARTICHOKES** (121)

FRENCH TOAST with Winter Fruit Compote

Use a variety of dried fruits in the compote, such as cherries, blueberries, currants, cranberries, apricots, dates, figs, raisins, and/or prunes.

MAKES 6 SERVINGS

WINTER FRUIT COMPOTE

¼ cup white port wine

1¾ cups dried fruits

1¼ cups apple cider

1 tsp cornstarch

1 tsp ground cinnamon

½ tsp grated nutmeg

FRENCH TOAST

2 large whole eggs

8 large egg whites

½ cup nonfat milk

¼ tsp ground cinnamon

2 tsp vegetable oil or unsalted butter

12 slices whole wheat Pullman loaf, ½ in thick

1. For the compote, pour the wine into a small bowl, add the dried fruits, and plump for 15 minutes. Drain, reserving the wine.

2. Bring the cider to a boil in a small saucepan.

3. Combine the cornstarch with 2 tablespoons of reserved wine to form a paste. Gradually add the cornstarch slurry to the cider and simmer until thickened, about 2 minutes. The cider should be the consistency of maple syrup. Add the dried fruits, cinnamon, and nutmeg to the thickened cider and simmer until heated through, about 1 minute more.

4. Beat together the whole eggs, egg whites, milk, and cinnamon.

5. Heat a nonstick skillet over medium heat and add a little of the oil. Dip the bread into the egg mixture and cook in the hot pan until golden brown on both sides, about 2 minutes on each side. Add more oil to the pan as needed while cooking the French toast.

6. Slice the toast on the diagonal and serve on a pool of warm winter fruit compote.

SEPARATING EGGS (219)

BREAKFAST BURRITOS

Burritos make a great walk-away breakfast. You can change the fillings to use up any tasty leftovers you might have on hand, such as very thinly sliced grilled steak or chicken, cooked corn kernels, or roasted peppers. As long as you can wrap your tortilla around it, you're good to go!

MAKES 4 SERVINGS

3 cups water

½ tsp kosher salt

1½ cups medium-grain brown rice

1 tsp canola oil

4 large eggs

Four 10-inch wheat tortillas

2 cups Vegetarian Refried Beans (page 114)

2 green onions, thinly sliced on the bias

½ cup grated cheddar cheese

¼ cup Tomato Salsa (page 304)

¼ cup sour cream

1. Bring the water and salt to a boil in a medium pot over high heat. Add the rice and bring to a simmer over low heat. Cover and cook until the rice is tender, 25 to 30 minutes.

2. Heat the oil in a sauté pan over medium heat. Add the eggs and cook, stirring frequently to scramble, about 3 minutes.

3. Preheat a griddle and add the tortillas to warm, about 20 seconds on each side. Transfer the tortillas to a work surface. Spread the refried beans on the tortillas and top with the scrambled egg and rice. Sprinkle with the green onions and cheese and finish with the salsa and sour cream. Fold the sides in about 1 inch, then roll up the burritos to completely enclose the filling.

STEAMING GRAINS (92)

PIPERADE WRAP

Whipping the eggs with milk before cooking makes for a lighter, fluffier scramble.

MAKES 4 SERVINGS

1 tsp olive oil

⅔ cup sliced onion

1¼ cups sliced red or green pepper

1 cup chopped tomatoes (peeled and seeded)

⅓ cup diced ham (optional)

¼ tsp ground white pepper, or as needed

4 large eggs

1 tbsp milk

Four 8-inch whole wheat tortillas

1. Heat a sauté pan over medium-high heat. Add the oil, swirling to coat evenly. Add the onions and sauté, stirring occasionally, until tender and golden, 8 to 10 minutes. Add the pepper and tomatoes and sauté until mixture is very hot and the peppers are tender, 6 to 8 minutes. Add the ham, if desired, and sauté just until the ham is hot, 2 to 3 minutes. Season with the white pepper.

2. Whisk the eggs and milk in a large bowl until foamy. Add the eggs to the pan and continue to cook, stirring constantly, until the eggs are scrambled.

3. Heat the tortillas in a skillet or over a grill until soft. Top each tortilla with the egg mixture and wrap into a cylinder. Serve immediately.

PEELING AND SEEDING TOMATOES (121)

BREAKFAST PIZZA

Baking stones or tiles give pizzas a wonderful crust texture. Chefs use a "peel," essentially a large, flat wooden paddle, to "shovel" the pizza into the oven. Scatter the peel with some cornmeal so the pizza won't stick to it. Some baking sheets have edges on only two or three sides. These sheets can be used as a peel if you want to bake the pizza on tiles or a baking stone. Use a quick, jerking motion and a flick of the wrist to slide the pizza from the peel or pan onto the tiles.

MAKES 8 SERVINGS

1 pound Semolina Pizza Dough (recipe follows)

½ cup cooked or canned black beans (page 94)

1 red pepper, roasted, peeled, seeded, and cut into strips

3 tbsp chopped cilantro

½ tsp kosher salt, or as needed

¼ tsp freshly ground black pepper, or as needed

4 large eggs

1 cup shredded Manchego cheddar or sharp cheese

1. Preheat the oven to 425°F. If you are using a pizza stone, place it on the bottom rack and let it preheat along with the oven.

2. Stretch or roll the pizza dough to fit the pizza pan or stone and transfer to a peel or pan. Let it rest at room temperature while preparing the toppings for the pizza.

3. Sprinkle the dough with the black beans, red pepper, and cilantro and season with the salt and pepper.

4. Beat the eggs with a fork in a small bowl and pour evenly over the pizza, being careful not to pour the eggs too near the edges. Sprinkle the cheese over the top. Bake the pizza until the edges are golden and the eggs are fully cooked, 15 to 18 minutes. Cut into squares or wedges and serve hot or warm.

COOKING DRIED LEGUMES (95) **ROASTING AND PEELING PEPPERS** (120), **USING YEAST** (259)

SEMOLINA PIZZA DOUGH

Adding a bit of semolina to the pizza dough makes a crust that has a great crisp texture and a wonderful flavor. If time is running short, however, try picking up a ball of dough at your favorite pizza parlor.

MAKES TWO 12-INCH PIZZAS OR 1 LARGE RECTANGULAR PIZZA

3½ cups bread flour

½ cup semolina or durum flour

1½ tsp active dry yeast

1½ cups water

3 tbsp olive oil, plus more as needed to coat dough

2 tsp salt

Cornmeal, as needed to coat pan or peel

1. Place the flours and yeast in the bowl of a mixer (or a large bowl if you are mixing by hand). Add the water, oil, and salt and mix on low speed for 2 minutes or until a dough is starting to form. Increase to medium speed and continue to mix until the dough is satiny and elastic but is still a little sticky, 4 minutes more. (If you are mixing by hand, transfer the dough to a floured work surface and knead until satiny, about 10 minutes.)

2. Transfer the dough to a clean bowl and rub the surface with oil. Cover with plastic wrap or damp towels and let rise until nearly doubled, about 30 minutes. Fold gently and allow the dough to relax another 30 minutes before cutting it into 2 pieces to make 2 pizzas, if you wish. Let the dough rest, covered, until relaxed, 15 to 20 minutes. (Or place the shaped dough on a baking sheet and let the dough rest overnight in the refrigerator. It will need to warm for about 30 minutes before shaping.)

3. Scatter a thin layer of cornmeal on a baking sheet.

4. To shape the dough, press the dough into a disk, stretching and turning the dough as you work. You may finish stretching the dough by flipping it: With the dough resting on the backs of your hands, simultaneously spin the dough and toss it into the air. As it falls back down, catch it on the backs of your hands once more. Continue until the crust is evenly thick, ⅛ to ¼ inch. If you prefer, you can pull and stretch the dough directly on a lightly floured work surface until it is an even thickness.

5. Transfer the pizza to a prepared baking sheet. Continue with the recipe as directed.

SPINACH SOUFFLÉ

The eggs for soufflés must be whipped just before baking, but that doesn't mean you can't plan ahead. The soufflé base may be cooled, refrigerated, and held for up to two days. Let the base warm up for half an hour at room temperature. Stir vigorously to loosen the base before folding in the beaten egg whites.

MAKES 6 SERVINGS

SOUFFLÉ BASE

2 tbsp unsalted butter

3 tbsp all-purpose flour

1¾ cups nonfat milk

¼ tsp kosher salt, or as needed

Pinch freshly ground black pepper, or as needed

5 egg yolks

Butter, soft, as needed

¼ cup grated Parmigiano-Reggiano

2¾ cups cooked, drained, and chopped spinach

6 large egg whites

1. For the soufflé base, melt the butter in a medium saucepan over medium heat. Add the flour and cook over medium-low heat, stirring frequently, until the roux is blond, 6 to 8 minutes. Add the milk, whisking constantly, until the mixture is very smooth. Add the salt and pepper and simmer over low heat, stirring constantly, until very thick and smooth, 15 to 20 minutes.

2. Blend about ½ cup of the hot base into the yolks to temper. Return the tempered yolks to the base mixture and continue to simmer, stirring constantly, 3 to 4 minutes. Do not allow the mixture to boil. Adjust the seasoning with salt and pepper, and strain through a sieve if there are lumps in the mixture. The base is ready to use, or it may be properly cooled and stored for later use.

3. For the soufflé, preheat the oven to 425°F. Brush six 6-ounce soufflé molds liberally with soft butter. Lightly dust the interior of each mold with some cheese.

4. Combine the soufflé base and spinach in a large bowl. Beat the egg whites in a mixer to medium-firm peaks. Gently fold the egg whites into the spinach mixture. Gently fill the soufflé molds with the finished batter and dust with a little of the remaining cheese. Bake until puffed and set, about 16 minutes. Serve at once.

PREPARING SPINACH AND LEAFY GREENS (121), **SEPARATING EGGS** (219)

TROPICAL FRUIT SMOOTHIES

The average blender can usually hold enough to make two servings of a smoothie at once, so if you are planning to make more, dice as much fruit as you need, then purée the smoothies in several batches.

MAKES 2 SERVINGS

1 cup diced pineapple

¼ cup diced mango (peeled and seeded)

¼ cup diced papaya (peeled and seeded)

¼ cup diced kiwi (peeled)

½ cup orange juice

¼ cup lowfat coconut milk

¼ cup plain nonfat yogurt (optional)

⅓ cup ice cubes

1 tbsp sugar, or as needed

¼ tsp vanilla extract

2 pineapple slices, for garnish

Toasted shredded unsweetened coconut, for garnish (optional)

1. Purée the pineapple, mango, papaya, kiwi, and ¼ cup of the orange juice in a blender until smooth. With the machine still running, add the remaining ¼ cup orange juice, the coconut milk, yogurt, if desired, ice, sugar, and vanilla. Blend until smooth and thick.

2. Serve the smoothies at once in chilled tall glasses, garnished with a pineapple slice and a sprinkle of toasted coconut, if desired.

PEACH SMOOTHIES

Try other fruit juices instead of peach juice or nectar. Cranberry, mango, apple, or pineapple juices are all good choices.

MAKES 2 SERVINGS

2 ripe peaches, peeled and pitted

1 banana, sliced

1 cup peach juice or nectar

½ cup plain nonfat yogurt

3 tbsp honey, or as needed

2 peach slices, for garnish

1. Purée the peaches, banana, peach juice, yogurt, and honey in a blender until smooth and thick.

2. Serve the smoothies at once in chilled tall glasses, garnished with a peach slice.

MANGO LASSI

This traditional Indian drink was originally made from yogurt, water, toasted cumin, salt, and chiles. Sweet lassis, such as this one, have become very popular in recent years. They are quite similar to smoothies. To make a mango purée, cut a very ripe mango and push the flesh through a fine-mesh sieve or a food mill. If you have any leftover purée, you can store it in the refrigerator or freezer.

MAKES 8 SERVINGS

4 cups mango purée (about 3 medium)

4 cups plain nonfat yogurt

½ cup nonfat milk

½ cup water

4 tsp lime juice

2 tsp honey, or as needed

¾ tsp ground cardamom

1. Whisk together the mango, yogurt, milk, water, lime juice, honey, and cardamom in a large bowl or pitcher. Taste the mango mixture and add more honey if needed.

2. Serve chilled as a beverage or as an early course in a meal.

JUICING CITRUS (285)

MANDARIN FRAPPÉ

To achieve the frothiest results, make one drink at a time.

MAKES 1 SERVING

Crushed ice, as needed

Juice of 1 lime

Juice of 1 mandarin orange

GARNISH

1 lime slice

1. Fill a cocktail shaker cup with crushed ice. Add the juices, cover the shaker cup with the top, and shake vigorously.

2. Fill a tall glass with more crushed ice. Strain the frappé into the ice-filled glass.

3. Rub the lime slice around the rim of the glass before garnishing.

ZESTING AND JUICING CITRUS (284)

Raspberry-Lime Rickey (page 247) and Mediterranean Cooler

MEDITERRANEAN COOLERS

A variety of fruit juices and nectars are now commonly available in most grocery stores and gourmet markets in the juice and beverage aisle. If you decide to use them instead of making your own juices, check the label to see if there are added sugars.

MAKES 6 SERVINGS

4 cups tangerine juice

2 cups pomegranate juice

2 cups club soda

Ice cubes (optional)

1. Combine the tangerine and pomegranate juices in a pitcher. Chill.

2. When ready to serve, pour the juice into 6 tall glasses, add the club soda, and stir to combine. Serve over ice, if desired.

JUICING CITRUS (285)

CANTALOUPE COCKTAIL

This drink highlights the almost creamy flavor of ripe cantaloupe,
which is complemented by the addition of vanilla extract.

MAKES 6 SERVINGS

1 medium cantaloupe, diced

2 cups orange juice

3 tbsp lime juice

¼ tsp vanilla extract

8 to 10 ice cubes

GARNISH

6 slices lime

Blend the cantaloupe, orange juice, lime juice, vanilla, and ice in a blender until very smooth. Serve in chilled glasses and garnish with the lime slices.

JUICING CITRUS (285)

CARROT-GINGER COCKTAIL

If you don't have a juicer, you can still make this delicious vegetable cocktail.
Replace the whole carrots called for here with 1½ cups carrot juice. You can
find carrot juice in larger markets or at natural foods stores.

MAKES 2 SERVINGS

4 medium carrots, trimmed and sliced

2 stalks celery, trimmed

2 apples, cored and chopped

1 slice peeled fresh ginger, about ¼ inch thick

1. Juice all of the ingredients in a juice machine following the manufacturer's instructions.

2. Stir the cocktail well to even out the flavor before serving. Serve at once in tall glasses.

PREPARING GINGER (284)

AGUA DE JAMAICA (Hibiscus Cooler)

Agua de jamaica is a delicious herbal tea from Mexico with a refreshing taste and a beautiful ruby red color that comes from hibiscus flowers. These flowers are known as *jamaica* in Spanish (pronounced ha-MAIK-ah). The flowers can leave stains, so use stainless-steel or glass containers instead of plastic, aluminum, or ceramic.

MAKES 8 SERVINGS

2 quarts (8 cups) water, or as needed

2 cups hibiscus flowers

1¼ cups sugar, or as needed

3 medium oranges, cut in half

1. Bring the water to a boil. Add the hibiscus and sugar and stir constantly until the mixture boils, about 1 minute.

2. Squeeze the juice from the oranges into a large, nonreactive bowl and add the orange halves. Pour in the hibiscus mixture and steep for 1 hour.

3. Strain through a sieve, pressing on the hibiscus and oranges to extract as much liquid as possible. Taste the liquid for strength and sweetness. If it is too pungent, add water. If it is too tart, add sugar. Cover and refrigerate in a pitcher until ready to serve.

RASPBERRY-LIME RICKEY

During berry season, you can make your own raspberry purée using fresh raspberries and adding sugar to taste. But this drink can be made year-round thanks to the unsweetened frozen raspberries available in the freezer section of most grocery stores and specialty markets.

MAKES 6 SERVINGS

¾ cup raspberries

1 tsp sugar (optional)

⅓ cup lime juice

Ice cubes, as needed (optional)

4 cups club soda or sparkling water

6 lime wedges, for garnish

1. Purée the raspberries in a blender until smooth. Strain to remove the seeds. Add the sugar to taste, if needed. Combine the raspberry purée and lime juice in a pitcher. Pour into 6 tall glasses, over ice if desired. Add the club soda and stir to mix well.

2. Serve, garnished with lime wedges.

JUICING CITRUS (285)

CHAI

Originally from India, *masala chai* or "spiced tea" is a flavorful tea brewed from black tea leaves and an array of spices, sweetened with honey.

MAKES 8 SERVINGS

3 cups water

12 Darjeeling tea bags

3 cinnamon sticks, broken into pieces

2 tbsp sliced ginger

1 tbsp cardamom pods

1½ tsp fennel seeds

¼ tsp cloves

3 or 4 black peppercorns

1 star anise

1 vanilla bean, split

3 tbsp honey, or as needed

3 cups low fat or skim milk

1. Bring the water to a boil in a medium saucepan over high heat. Add the tea bags, cinnamon, ginger, cardamom, fennel, cloves, peppercorns, star anise, and vanilla. Reduce the heat to low and simmer, stirring occasionally, until aromatic and the mixture is a rich caramel brown, about 10 minutes. Add the honey and milk and stir to dissolve the honey. Bring to a boil and remove from the heat.

2. Strain the liquid through a sieve, pressing on the tea bags and spices to extract as much liquid and flavor as possible. Taste the liquid for sweetness, and add more honey if needed.

3. Serve the chai immediately as a hot drink, or chill and serve over ice.

PREPARING GINGER (284)

Chai spices include cardamom, ginger, star anise, cinnamon, fennel, and peppercorns.

HOT MULLED CIDER

Mulled cider is a classic late fall and winter beverage that includes both fresh cider and citrus. For more citrus flavor, add additional orange zest.

MAKES 6 SERVINGS

4 cups apple cider

1 cinnamon stick

3 or 4 cloves

3 or 4 allspice berries

Zest of 1 orange

6 orange slices, for garnish

1. Combine the cider, cinnamon stick, cloves, allspice, and orange zest in a small saucepan. Simmer until the flavor of the spices and orange peel are infused into the cider, about 20 minutes.

2. Strain the cider and serve in heated mugs or glasses. Garnish each portion with an orange slice.

JUICING CITRUS (285)

CHAPTER NINE

Desserts and Baked Goods

One of the greatest challenges in healthier eating is desserts and baked goods. These items are often high in fat, sugar, and salt, without much in the way of beneficial nutrients. We still enjoy something sweet after a meal, a bit of bread with our meals, or even a baked good as the main part of a meal like breakfast.

Fruits, chocolates, nuts, reduced- or nonfat dairy, and whole grains are the basis of the recipes in this chapter. These ingredients all have positive nutritional benefits that give you more flexibility than you might imagine. Cornmeal, for instance, makes a great cornbread as well as an indulgent pudding-style cake. Including some prune purée in chocolate cookies makes them fudgy and rich, as well as higher in fiber, vitamins, and minerals than a typical cookie.

Cutting back on sugars and fats in baked goods calls on the cook to use some inventive strategies to keep desserts and baked goods moist and flavorful. Ingredient selection is the first step. Look for ripe, seasonal fruits, high-quality dark chocolates, and a selection of raw nuts to keep on hand. Low-fat ricotta and Greek-style yogurt fill in for sour or heavy cream; they have rich, appealing flavors and textures of their own, unlike other low-fat or low-calorie substitutions. Use herbs and spices as an accent or to deepen flavors. Use textures to your advantage too; phyllo dough can stand in for a traditional pie dough to make galettes and turnovers.

Chocolate and Cocoa

Chocolate is produced from cocoa beans harvested from the cacao tree. Commonly associated with sweets and desserts, you can also use chocolate in savory entrées, as is the case in Mexico, where chocolate appears particularly in moles.

Chocolate is naturally bitter, so sugar is added to make it palatable. Most chocolate contains varying amounts of cocoa butter, the vegetable fat that occurs naturally in chocolate. Cocoa powder, on the other hand, is usually unsweetened. Dutch-process cocoa powder, mostly used in baking, is treated with an alkali to reduce its acidity.

WORKING WITH CHOCOLATE

Good-quality chocolates and cocoas are showing up everywhere. With a little information about labels and the information they contain, you'll be able to find a brand that has the perfect texture, aroma, and taste.

IS CHOCOLATE HEALTHY?

Chocolate and cocoa powder contain antioxidants, including catechins, the compounds that make tea so beneficial. Dark chocolate has more catechins than milk chocolate. Chocolate also has minerals such as copper, iron, and zinc. Even though rich with nutrients, however, chocolate is also high in fat and sugar and so should be eaten in moderation.

Store chocolate, well wrapped, in a cool, dry, ventilated area. Refrigerate only if outside temperatures are hot and humid; refrigeration can cause moisture to condense on its surface. That can affect the way it melts as well as its appearance, giving it grayish streaks.

According to health experts and nutritionists, chocolate may actually be good for us. But there is a catch: Only a small quantity of chocolate is good for us. And further, experts generally consider darker chocolates to have the upper hand. The benefits of chocolate are related to the quantity of antioxidants and other heart-healthy compounds found in cocoa beans, but many of these compounds are destroyed during processing.

Chocolate Labels

Many chocolate brands include a percentage on the label these days. The higher the number, the more chocolate liquor and butter the product contains. The percentage doesn't really tell you much more about the chocolate in terms of its quality. Some chocolates also indicate their geographic origin, as well as the variety of cocoa bean in the product.

Until 2004, the term *white chocolate* was not acceptable for use on a product label. The FDA does currently accept the name. The minimum requirement for something to be labeled white chocolate is that the product contains at least 20 percent cocoa butter, 14 percent milk solids, 3.5 percent butterfat, and not more than 55 percent sugar.

Cocoa Powder

Cocoa powder is produced when chocolate liquor (ground cocoa beans with no added sugar or other ingredients) is pressed to extract as much cocoa butter as possible. The solids left behind are ground into a power known as cocoa. Some cocoa powders contain more than 22 percent fat, and others contain less than half that amount. Dutch-process cocoas have been treated with an alkali to neutralize acids and eliminate any sour flavors in the cocoa. This process also makes the cocoa darker but doesn't have any effect on the depth of "chocolatey-ness" of the cocoa.

Melting Chocolate

Because of the types of fats found in chocolate, it can be tricky to melt chocolate without having it turn lumpy or stiff—the automatic results of letting water come in contact with the chocolate or letting it get too hot. To melt chocolate on the stovetop, use a bain marie, or better yet, a metal bowl that fits down into a sauce pot and is wider than the opening of the pot (that will keep water droplets from getting into the chocolate), such as a double boiler. Chop the chocolate, add it to the bowl, and let the heat from the barely simmering water beneath it warm and melt the chocolate. You can also melt chocolate successfully in a microwave, as long as you use a low to moderate setting. Work in short "bursts" and stir the chocolate between each burst to melt it evenly.

Fruits in Desserts

Customarily used in sweet dishes, fruits are used in desserts such as galettes and ice creams, or served with or without cheese as a classic finale to a meal.

Fruits can be used to great advantage on their own. Consider broiling fresh citrus or other fruit to caramelize the natural sugars.

GRILLING OR ROASTING FRUITS

Fruits are usually softer than vegetables, and you may need to give them a very light coating of oil or put them in a hand rack or grill basket when you grill them so they don't stick or tear when you turn them over. Pineapple has a lot of natural sugar and is quite juicy. Be sure the heat is high enough to quickly mark the outside. The grill marks add color and some texture, as well as a pleasantly smoky, bitter taste.

Roasted fruits are prepared by slicing the fruit thin enough so that it cooks to the texture and flavor you want. Like grilling, roasting amplifies some of the fruit's natural flavors. It also has a more noticeable effect on the fruit texture, drying it until it is almost leathery. Fruits can be roasted at a low temperature for short periods to soften them slightly, or for a longer period to create crunchy or chewy textures. Roasted fruits are a good garnish for fruit desserts or salads, or they can be used as an element in a sauce, compote, or salsa.

Quick Breads, Cookies, and Simple Cakes

The basic mixing methods used for baked goods in this chapter include the straight mixing method, in which wet ingredients are added to dry ingredients in a single step; liquids such as buttermilk take the place of oils and melted butter. The foaming mixing method takes advantage of egg whites to produce a delicate cake perfect for pairing with fruit.

THE STRAIGHT MIXING METHOD

The straight mixing method is one of the most common techniques for mixing quick breads and simple cakes.

Combining the Dry Ingredients

The dry ingredients—such as flour, salt, and baking powder or soda—are evenly blended by either sifting or whisking them together. You may sift them together, or simply measure the ingredients into a bowl and then use a whisk to stir them. This will break up any lumps and distribute the leaveners more evenly. When a recipe calls for both baking powder and baking soda, the baking soda's main purpose is to neutralize an acid in the batter, while the baking powder provides the majority of the leavening action.

Combining the Wet Ingredients

Wet ingredients usually include milk, buttermilk, cream, water, fruit juice, oil, or melted butter. Eggs are also considered a liquid. All of these ingredients should be properly measured and, when necessary, warmed enough to blend easily with the other wet ingredients. Batters blend most evenly when the liquid ingredients are all close to room temperature. Use a whisk or a table fork to blend the wet ingredients together until they are smooth.

Combining the Dry and Wet Ingredients

Most batters made with the straight mixing method are best mixed by hand. They are usually not heavy enough to make stirring difficult, and a short mixing time produces the most tender baked goods. Combine the wet and the dry ingredients all at once. Use a wooden spoon or a spatula to stir and fold the batter until the dry ingredients are evenly moistened. As soon as the batter is mixed, transfer it to prepared pans and bake at once (unless a recipe directs otherwise). If the batter sits for too long after mixing, the chemical leaveners can lose their leavening power.

THE FOAMING MIXING METHOD

The foaming mixing method gives angel food and sponge cakes their delicate, light texture.

Whipping the Eggs

The mixing method, used primarily for angel food cakes, calls for eggs (whole or separated) to be whipped with sugar until they make a thick, relatively stable foam. Use a large, round balloon whisk or the wire whisk attachment of a stand mixer to incorporate as much air as possible. Begin whipping at a slow to moderate speed, until the whites loosen and become foamy. Ingredients like sugar or cream of tartar are gradually added starting at this point. Increase the speed to high and continue to whip. As more air is beaten into the whites, the texture becomes very smooth and the foam thickens enough to mound slightly. As you keep whipping, you will see the whisk start to leave track marks in the egg whites. "Soft peak" describes the point at which the foam is still very glossy and moist, and when you pull the whisk out of the bowl and turn it upright, the whites slump over to one side in rounded peaks. A "medium peak" stays upright, but the tip folds over. "Stiff peaks" stand up straight.

Folding In the Dry Ingredients

Once the foam is prepared, work quickly to keep as much air in the foam as possible. Scatter the dry ingredients over the entire surface of the batter. Use a smooth, circular motion to fold the batter together: Sweep a rubber spatula down along one side of the bowl and toward the center, then lift the spatula up through the center of the batter. Give the bowl a quarter turn periodically as you fold to mix the batter evenly.

Adding Fat without Losing Volume

Adding a small amount of melted butter or oil to a foam provides moisture and tenderness, but as you add these ingredients you want to avoid weighing down the foam so much that it collapses. Both the foam batter and the fat should be at room temperature. Add a few dollops of batter to the fat and fold them together before adding the tempered fat mixture back into the batter, folding swiftly and carefully.

DETERMINING DONENESS

As muffins, quick breads, scones, and biscuits bake, they increase in volume, puffing up as the chemical leaveners do their work. When fully baked, they have a golden brown color.

Testing for Doneness

Use the suggested time range in recipes as a general guideline, but also use as many of the following tests as possible to test baked items for doneness.

Quick breads and cakes prepared in a skillet or on a griddle, like crêpes or pancakes, are cooked on the first side until the edges just start to set and small bubbles break through the upper surface. When fully cooked, the cakes are browned on both sides and the sides appear set and no longer wet. Test thick pancakes by pressing them lightly with your fingertip. You should feel relatively little give.

Test simple cakes and loaf-style quick breads for doneness by gently pressing them near the center with the pad of your index finger. When fully baked, the cake springs back, leaving no indentation. Another common test calls for inserting a wooden skewer or toothpick near the center of the cake; the skewer should come out of the cake clean or with only a few moist crumbs clinging to it. Test biscuits and scones by tapping them on the bottom with your fingertips and listening for a hollow sound.

Frozen Desserts

Frozen desserts range from a churned glacé, similar in many respects to ice cream but with a flavor and texture all its own, to a Bavarian-style cream to an icy sorbet. Churned frozen desserts call for an ice cream machine, but still-frozen desserts are simply placed in a mold and allowed to freeze until firm.

MAKING CHURNED FROZEN DESSERTS

Our Maple-Ricotta-Yogurt Cream (page 268) and Champagne and Lemon Sorbet (page 271) are churned frozen desserts, made in an ice cream maker. The churning action introduces air for a light texture that can be scooped even when fully frozen. It also keeps the ice crystals from getting so large, for a delicate, creamy consistency.

Flavoring and Ripening the Base
It is good practice to refrigerate the base mixture for at least 4 hours and preferably overnight before freezing it. If the base is not chilled completely before you put it into an ice cream maker, it may not freeze properly.

Likewise, allowing the finished glacé or sorbet to "ripen" or set in the freezer for at least 3 or 4 hours before you serve gives it a chance to fully set. This makes the dessert easier to scoop and slower to melt. Flavor also continues to develop and mellow during ripening.

Serving Churned Frozen Desserts
To serve a frozen dessert, make sure that your scoop is clean and dry. If the scoop is wet, it can introduce ice crystals that will give your ice cream or other dessert an unpleasant gritty texture. You can also use a large, sturdy spoon to scrape curls of glacé from the top of a large block. If your glacé or sorbet is too firm to scoop or scrape easily, let it rest in the refrigerator for about 30 minutes before serving.

MAKING MOLDED FROZEN DESSERTS

Still-frozen desserts are molded before they go into the freezer. The mold gives these desserts their distinctive shapes. Frozen soufflés mimic hot soufflés in appearance; a paper collar secured around the mold allows you overfill it, creating the illusion that the mixture has risen like a hot baked soufflé. Parfaits can be piped or spooned into attractive molds; a glass mold practically begs you to use layers of different flavors and colors to make a beautiful presentation.

Preparing the Mold
Some frozen desserts are served directly from the mold. Others are frozen in the mold and then unmolded before they are served. Mold options include glasses or stemware, loaf pans, bowls, cups, and molds made specifically for frozen desserts. Prepare the mold by spraying it with cooking spray or lining it with plastic wrap so that you can easily unmold the dessert before you serve it, but you can opt to serve it right in or from the molds, and then the mold does not have to be treated.

For frozen soufflés or parfaits that will look like hot soufflés, spray the mold with flourless cooking spray. Cut a piece of parchment paper long enough to wrap completely around the outside of the mold; it should rise about 2 inches above the mold. Tape the ends of the paper down to secure it in place or wrap a piece of string around the mold and tie it to hold the paper around the mold. Pour the filling into the mold so that it rises above the mold's rim. The parchment holds the filling in place as it freezes.

Filling the Mold

To fill the mold evenly without any air pockets, be certain the ice cream or mousse is soft enough to pour or spoon easily. Use the back of a spoon or a small palette knife to spread the mixture in an even layer and press out any air bubbles. You can add a variety of ice creams and mousses with different flavors and colors to create a variegated frozen dessert, or add layers of garnish items, like crushed cookies, a fruit purée, or ganache. To settle the ice cream or mousse into the mold and fill every corner, gently tap the filled mold on the countertop.

Freezing and Unmolding

Put the filled mold in the freezer and let the dessert firm up for at least 3 hours; most molded frozen desserts can be held for 2 or 3 days if they are properly wrapped. Be certain that the mold is sitting level on the shelf. Most frozen desserts benefit from a short period of tempering before you serve them. Transfer the frozen dessert to the refrigerator for about 30 minutes so that it softens evenly and the flavors open up. To unmold, fill a big bowl or pan or the sink with a few inches of hot water. Lower the mold into the water for a few seconds, then put a plate over the top of the mold. Hold the plate in place with one hand and invert the plate and mold. Lift the mold up and away from the dessert to release it onto the plate. Peel away the plastic wrap, if used.

WORKING WITH GELATIN

Gelatin gives mousses, whipped cream, and other soft, relatively liquid items extra body.

SOFTENING OR "BLOOMING" GELATIN

Place a small amount of cold liquid in a small bowl, usually about ¼ cup for 1 envelope (2¼ teaspoons or ¼ oz) powdered gelatin, and scatter the gelatin over the surface. Stir briefly with a fork to break up any clumps. As the gelatin sits in the liquid, it will swell, a process known as blooming.

MELTING GELATIN

After the gelatin has bloomed, melt it in a double boiler over barely simmering water until the mixture is clear. Alternatively, microwave it on low power for 20 seconds. Once melted, add it immediately to the liquid to be thickened. Stir it well, or the gelatin may sink to the bottom.

Phyllo Dough

Phyllo dough is made from a simple mixture of flour and water. The dough is worked until it develops enough gluten to stretch into very thin sheets, sometimes called leaves. Although it doesn't rise quite as dramatically as puff pastry, stacking sheets up with a layer of melted butter in between each sheet gives the finished pastry a similarly flaky texture. Phyllo dough is readily available frozen.

USING PHYLLO DOUGH

Phyllo dough is available in the freezer section of well-stocked supermarkets and in Greek or Middle Eastern groceries.

Thawing and Layering
Thaw frozen phyllo dough either overnight in the refrigerator or at room temperature for 2 hours. Once thawed, the individual sheets should pull apart easily and be very flexible. However, contact with the air soon dries out phyllo unless it is covered.

Setting Up a Work Flow
Set up your work area so that your phyllo stays moist and flexible as you work with it. Place a large baking sheet or a piece of plastic wrap on your work surface, remove the phyllo from the box, and unroll enough sheets to make your recipe. Set the sheets flat on the baking sheet or plastic wrap. Cover the sheets completely with another large piece of plastic wrap, then lay lightly dampened paper towels or a barely moistened kitchen towel over the plastic to keep the air around the phyllo moist.

Stacking the Sheets
Transfer one sheet of the phyllo at a time to your flat work area and immediately re-cover the remaining sheets. Brush or spray the entire sheet with butter or oil. For a very flaky texture and extra flavor in the finished dish, you can scatter bread crumbs or sugar over the sheet next. Keep working this way, one sheet at a time, until you have the correct number of layers for your recipe.

Yeast Bread

Our naan recipe (page 265) as well as our recipes for pizza dough (pages 77 and 239) are made with yeast. If you've never worked with yeast before, naan is an excellent and forgiving introduction to the technique.

USING YEAST

Yeast is an organic, living leavening agent that requires a food source, moisture, and a moderate temperature in order to grow and reproduce. It is that activity that gives yeasted baked goods their lighter texture and complex flavors.

Creating the Proper Environment

Yeast thrives when temperatures are moderate (75° to 80°F is ideal). The liquid you use in a bread recipe should be at room temperature (somewhere between 68° and 76°F) for most breads; it will feel slightly cool but not cold. Warm or hot water is generally not needed unless your kitchen and the ingredients are very cold. Similarly, if the kitchen is very warm, you may want to use slightly cooler water (60° to 70°F) to prevent the dough from rising too quickly.

KNEADING

Kneading dough stretches the gluten in the flour, making it strong, flexible, and elastic.

Gathering Into a Shaggy Mass

Whether you are mixing dough with a stand mixer or by hand, look for the dough to become heavy, stiff, and shaggy in appearance. It is now ready to move from the mixing stage into the kneading stage.

To knead by machine, simply increase the machine's speed. If your machine starts to "walk" across the counter as it kneads the dough, you should finish kneading by hand, incorporating the additional flour as needed.

To knead by hand, turn the dough out of the bowl onto a floured work surface and follow the steps below.

Kneading the Dough

Transfer the dough to a lightly floured work surface and gather it into a ball. Press the heels of your palms into the dough and push the dough away from you. Give the ball of dough a quarter turn as you fold the far edge back over onto the dough. As you continue to push and pull the dough, stretching it evenly in all directions, dust the dough, the work surface, and your hands lightly with flour to prevent sticking.

The First Rise

When the dough is smooth and elastic, it is ready for the first rise. Shape the dough into a ball and place it in a bowl that you've rubbed very lightly with oil. Cover the bowl with plastic wrap and let the dough double in volume. The warmer your kitchen, the faster this will happen. Typically, it takes 1 to 1½ hours. You'll know it's ready when you press the dough with a fingertip; it should leave behind an indentation that does not fill in again rapidly.

Folding Over the Dough

Instead of "punching" the dough as some cookbooks recommend—a little too vigorous for most doughs—gently fold the dough over on itself from the edges to the center and gently press down. You should be able to hear and feel the gases release. Once folded, some doughs are given a second rise, whereas some are simply rested briefly before dividing or shaping them.

BLACK PEPPER BISCUITS

Black pepper gives the biscuits a fair amount of heat, but they are a perfect accompaniment to grilled or roasted foods and a great option for simple sandwiches made with fresh or roasted vegetables and a bit of goat cheese.

MAKES 6 SERVINGS

2 cups all-purpose flour, or as needed

1 tbsp sugar

1½ tsp coarsely ground black pepper

1½ tsp baking powder

¼ tsp baking soda

¼ tsp kosher salt

2 tbsp cold unsalted butter

¾ cup buttermilk

Milk, as needed

1. Preheat the oven to 375°F. Lightly spray a baking sheet with cooking spray.

2. Combine the flour, sugar, pepper, baking powder, baking soda, and salt in a large bowl. Cut the butter into the dry ingredients using a pastry cutter or two table knives until the mixture looks like a very coarse meal.

3. Make a well in the center and pour the buttermilk into the well all at once. Stir the ingredients together with a fork just until the dry ingredients are evenly moistened. The dough will be quite heavy but should not be dry.

4. Dust the work surface and rolling pin lightly with flour. Transfer the dough to the work surface and roll out to a 1-inch thickness. Fold the dough in half and turn it 90 degrees. Roll it out, fold, and turn twice more. The dough should be about 1 inch thick. Cut the dough into rounds using a 2-inch biscuit cutter. Cut as many biscuits as you can, then gather up the scraps, press the dough into a ball, and roll it out once more to a 1-inch thickness. Cut more biscuits until all the dough is used up.

5. Arrange the biscuits on the baking sheet in even rows, leaving about 1 inch between them. Lightly brush the tops of the biscuits with milk and bake until golden brown, 12 to 15 minutes. Cool the biscuits on wire racks, and serve warm or a room temperature.

THE STRAIGHT MIXING METHOD [255], **DETERMINING DONENESS** [256]

COUNTRY CORN BREAD

This recipe does contain a little sugar, but you can eliminate that if you prefer a more traditional Southern flavor. If you have a 10-inch cast-iron skillet, use that to bake the corn bread to get a rich, flavorful, crunchy crust. Let the pan get hot in the oven as it preheats. If you have corn stick pans, treat them the same way as you would your cast-iron skillet. The baking time will be reduced by five to six minutes.

MAKES 6 SERVINGS

Butter, soft, as needed

1 cup yellow cornmeal

1 cup all-purpose flour

1 tbsp sugar

2 tsp baking powder

½ tsp baking soda

¼ tsp kosher salt

1½ cups buttermilk

2 large eggs

2 tbsp canola oil

1. Preheat the oven to 425°F. Rub a 9-inch square baking pan with butter.

2. Stir together the cornmeal, flour, sugar, baking powder, baking soda, and salt with a fork in a large bowl.

3. Whisk together the buttermilk, eggs, and oil in another bowl.

4. Add the wet ingredients to the dry ingredients and stir just until the dry ingredients are evenly moistened.

5. Spread the batter in an even layer in the baking pan. Bake until the top crust is golden brown and a wooden skewer inserted in the center of the corn bread comes out clean, about 25 minutes.

THE STRAIGHT MIXING METHOD (255), **DETERMINING DONENESS** (256)

Country Corn Bread (rear), Black Pepper Biscuits (page 261; front)

Grilling the eggplant makes the flesh tender for puréeing and gives the purée a delicious charred flavor.

Grilled Naan with Eggplant Purée and Red Pepper Coulis (page 298)

GRIDDLED NAAN with Eggplant Purée

Naan is the perfect accompaniment to Indian food, but we also like it with grilled eggplant purée. Sometimes, we fold a whole naan around the eggplant filling to enjoy as a sandwich.

MAKES 8 PIECES

NAAN

1 package active dry yeast

1 cup warm water

3 cups bread flour

¼ tsp kosher salt

¼ cup plain yogurt

2 tbsp olive oil

1 large egg, lightly beaten

1 cup Eggplant Purée (recipe follows)

½ cup Red Pepper Coulis (page 298)

---

1. Combine the yeast and warm water in a small bowl and stir to moisten the yeast. Let the mixture rest until there is a thick foam on the surface, about 30 minutes.

2. Combine 2 cups of the flour and the salt in a large bowl and make a well in the center. Add the yeast mixture, the yogurt, oil, and egg into the center of the dry ingredients and stir with a wooden spoon until a heavy dough forms. Turn the dough out onto a floured work surface and knead the dough by hand until it is soft but smooth and resilient, adding ¼ cup of the remaining flour at a time as needed.

3. Gather the dough into a ball and place in a lightly oiled bowl. Cover with a clean towel and let it rise until it is nearly doubled, about 1 hour. Press the dough with your fingertips to release the gases. Place the dough on a lightly floured work surface. Cut the dough into 8 pieces of equal size with a sharp knife. Shape the pieces into disks and let them rest for 15 minutes.

4. Heat a cast-iron skillet or griddle over medium-high heat. (If the pan is not well seasoned, you should brush it very lightly with a bit of oil to keep the naan from sticking.)

5. Stretch or roll the pieces of dough into thin circles (about ¼ inch). As you lift the dough to transfer it to the skillet or griddle, pull on one side to make a teardrop shape. Cook the naan on the first side until blistered and light golden. Turn the dough and finish cooking.

6. Serve the naan with the eggplant purée.

USING YEAST (259), **KNEADING** (260)

EGGPLANT PURÉE

MAKES 2 CUPS

1 eggplant, whole	1 tsp minced green chiles
¼ tsp kosher salt	1 tbsp yogurt
½ cup minced onion	

Prepare a grill for a medium fire. Grill the eggplant, turning as necessary until soft and well browned on all sides, about 20 minutes. Remove the skin and place the pulp in a bowl. Mash the pulp thoroughly. Add the remaining ingredients and mash and stir to make a thick purée.

CHOCOLATE-RICOTTA BAVARIAN

Serve this rich, creamy dessert with Almond-Anise Biscotti (281), fresh berries, and a little drizzle of Caramel Sauce for a delicious plated dessert.

MAKES 6 SERVINGS

Powdered sugar, as needed

1½ tsp gelatin

2 tbsp water

1⅓ cups Maple-Ricotta-Yogurt Cream (page 268)

2 oz semisweet chocolate, chopped

½ cup cocoa powder

2 tbsp sugar

5 large egg whites

6 Almond-Anise Biscotti (page 281)

½ cup Caramel Sauce (recipe follows)

1. Spray the inside of six 3-inch molds with vegetable oil and dust with powdered sugar. Place the molds on a baking sheet lined with plastic wrap. Place in the refrigerator until needed.

2. Meanwhile, combine the gelatin and water and bloom, about 5 minutes. Melt the gelatin in a double boiler.

3. Combine the cream with the chocolate and heat very gently in the double boiler, 3 to 4 minutes. Add the dissolved gelatin and cocoa powder to the chocolate mixture and whisk until smooth. Remove from the heat and cool to room temperature.

4. Warm the sugar and egg whites in the double boiler until they are warm to the touch (100°F). Remove from the double boiler, whip the mixture to medium peaks with a mixer, and fold into the chocolate mixture.

5. Fill a pastry bag with the chocolate mousse and pipe the mixture into the molds. Cover with plastic wrap and chill for at least 2 hours.

6. Dip the molds into the hot water long enough to warm the mold. Hold a plate on top of the mold, and turn the mold and plate over so that the Bavarian drops out of the mold onto the plate. Serve with the biscotti and sauce.

MELTING CHOCOLATE (254), **WORKING WITH GELATIN** (258), **SEPARATING EGGS** (219)

CARAMEL SAUCE

MAKES ¾ CUP

2 tbsp unsalted butter	¼ cup evaporated skim milk
3 tbsp water	1 tsp cornstarch
½ cup sugar	1 tbsp dark rum, Kahlúa, or brandy

1. Combine the butter, water, and sugar in a medium sauce pot over medium-low heat and cook, stirring frequently, until the mixture turns a dark brown color, about 5 minutes. Remove from the heat.

2. Combine the milk, cornstarch, and liqueur in a small bowl. Add to the caramelized sugar and stir well. Return the sauce to low heat and boil gently until lightly thickened, about 2 minutes. Remove from the heat and cool. The sauce is ready to serve, or it may be stored in the refrigerator for 2 to 3 days.

RICE PUDDING

Letting the rice cook slowly and gently in sweetened milk produces a comforting, creamy dessert. We've opted for a round-grain brown rice for extra flavor and texture.

MAKES 6 SERVINGS

⅔ cup round-grain brown rice

1¾ cups water

⅔ cup golden raisins

Pinch grated nutmeg

Pinch ground cinnamon

Pinch kosher salt

¼ cup sugar

1 tsp lemon juice

⅓ cup part-skim ricotta cheese, puréed

1 tsp vanilla extract

1. Combine the rice, water, raisins, nutmeg, cinnamon, salt, sugar, and lemon juice in a medium saucepan over medium heat. Cover and simmer until the rice is tender and has absorbed the liquid, 25 to 30 minutes.

2. Transfer the rice to a 13 by 9 by 2-inch dish. Fold the ricotta and vanilla into the rice. Let the rice pudding chill for at least 3 hours before serving.

JUICING CITRUS (285), **STEAMING GRAINS** (92)

MAPLE-RICOTTA-YOGURT CREAM

You can add a number of flavors to this cream, like fresh or puréed fruits, nuts, spices, or coffee.

MAKES 6 SERVINGS (2⅔ cups)

1¼ cups part-skim ricotta cheese

¾ cup plain nonfat yogurt

⅔ cup maple syrup

2 tsp vanilla extract

1. Purée the ricotta in a food processor or blender until smooth.

2. Add the remaining ingredients and process until incorporated and very smooth. The base is ready to use now in other preparations, or it may be flavored (see variations below).

3. For frozen ricotta cream (glacé), freeze in an ice cream machine following the manufacturer's instructions.

Variations
FRESH BERRY GLACÉ: Add 1 part berries to 3 parts Maple-Ricotta-Yogurt Cream. The fruit may be whole, sliced, or puréed.

PUMPKIN GLACÉ: Add 1 cup pumpkin purée, ½ tsp ground cinnamon, and ¼ tsp grated nutmeg to 1 cup of Maple-Ricotta-Yogurt Cream.

MAKING CHURNED FROZEN DESSERTS (257)

CHOCOLATE CRÊPES

Crêpes are easily made in advance. Make stacks of five or six crêpes, separating them with parchment or waxed paper between them. Wrap well in plastic wrap and refrigerate or freeze for later use. Fill these crêpes with berries, bananas, or caramel sauce.

MAKES 12 CRÊPES

2 large eggs

1 cup nonfat milk

1 tbsp unsalted butter, melted

¾ cup all-purpose flour

¼ cup cocoa powder

2 tbsp sugar

¼ tsp kosher salt

1. Process or blend the eggs, milk, butter, flour, cocoa powder, sugar, and salt in a food processor or blender for 1 minute. Scrape down the sides and process an additional 30 seconds. Allow the batter to rest at room temperature for 15 minutes.

2. Heat a crêpe pan or a small nonstick skillet over medium-high heat. When the pan is hot, spray it lightly with vegetable oil. Ladle about ¼ cup of the batter into the pan and cook on the first side until the edges start to look dry, 1 to 2 minutes. Turn the crêpe once and cook briefly on the second side, about 30 seconds. Remove the crêpe to a plate and continue until all of the batter is used. Separate the crêpes with squares of waxed or parchment paper.

3. The crêpes are ready to fill, or tightly wrap (still separated by paper) and refrigerate for up to 4 days or freeze for up to 8 weeks.

MAKING CRÊPES (220)

BAKED FIGS

This is a fantastic dish to try when fresh figs are available, in late June through mid-August and sporadically throughout the fall. Substitute peeled and cored pears or apples when figs are not available.

MAKES 6 SERVINGS

6 fresh medium figs, stemmed

2 tbsp almond paste

6 sheets phyllo dough

1 tbsp unsalted butter, melted

2 tbsp powdered sugar

1. Preheat the oven to 300°F.

2. Score each fig down its length, letting the blade cut only two-thirds of the way into the fig.

3. Roll the almond paste into 6 equal balls. Press one ball into the opening of each fig.

4. Cut each phyllo sheet into quarters and brush with the melted butter. Stack four of these quarter pieces, staggering the corners. Place the fig on the center of the stack and wrap the sheets around the fig, making a beggar's purse.

5. Bake the figs until the figs are soft and the phyllo is golden brown, about 30 minutes. Dust with powdered sugar and serve.

USING PHYLLO DOUGH (259)

White Chocolate Cheesecake (background; page 275)
Chocolate-Yogurt Mousse, Champagne and Lemon Sorbet with Lace
Triangle Cookies (page 280), and Berry Cobbler (page 274)

CHAMPAGNE AND LEMON SORBET

Serve this sorbet between courses to cleanse the palate, or as a dessert with a selection of seasonal fruits and a few cookies. For an elegant presentation, scoop the sorbet into champagne saucers or flutes. You can use other dry sparkling wines, sparkling water, or still water to replace the Champagne if desired.

MAKES 1½ QUARTS

2 cups water

1⅓ cups sugar

1½ cups Champagne

2¼ tsp grated lemon zest

½ cup lemon juice

1. Bring 1 cup of the water and the sugar to a boil in a small saucepan over medium heat, stirring occasionally, until the sugar is dissolved. Remove from the heat and let cool to room temperature, about 1 hour.

2. Stir in the remaining 1 cup water, the Champagne, lemon zest, and lemon juice.

3. Refrigerate for at least 4 hours or up to overnight. Freeze in an ice cream machine according to the manufacturer's instructions. Pack the sorbet in containers and let ripen in the freezer for 3 to 4 hours before serving. (It keeps well in the freezer for up to 1 month.)

ZESTING AND JUICING CITRUS (284), **MAKING CHURNED FROZEN DESSERTS** (257)

CHOCOLATE-YOGURT MOUSSE

Use good-quality cocoa powder to make this mousse. It will give rich flavor to offset the tartness of the yogurt.

MAKES 6 SERVINGS

1⅓ cups plain nonfat yogurt, room temperature

¼ cup chopped dark chocolate, melted

⅓ cup cocoa powder

5 large egg whites

⅓ cup sugar

6 tbsp Caramel Sauce (page 266; optional)

White chocolate curls (optional)

Fresh seasonal berries (optional)

1. Drain the yogurt in a sieve lined with cheesecloth placed over a bowl in the refrigerator for 24 hours. When you are ready to make the mousse, bring the yogurt to room temperature.

2. Combine the yogurt with the chocolate.

3. Sift the cocoa powder twice. Fold it into the yogurt mixture.

4. Combine the egg whites and sugar in a stainless-steel bowl. Heat to 135°F in a double boiler. Remove from the heat and beat with a mixer until the whites form medium peaks.

5. Fold the meringue into the yogurt mixture, pour it into cups, glasses, or molds, and chill in the refrigerator until firm, at least 3 and up to 24 hours. To serve, unmold the mousse onto a plate and serve with the sauce or other garnishes: white chocolate curls or fresh berries.

MELTING CHOCOLATE (254), **SEPARATING EGGS** (219), **FILLING THE MOLD** (258)

INDIVIDUAL PEACH AND BLUEBERRY GALETTES

While not essential, a layer of cake crumbs in a galette absorbs some of the juices from the fruit during baking so that the crust stays crisp. Crumble store-bought ladyfingers (found in the cookie aisle of most grocery stores) with your hands or grind them in a food processor to achieve fine crumbs.

MAKES 6 GALETTES

8 oz Sweet Ricotta Pastry (recipe follows)

1⅔ cups sliced peaches (peeled)

½ cup fresh blueberries

Water, as needed

1. Preheat the oven to 350°F.

2. Portion the dough into six pieces and roll into balls. Retaining a round shape, roll out each piece of dough on a floured surface to about ⅛ inch thick.

3. Arrange peaches and blueberries on each round of pastry dough, leaving a ½-inch border around the edge of the dough.

4. Working gently, fold the edges of the dough up and slightly over the fruit, overlapping the edges and leaving the fruit exposed in the center of the pastry. If desired, brush a small amount of water onto the dough once each section is folded over to help the overlapping section adhere to it. Each time you roll a bit of pastry, try to catch the previous fold underneath the one you are rolling to get the coiled look in the accompanying photograph.

5. Gently place the galettes onto a parchment-lined sheet pan, spacing them evenly on the pan. Bake the pastries until the edges are golden brown, about 25 minutes. Allow them to cool slightly before serving. The baked galettes can be stored in an airtight container at room temperature for up to 2 days.

SEPARATING EGGS (219)

SWEET RICOTTA PASTRY

MAKES ABOUT 8 OUNCES

1 cup all-purpose flour	2 tbsp nonfat milk, cold
3 tbsp sugar	1 large egg white, cold
1 tbsp baking powder	2 tbsp unsalted butter, diced, cold
Pinch kosher salt	1 tsp vanilla extract
¼ cup part-skim ricotta cheese, cold	

1. Process or blend the flour, sugar, baking powder, and salt in a food processor or blender briefly to evenly mix the ingredients.

2. Add the ricotta, milk, egg white, butter, and vanilla and pulse just until a dough forms. Gather the dough into a ball and wrap tightly with plastic wrap. Refrigerate the dough until firm, at least 1 hour. The dough is ready to roll out, or it may be stored in the refrigerator for up to 2 days.

BERRY COBBLER

Cobblers are part of a robust repertoire of fruit-based desserts enjoyed throughout the United States. Different parts of the country prefer their own interpretations of the dish. Some cobblers feature a cakelike batter, as we have here, while others include either a pastry crust or a biscuit topping.

MAKES 6 SERVINGS

1 cup all-purpose flour

2 tbsp sugar

¾ tsp baking powder

¼ tsp kosher salt

3 tbsp unsalted butter, cold

¾ cup buttermilk

3 cups blueberries, raspberries, or blackberries

1. Preheat the oven to 350°F. Lightly spray a 2-quart baking dish with oil.

2. Combine the flour, sugar, baking powder, and salt in a large bowl. Cut the butter into the dry ingredients using a pastry cutter or two table knives until the mixture looks like a very coarse meal. Make a well in the dry ingredients and pour the buttermilk into the well all at once. Stir the ingredients together with a fork just until all of the dry ingredients are evenly moistened. The batter will be quite heavy but soft enough to drop from a spoon.

3. Add the fruit to the baking dish. Drop spoonfuls of the topping onto the surface of the fruit. Bake the cobbler until the berries are very juicy and hot and the topping is completely baked, about 30 minutes.

4. Remove the cobbler from the oven and let it rest for 10 minutes before serving.

THE STRAIGHT MIXING METHOD (255), **DETERMINING DONENESS** (256)

ANGEL FOOD CAKE

In order to reach a lofty height, angel food cake needs to cling to the sides of the pan, both as it bakes and while it cools. This is why the pan is ungreased and the cake is cooled upside down.

MAKES ONE 10-INCH CAKE, 10 TO 12 SERVINGS

1¾ cups cake flour

1 tsp baking powder

1⅔ cups egg whites, about 10 large

⅔ cup powdered sugar

1 tsp cream of tartar

2 tsp vanilla extract

1. Preheat the oven to 325°F.

2. Sift the cake flour and baking powder together twice.

3. Whip the egg whites with a mixer until thick and foamy but do not hold a peak, about 3 minutes. Gradually incorporate the sugar and cream of tartar and continue beating to medium peaks. Gently fold the flour mixture into the beaten egg whites. Gently fold in the vanilla.

4. Pour the batter into an ungreased tube pan. Bake until the cake springs back when pressed with a fingertip and it has a golden brown top, about 30 minutes. Remove the cake from the oven and turn the pan upside down. Let the cake cool completely in the pan before removing it (this will prevent the cake from deflating).

SEPARATING EGGS (219), **THE FOAMING MIXING METHOD** (255), **DETERMINING DONENESS** (256)

WHITE CHOCOLATE CHEESECAKE

Select a good-quality white chocolate with at least 20 percent cocoa butter for this recipe. It will give the cheesecake great flavor, and the finished cake will be extremely smooth.

MAKES ONE 10-INCH CAKE, 10 TO 12 SERVINGS

5 oz chopped white chocolate

6 oz Neufchâtel or low-fat cream cheese (12 oz)

1½ cups fresh ricotta (part-skim)

2 tbsp sugar

1 large egg

2 large egg whites

1 tsp vanilla extract

1. Preheat the oven to 325°F.

2. Melt the chocolate in a double boiler.

3. Beat the cream cheese and ricotta with a mixer until soft. Add the sugar to the cream cheese and mix well.

4. With the mixer on low speed, pour the chocolate, egg, egg whites, and vanilla into the cream cheese mixture. Mix until smooth.

5. Spray a 10-inch springform cake pan lightly with vegetable oil and place on a baking sheet lined with parchment paper. Pour the cheese mixture into the pan and bake until set, about 30 minutes. Allow the cheesecake to cool completely before releasing and removing the sides of the pan. Refrigerate the cheesecake for at least 4 hours before slicing and serving.

MELTING CHOCOLATE (254)

CHOCOLATE POLENTA PUDDING CAKE

Top the finished cake with a sifting of powdered sugar or cocoa powder.
Instead of the sauce here, you could also top it with a dollop of whipped cream,
Maple-Ricotta Cream (page 268), or Raspberry Sauce (page 281).

MAKES 6 SERVINGS

4 cups nonfat milk

1 large piece orange peel

⅓ cup sugar

¼ cup cocoa powder

⅓ cup cornmeal

¼ cup chopped bittersweet chocolate

3 large egg whites

½ cup Raspberry Sauce (page 281)

1. Bring the milk and the orange peel to a boil in a small pot over medium-high heat. Remove from the heat, cover, and steep for 30 minutes. Discard the peel and pour the milk into a medium pot.

2. Bring the milk to a simmer over medium heat. Add half of the sugar and all of the cocoa powder. Slowly add the cornmeal, stirring constantly.

3. Add the chocolate and continue to simmer, stirring constantly, until the mixture pulls away from the sides of the pot, about 20 minutes. Transfer the mixture to a 13 by 9 by 2-inch pan. Spread thinly, cover with parchment paper, and cool to room temperature.

4. Preheat the oven to 400°F. Brush six 6-ounce soufflé dishes with butter and dust with 2 teaspoons of the sugar. Place in the refrigerator until ready to use.

5. Beat the egg whites in a mixer to soft peaks. Gradually add the remaining 2 tablespoons sugar and continue to beat to stiff peaks. Fold the egg whites into the polenta.

6. Fill the soufflé dishes three-quarters full. Place them in a pan and add about 1 inch of water to the pan. Bake until well risen, about 25 minutes. Serve warm with raspberry sauce.

SEPARATING EGGS (219), **ZESTING CITRUS** (284)

Gently folding the egg whites into the chocolate polenta gives this cake a light, airy texture.

CARROT CAKE with Cream Cheese frosting

If you have a Mouli-style rotary grater or grating and shredding disks for your food processor, you can select how coarse or fine you want your grated carrots. The more finely you grate your carrots, the finer the texture of the finished cake will be. Coarsely grated carrots remain more visible in the baked cake, for an appealing flecked appearance and a delightfully rustic texture.

MAKES 10 TO 12 SERVINGS

1⅓ cups whole wheat flour

1 tsp baking soda

1 tsp baking powder

1 tsp ground cinnamon

½ cup vegetable oil

1 cup sugar

2 large whole eggs

¾ cup diced pineapple (peeled and cored)

4 cups grated carrot (3 large)

⅔ cup raisins

2 large egg whites

Cream Cheese Frosting (recipe follows)

1. Preheat the oven to 350°F. Line a jelly roll pan with parchment or brush it lightly with oil.

2. Combine the flour, baking soda, baking powder, and cinnamon in a large bowl.

3. Beat the oil, sugar, and whole eggs with a mixer until smooth. Add the dry ingredients to the egg mixture and beat to blend well. Stir in the pineapple, carrot, and raisins.

4. Beat the egg whites in the mixer to medium peaks and fold into the batter.

5. Pour the batter into the pan and bake until a skewer poked into the center of the cake comes out with just a few moist crumbs, about 30 minutes. Cool in the pan on a rack.

6. Cut the cooled cake in half horizontally. Spread the frosting on the cut side of one half of the cake and top with the second half. Cut into pieces and serve, or wrap the cake and store it in the refrigerator for up to 6 days.

DICING (119), **SEPARATING EGGS** (219), **DETERMINING DONENESS** (256)

CREAM CHEESE FROSTING

MAKES 1¼ CUPS

1½ cups Neufchâtel or nonfat cream cheese, softened (12 oz)

¾ cup powdered sugar, sifted

2 tsp vanilla extract

Mix all the ingredients in a food processor, blender, or mixer until smooth. The frosting is ready to use, or store in a covered container in the refrigerator for up to 2 weeks.

GLAZED PINEAPPLE MADAGASCAR

Glazing the pineapple allows the flavors of the orange juice, honey, and rum
to caramelize in the pan along with the pineapple's natural sugars.

MAKES 6 SERVINGS

1 tsp brined green peppercorns, rinsed

1¾ cups sliced pineapple (peeled and cored)

2 tbsp sugar

1⅓ cups orange juice

1 tbsp honey

¼ cup light rum

1. Crush the peppercorns using the back of a wooden spoon. Rub the peppercorns over the pineapple slices and sprinkle with the sugar.

2. Combine the orange juice, honey, and rum in a small bowl.

3. Heat a large sauté pan over high heat. Add the pineapple slices to the pan and cook until the sugar on both sides of the slices caramelizes.

4. Remove the browned slices from the pan and add the juice mixture to the pan. Reduce the liquid to a maple syrup consistency and pour over the pineapple.

JUICING CITRUS (285), **SAUTÉING** (124)

LACE TRIANGLE COOKIES

You must work quickly to cut these cookies into the desired shape, as they will get
more brittle as they cool. Use a sharp knife to achieve the best results.

MAKES 12 COOKIES

3 tbsp sugar

2 tbsp unsalted butter

1 tbsp light corn syrup

¼ cup all-purpose flour

1 tsp coarsely chopped toasted hazelnuts

1. Preheat the oven to 375°F.

2. Bring the sugar, butter, and corn syrup to a boil in large pot over medium heat. Remove from the heat and stir in the flour and hazelnuts. Pour the batter into a baking dish to cool.

3. Spray an inverted baking sheet with vegetable oil.

4. When cool enough to handle, roll the dough into small balls (see Note). Flatten the balls into disks about ⅛ inch thick and place on the baking sheet.

5. Bake until the cookies stop bubbling completely, about 10 minutes.

6. Remove from the oven. When each cookie is set but still flexible, lift from the pan and cut into 6 triangle-shaped pieces. If you wish, you can drape them over a rolling pin or inside a coffee cup to make a curved cookie. Store the cookies between parchment paper in a covered container in a cool, dry place.

NOTE The unbaked batter will keep refrigerated for 1 week.

TOASTING SPICES, NUTS, AND SEEDS (290)

ALMOND-ANISE BISCOTTI

Biscotti are crisp, dry cookies that are thought to have originated in the Prato region of Tuscany. They are often served with coffee or cappuccino, or with a glass of *vin santo*, one of Tuscany's famous dessert wines. Their crisp texture makes biscotti perfect for dunking without disintegrating.

MAKES 12 COOKIES

1 cup all-purpose flour

¼ cup sugar

1 tsp baking powder

2 tbsp unsalted butter

2 large egg whites

½ tsp vanilla extract

¼ tsp almond extract

3 tbsp chopped almonds

½ tsp anise seeds

1. Preheat the oven to 350°F. Spray a baking sheet lightly with cooking spray or brush with oil.

2. Combine the flour, sugar, and baking powder in a large bowl. Cut the butter into the dry ingredients using a pastry cutter or two table knives until the mixture looks like a coarse meal. Stir in the egg whites and vanilla and almond extracts. Fold in the almonds and anise seeds.

3. Roll two equal-size oval logs of dough and place them on the baking sheet, spacing them at least 3 inches apart. Bake until the logs are golden brown and spring back when lightly pressed with a fingertip, about 25 minutes.

4. Cool for 10 minutes. Cut each log into ¼-inch-thick slices. Place the slices back on the baking sheet and return them to the oven. Bake until the biscotti are very dry, 15 minutes more.

5. Cool the biscotti on cooling racks. They may be served now or stored in an airtight container at room temperature for up to 6 days.

SEPARATING EGGS (219)

RASPBERRY SAUCE

MAKES 1 CUP

½ lb fresh or frozen raspberries

¼ cup sugar, or as needed

1 tsp fresh lemon juice, or as needed

1. Combine the raspberries, sugar, and lemon juice in a saucepan over low heat. Simmer gently, stirring, until the sugar has dissolved, about 10 minutes. Press the sauce through a fine-mesh sieve to remove the seeds.

2. Taste the sauce and add more sugar and/or lemon juice if necessary. The sauce is ready to serve now, or it can be stored in a covered container in the refrigerator for up to 1 week.

CHOCOLATE FUDGE COOKIES

Though it seems strange, the puréed prunes and chestnuts are what give this cookie its wonderfully fudgy texture. They also provide subtle sweetness and nuttiness that enhance the chocolate's flavor.

MAKES 12 COOKIES

⅓ cup chopped prunes

3 tbsp chestnut purée

2 tbsp water

1 tbsp rum

2½ tsp sugar

2 tbsp cocoa powder

3 tbsp chopped dark chocolate

¼ cup all-purpose flour

½ tsp baking powder

1. Preheat the oven to 350°F. Spray a baking sheet lightly with vegetable oil.

2. Purée the prunes in a food processor or blender until smooth. Combine the prune and chestnut purées and strain through a fine-mesh sieve. Set aside.

3. Combine the water, rum, sugar, and cocoa powder in a small sauce pot over medium heat. Heat to dissolve the sugar, about 1 minute.

4. Melt the chocolate in a double boiler.

5. Combine the prune-chestnut purée, the cocoa mixture, and the melted chocolate in a mixing bowl and stir until smooth. Add the flour and baking powder and stir until just combined.

6. Drop teaspoon-size balls of dough onto the baking sheet and bake until the edges are set, about 10 minutes. Remove the cookies from the baking sheet and cool on a cooling rack. Store in an airtight container at room temperature for up to 6 days.

MELTING CHOCOLATE (254)

OATMEAL-PEAR COOKIES

Any dried fruit could be substituted for the pears. Be careful not to overbake the cookies; if overbaked, they could lose their delightfully chewy texture.

MAKES 18 COOKIES

½ cup brown sugar, tightly packed

⅓ cup honey

2 tsp unsalted butter, soft

2 tsp evaporated nonfat milk

1 tsp vanilla extract

½ cup rolled or quick-cooking oats

⅔ cup all-purpose flour

⅓ cup diced dried pears

1. Preheat the oven to 350°F. Spray a baking sheet lightly with vegetable oil.

2. Cream together the sugar, honey, and butter by hand with a wooden spoon. Add the milk and vanilla to the creamed mixture. Fold in the oats and flour. Stir in the pears.

3. Drop teaspoon-size balls of dough onto the baking sheet and bake until the edges are a light brown, about 10 minutes. Remove the cookies from the baking sheet and cool on a cooling rack. Store in an airtight container at room temperature for up to 6 days.

DICING (119)

CHAPTER TEN

Basic Recipes and Techniques

A well-stocked pantry is infinitely useful to any home cook. This chapter includes a number of the basics: broths, dressings, sauces, and condiments, as well as preserved items such as pickles. Experiment using new and unique ingredients when using these recipes: They can be used as a base to get creative with everyday pantry staples.

Aromatic Flavoring Ingredients and Preparations

The flavors that you build into your dishes are an important part of great healthy cooking. They add more than flavor, of course. The fact that they are so flavorful also means that they contain a wide range of substances that are both good for our palate and good for our health. These aromatic ingredients—garlic, mushrooms, onions, leeks, lemongrass, ginger, and citrus—are the very foundations of flavor. You find them in every culture and in every cuisine.

PREPARING GARLIC

Depending on how it is prepared, garlic contributes distinctly different flavors. For the best flavor, prepare garlic as close to the time of cooking as possible and cut away any green sprouts in the cloves. Lay the cloves on a cutting board and smash them well, pressing down firmly with the side of your knife blade. Smashing the cloves loosens the skin so you can pull it away. Use a rocking motion to chop or mince the garlic to the desired fineness.

Roasting Garlic
Cut off the tip of a head of garlic to expose the cloves. Rub lightly with olive oil, set the garlic on a bed of kosher salt, and then roast in a 350°F oven until soft, 30 to 45 minutes. Squeeze out the roasted garlic or pass the cloves through a food mill. Use the roasted garlic in soups, vegetable purées, sauces, and vinaigrettes, or as a spread on sandwiches or grilled bread.

Roasting Shallots
Roasting shallots adds an extra dimension of flavor to dishes like soups, stews, and sauces. To roast shallots, place them, still in their skins, in a baking dish and place them in a hot oven (the exact temperature doesn't really matter; you can roast some shallots anytime you have the oven on for something else). Let the shallots roast until they feel soft and smell sweet, 15 to 30 minutes depending on how hot the oven is. When they are cool enough to handle, cut the ends off and peel the shallots. Cut the shallots into slices and pull the slices apart into individual rings. They can be stored in a covered container in the refrigerator for up to 5 days.

PREPARING GINGER

Sliced ginger is often used to infuse stock soups, broths, and poaching liquids. Thicker pieces hold up well for long simmering, whereas thin slices release flavor quickly in shorter cooking times. Use a vegetable peeler or a coffee spoon to remove the tan skin of fresh ginger, peeling only as much as you will need at a time. Peel off as thin a layer as possible, since much of the flavor of ginger lies just beneath its skin. You will notice, particularly in older ginger, a distinct "grain" that makes it easier to slice cleanly in one direction, producing shreds in the other.

To mince ginger, cut it into thin slices against the grain, then chop it finely as you would garlic. For a moist, fine purée, use a ginger grater, a small ceramic dish lined with tiny points or pyramids, or a flat, file-like metal grater to reduce the fibers of gingerroot into a softer texture.

ZESTING AND JUICING CITRUS FRUITS

The flavors of citrus can go a long way toward brightening up a dish without adding extra sodium.

Zesting Citrus
When selecting citrus fruits for their zest, choose those with bumpy skin rather than very shiny, smooth peels, as the rough skins will provide more zest and are easier to shave or grate. If possible, choose organic fruit for zesting, since pesticides accumulate in the peel.

Depending on how the zest will be used in a recipe, you may remove it in wide pieces, thin strips, or fine shavings. To infuse milk, sugar syrups, or liqueurs, use a vegetable peeler to peel away long, 1-inch-wide pieces of the zest that may be removed easily from a liquid later. Take care not to cut into the pith, and use a paring knife or the edge of a spoon to scrape away any pith that remains on the zest. You may also cut these pieces crosswise for thin strips.

Specially designed zesters will create thin, delicate strips of zest for sauces or garnish. For finely grated zest, use a grater with very small holes and rotate the fruit frequently as you grate to avoid removing the bitter pith beneath the zest. Alternatively, you may remove the peel with a vegetable peeler and then mince the zest very finely with a knife.

Juicing Citrus

A citrus fruit at room temperature gives more juice than chilled fruit. Before cutting and juicing it, roll the fruit firmly beneath your palms to crush its pulp. Use a fluted reamer or a mechanical juicer to extract as much juice as possible.

SUPPORTING FLAVORS

Select additional ingredients to add flavor, aroma, and color to a soup, sauce, stew, or braise. Aromatic herb and vegetable combinations such as mirepoix (usually two parts onion, one part carrot and one part celery), sachet d'épices or spice sachet (generally consisting of parsley stems, thyme, cracked black pepper, and bay leaves), or bouquet garni (similar to a sachet d'épices but wrapped in leek leaves) are traditional. Other traditional bases of flavor include the Cajun trinity (onions, peppers, and celery) and soffrito (tomatoes, onions, and garlic cooked down to a flavorful paste). Contemporary broths may call for such ingredients as dried tomatoes, lemongrass, wild mushrooms, or ginger to give the broth a unique character.

The degree to which the aromatics are cooked has a strong influence on a dish's final flavor and color. Some recipes ask you to cook them until they are just limp and translucent; professionals refer to this as "sweating" the vegetables because the vegetables actually start to release some of their own moisture. If you cover the pot, it helps to cook the aromatics a little more quickly; this technique is known as "smothering." Other recipes may instruct you to cook the aromatics until they develop a golden color or even become a rich golden brown. Cooking the aromatics to this darker, caramelized stage is referred to as pincé or creating a pinçage. A pinçage often includes tomato product such as tomato paste, which is cooked to a deeper, brick red color before the liquid is added.

Making a Spice Sachet

These bundles of herbs and spices are used to add flavor to a simmering broth, soup, or stew.

A basic sachet that will flavor 2½ to 3 quarts of liquid contains 5 or 6 cracked peppercorns, 3 or 4 parsley stems, 1 sprig fresh thyme or ½ teaspoon dried thyme, and 1 bay leaf. Add or substitute other spices to complement the flavors in a specific dish. For example, use cardamom, chiles, or star anise to flavor an Asian-style soup. Place the herbs and spices on a square of cheesecloth large enough to contain them. Twist the corners of the cheesecloth together and tie securely with one end of a long piece of kitchen string. When adding to the pot, tie the other end of the string to the pot handle for easy removal later. At the end of cooking, gently pull out the bundle, untie the string from the pot handle, and discard. If you prefer, enclose the herbs and spices in a large tea ball in place of the cheesecloth and hook it to the side of the pot.

Making a Bouquet Garni

A bouquet garni is made from a selection of fresh herbs and aromatic vegetables. Typically, you'll use a few sprigs of parsley, a sprig of thyme, a bay leaf, garlic clove, and a few peppercorns wrapped up in a leek leaf or packed between a few long pieces of parsley, along with a bit of carrot. This is tied up in a bundle and added to the dish as it simmers. The bouquet will flavor and perfume the dish within 30 to 45 minutes of adding it to the dish, but if the flavor starts to overwhelm the other ingredients, take it out earlier.

Spices:	Are derived from the bark, root, fruit, or berry of perennial plants. Examples: • Cinnamon from the bark • Pepper from the berry • Ginger from the root • Nutmeg from the fruit
Herbs:	Are the leaves of annual and perennial low-growing shrubs
Aromatic seeds:	Are the seeds of graceful lacy annual plants (anise, caraway, coriander)

Name:	Allspice
Type:	Dried berry of evergreen tree in myrtle family
Origin:	Jamaica, Mexico, and Central America
Traditional Uses:	Savory dishes in the Caribbean, Mexico; cakes; cookies; puddings; pies; and pickling liquids

Name:	Aniseed
Type:	Seed from plant in parsley family
Origin:	Asia Minor and Egypt, now cultivated in countries of temperate zone
Traditional Uses:	Savory dishes in northern Europe; confections; coffee cakes; flavoring for liqueurs

Name:	Caraway seed
Type:	Seed from plant in dill family
Origin:	Europe and Asia Minor, related to carrot
Traditional Uses:	Savory dishes in North Africa; breads, rolls, and biscuits

Name:	Cardamom
Type:	Pod of perennial plant of the ginger family
Origin:	Native to India, cultivated in Malabar and Ceylon
Traditional Uses:	Savory dishes in India, northern Europe, Asia; cakes, Danish, and cookies

Name:	Cinnamon There are three types of cinnamon: Ceylon: Mild pungency, not that popular in the United States Saigon Cassia: China, Indochina, and Vietnam, warm bittersweet aromatic taste, better quality Batavia Cassia: Indonesia, flavor inferior to Saigon, used for sticks
Type:	Stripped dried bark of evergreen tree in laurel family
Origin:	Far East
Traditional Uses:	Savory foods in North Africa, India, Asia, Mediterranean Levant, United States; baked goods; entrées; puddings

Name:	Cloves
Type:	Unopened dried buds from an evergreen
Origin:	Spice Islands, cultivated in West Indies, Zanzibar, Madagascar, and tropical Africa
Traditional Uses:	Savory foods in North Africa, India, Asia, Mediterranean Levant, United States, Mexico; cakes, cookies, and other baked goods; meats; sauces; and vegetables

Name:	Coriander
Type:	Seed from plant of the parsley family
Origin:	Mediterranean, Morocco (supplies most coriander)
Traditional Uses:	Savory foods in North Africa, India, Asia, Mediterranean Levant, United States, Mexico; pastry; sausage; breads and desserts; pickles

Name:	Dill seed
Type:	Seed from plant in anise family
Origin:	Asia Minor and Europe, most comes from India
Traditional Uses:	Savory dishes in Mediterranean, northern Europe; appetizers; fish; pickling; breads and rolls

Name:	Ginger
Type:	Root from plant of tropical Asia that looks similar to young corn
Origin:	Tropical Asia, now cultivated in Africa, Jamaica, India. Jamaican ginger is the finest quality.
Traditional Uses:	Savory dishes in Asia, northern Europe, Mediterranean; cakes; pies; meats; pickling

Name:	Mace
Type:	Membrane covering of nutmeg from an evergreen tree
Origin:	Spice Islands, now cultivated in Grenada, West Indies
Traditional Uses:	Savory dishes in northern Europe, Asia, Caribbean; baked goods; pies

Name:	Mint (spearmint, peppermint)
Type:	Leaf from herb
Origin:	Mediterranean region, cultivated in Europe and United States
Traditional Uses:	Savory dishes in Mediterranean, Southeast Asia, eastern Mediterranean, Mediterranean Levant; baked items; fruit; meats; sauces; oil used for flavoring and scent

Name:	Nutmeg
Type:	Nut from evergreen tree
Origin:	Spice Islands, now cultivated in Grenada, West Indies
Traditional Uses:	Savory dishes in the Caribbean; baked goods; sauces; potatoes; meats

Name:	Poppy seed
Type:	Seed from poppy flower
Origin:	Southwestern Asia, cultivated in Holland, Poland, Iran, Turkey, and Argentina
Traditional Uses:	Savory dishes in Asia; bread and rolls

Name:	Sesame seed
Type:	Seed or paste or oil
Origin:	South-central Asia, cultivated in southwest United States, South America, China, Africa, and India
Traditional Uses:	Savory dishes in Asia, Mexico, Mediterranean, Eastern Mediterranean; baked goods; breads and rolls

Name:	Vanilla bean
Type:	Fruit, dried pod of delicate orchid
Origin:	Tropical America, cultivated in Madagascar and Mexico
Traditional Uses:	Ice cream, desserts, and confections

SELECT SPICE MIXTURES OF THE WORLD

MIXTURE	COUNTRY OF ORIGIN	TRADITIONAL USE	FORM	CHARACTERISTIC SPICES
Bumbu	Indonesia	Used to flavor rendangs and gulais, spicy dishes served with sauce	Dry spice mixture is combined with coconut milk prior to use	Ginger, turmeric, chiles, cinnamon, cloves, coriander, black peppercorns
Ras al Hanout	Morocco	All-purpose flavoring powder	Whole spices ground together	10 to 15 ingredients, usually including allspice, cloves, cumin, cardamom, chiles, ginger, peppercorns, mace, turmeric, and caraway seeds
Berbere	Ethiopia	Cure for meats, added to condiments and stews	Ingredients are mixed together, then simmered prior to use	Chiles, cardamom, cumin, black pepper, fenugreek, allspice, ginger, cloves, coriander
Harissa	Tunisia, Morocco, Algeria	All-purpose condiment, also used to flavor stews and sauces	Whole spices are ground together, then mixed with olive oil to moisten	Chiles, caraway, cumin, coriander, garlic
Baharat	Middle East (Lebanon, Syria, Gulf States, Saudi Arabia)	Whole spices ground together	Widely used to flavor all types of dishes, particularly soups and stews	Cloves, nutmeg, cinnamon, coriander, black pepper, paprika
Curry Powder	Southern India	Used to flavor thin, soupy sauces	Freshly ground spices are sautéed in oil at beginning of cooking process	Curry leaves, turmeric, chiles, coriander, black pepper, and sometimes cumin, ginger, fenugreek, cinnamon, cloves, nutmeg, and fennel seeds
Garam Masala	Northern India	Usually added at end of cooking to complete seasoning	Spices are roasted whole, then ground into a powder	Cinnamon, cardamom, cloves, cumin seeds, coriander, black peppercorns, nutmeg, mace
Panch Phoron (Indian Five-Spice Mix)	Eastern India— Bengal	All-purpose flavoring for vegetable dishes	Sautéed in hot oil prior to cooking	Whole cumin seeds, fennel seeds, fenugreek, parsley seeds, black mustard seeds
Gaeng Wan (Green Curry Paste)	Thailand	All-purpose flavoring, widely used in soups and sauces	Ingredients are ground together in mortar and pestle to form a wet paste	Green chiles, turmeric, lemongrass, ginger, coriander, cumin, white peppercorns
Mussaman Paste	Thailand	All-purpose flavoring, widely used in soups and sauces	Ingredients are ground together in mortar and pestle to form a wet paste	Chiles, coriander, cumin, cinnamon, cloves, star anise, cardamom, white peppercorns
Recado	Yucatan Peninsula of Mexico	Rubbed on food prior to cooking, also used as all-purpose flavoring for sauces and stews	Spices are pounded to a paste in combination with vinegar, garlic, and herbs	Achiote, cloves, black pepper, chiles, allspice, cinnamon

SELECT SPICE MIXTURES OF THE WORLD

MIXTURE	COUNTRY OF ORIGIN	TRADITIONAL USE	FORM	CHARACTERISTIC SPICES
Five-Spice Powder	China	Used as flavoring in wide variety of Chinese dishes; frequently used in marinades	Whole spices are ground into a raw powder	Anise, fennel seeds, cloves, cinnamon, peppercorns
Quatre Epices	France	Most often used in pâtés	Spices are combined and then ground into a powder	Pepper, nutmeg, cloves, ginger, sometimes cinnamon
Pickling Spices	Europe	Used to add flavor to pickles and certain liquids	Raw whole spices	Mustard seeds, cloves, coriander seeds, mace, black peppercorns, allspice, ginger, chiles
Cajun Blackening Spices	Louisiana, USA	Used to coat fish prior to cooking	Ground raw spices	Mustard seeds, cumin, paprika, cayenne pepper, black pepper
Crab or Shrimp Boil	Chesapeake Bay, USA	Thrown in water used for boiling crab or shrimp	Ground raw spices	Peppercorns, mustard seeds, coriander, salt, cloves, ginger, ground bay leaves
Barbecue Rub	Southern and Western USA	Rubbed on meats prior to cooking	Ground raw spices	Any combination of cumin, chiles, cloves, cinnamon, mustard seeds, paprika and brown sugar

Toasting Spices, Nuts, and Seeds

Spices, nuts, and seeds store best if they are purchased whole and untoasted. To bring out their rich, aromatic flavors, toast them as close to the time that you want to use them as possible. You can toast more than one ingredient at a time, as long as you don't overcrowd the pan. There should be just a thin, relatively even layer. If the pan is crowded, the spices won't toast evenly. If there are too few to fill the pan, the pan could heat unevenly and increase your chance of scorching them. Toast small amounts in a dry skillet. For large quantities, use the oven.

For stovetop toasting, preheat a dry skillet; cast iron is a good choice because it holds and releases its heat evenly. Once the pan is hot, scatter the spices, nuts, or seeds in a single layer, leaving enough room to swirl them around in the pan. Gently swirl the pan or stir the frequently so they toast evenly.

For larger quantities of nuts, spices, or seeds, preheat the oven to 325°F. Spread the nuts on an ungreased baking sheet and toast them until golden brown and fragrant, 7 to 15 minutes depending on the size of the items you are toasting. Stir occasionally as they toast in the oven; those on the edges of the baking sheet will tend to brown more quickly.

Once they have reached the color you want, immediately transfer them from the skillet or baking sheet to a cool container. This keeps them from continuing to brown. Toast nuts before chopping them for the best results. Even if a recipe does not specifically call for toasting the nuts, you may choose to do so. Toasting brings out the best flavor in nuts and improves the entire dish.

CURRY SPICE BLEND

This recipe makes more than enough spice blend for the Pumpkin, Zucchini, and Chickpea Tagine on page 133, so you can use it in other dishes, including the Bombay-Style Potatoes on page 149. **MAKES ABOUT ¼ CUP**

2 tsp cumin seeds

2 tsp coriander seeds

2 tsp cardamom pods

1 piece cinnamon stick (about 1 inch long)

½ tsp black peppercorns

2 tsp Spanish paprika

1 tsp ground turmeric

1 tsp dry mustard

⅛ tsp cayenne

1. Heat a small sauté pan over medium heat. Add the cumin, coriander, cardamom, cinnamon, and peppercorns and toast the spices, swirling the pan to keep them in motion. When the spices are aromatic, 1 or 2 minutes, (they may even begin to "pop"), pour them from the pan onto a cool plate to stop them from overtoasting.

2. Combine the toasted spices, the paprika, turmeric, mustard, and cayenne in a spice grinder or mortar and pestle and grind to a powder. The spice blend is ready to use, or it may be stored in a covered container in a cool, dark cupboard for up to 3 weeks.

ETHIOPIAN CURRY POWDER

MAKES ABOUT 4 TEASPOONS

1 cinnamon stick, broken into pieces

1 tsp fenugreek seeds

½ tsp cumin seeds

¼ tsp cardamom seeds

¼ tsp ground turmeric

½ tsp grated nutmeg

1 clove

1. Heat a dry skillet over medium heat. Add the cinnamon stick, fenugreek, cumin, and cardamom and toast the spices, swirling the pan to keep them in motion. When the spices are aromatic, 1 or 2 minutes, (they may even begin to "pop"), pour them from the pan onto a cool plate to stop them from overtoasting.

2. Grind the toasted spices, the turmeric, nutmeg, and clove in a spice or coffee grinder to a fine powder. The curry powder is ready to use, or it may be transferred to a jar or bottle, tightly capped, and stored in a cool, dark cupboard for up to 1 month.

RED CURRY PASTE

Red curry paste can also be used to flavor a variety of dishes, such as stir-fries, or stews of chicken, fish, or seafood. **MAKES 1 CUP**

1 tsp coriander seeds

½ tsp fennel seeds

½ tsp cumin seeds

½ tsp black peppercorns

1 stalk lemongrass

2 red peppers, roasted, peeled, and seeded

3 jalapeños, seeded

1 canned chipotle

2 tbsp olive oil

1 shallot, minced

3 garlic cloves, minced

1 tbsp minced ginger

¼ tsp grated nutmeg

Zest of 1 lime

½ tsp kosher salt

1. Preheat an oven to 350°F. Combine the coriander, fennel, cumin, and peppercorns in a small baking dish and toast in the oven for 5 minutes. Remove and cool slightly. Grind in a spice or coffee grinder or mortar and pestle to a powder.

2. Cut away the bottom 4 inches of the lemongrass, peel away the tough outer layer, and mince or chop the inside stalk.

3. Purée the toasted spices, chopped lemongrass, peppers, jalapeños, chipotle, oil, shallot, garlic, ginger, nutmeg, lime zest, and salt in a food processor or blender until a fine paste forms. Store the paste in a clean jar or dish, cover tightly, and refrigerate. It will keep well for at least 3 weeks.

JERK RUB

MAKES ABOUT ½ CUP

1 tbsp allspice berries

½ cinnamon stick

½ tsp grated nutmeg

2 green onions, minced

¼ cup minced onion

½ Scotch bonnet chile, minced

2 tsp dark rum

½ tsp kosher salt

½ tsp freshly ground black pepper

1. Grind the allspice berries, cinnamon, and nutmeg to a powder in a spice mill or mortar and pestle.

2. Purée the ground spices, green onions, onion, chile, rum, salt, and pepper in a food processor until a thick paste forms. (This can be done entirely in the mortar and pestle, if you are using one.) The jerk rub is ready to use, or it may be stored in a tightly capped jar in the refrigerator for up to 5 days.

MOROCCAN-STYLE SPICE PASTE

MAKES ¼ CUP

1 tsp coriander seeds

1 tsp cumin seeds

1 tsp caraway seeds

1 tsp cardamom seeds

1 tsp anise seeds

1 tsp black peppercorns

3 tbsp light sesame oil

Grind the coriander, cumin, caraway, cardamom, anise seeds, and black peppercorns in a spice grinder to a coarse powder. Combine the ground spices and oil in a small bowl. The paste is ready to use, or it may be stored in a container at room temperature for up to 3 days.

VINAIGRETTE-STYLE DRESSING

This dressing can be flavored in a myriad of ways. Try adding mustard, chopped fresh herbs, capers, onions, garlic, or citrus zest. Fruit and vegetable juices can be used in place of the broth for a more intense flavor. Special vinegars such as balsamic, sherry, or red wine will give the dressing distinct character. Oils other than olive may be used, including various nut and seed oils (peanut, sesame, or walnut), canola oil, or other mono- or polyunsaturated oils. Refrigerated, this dressing may be stored for up to a week.

MAKES 2 CUPS

1½ tsp cornstarch

1 cup Chicken or Vegetable Broth (page 294)

½ cup red wine vinegar

½ cup extra-virgin olive oil

¼ tsp kosher salt, or as needed

¼ tsp freshly ground black pepper, or as needed

1. Combine the cornstarch with 2 tablespoons of the broth to form a paste. Bring the remaining broth to a boil in a small pot over medium-high heat. Remove the broth from the heat.

2. Gradually add the cornstarch slurry to the broth. Bring the mixture back to a boil over medium heat, whisking constantly, until the broth has thickened.

3. Remove from the heat, stir in the vinegar, and cool completely. Transfer the mixture to a small bowl. Gradually whisk in the oil. Taste and add the salt and pepper as needed.

BALSAMIC VINAIGRETTE

Use good extra-virgin olive oil and balsamic vinegar for the best flavor. **MAKES 2 CUPS**

1½ tsp cornstarch

1 cup Chicken or Vegetable Broth (page 294)

½ cup balsamic vinegar

½ cup extra-virgin olive oil

¼ tsp kosher salt

¼ tsp freshly ground black pepper

1 tbsp chopped basil

1. Combine the cornstarch with 2 tablespoons of the broth to form a paste. Bring the remaining broth to a boil in a small pot over medium-high heat. Remove the broth from the heat.

2. Gradually add the cornstarch slurry to the broth. Bring the mixture back to a boil over medium heat, whisking constantly, until the broth has thickened.

3. Remove from the heat, stir in the vinegar, and cool completely. Transfer the mixture to a small bowl. Gradually whisk the oil. Stir in the salt, pepper, and basil. Refrigerated, this dressing will thicken and may be stored for up to 1 week.

GINGER-SESAME VINAIGRETTE

MAKES 1 CUP

¼ cup rice wine vinegar

¼ cup reduced-sodium soy sauce

1 tbsp minced ginger

1 tsp minced garlic

Pinch kosher salt

Pinch freshly ground black pepper

1 tbsp honey

1 tbsp rinsed and chopped fermented black beans

Dash Tabasco sauce

2 tbsp lemon juice

2 tbsp peanut oil

1 tbsp sesame oil

Combine the vinegar, soy sauce, ginger, garlic, salt, pepper, honey, beans, Tabasco, and lemon juice in a small bowl. Slowly whisk in the oils. Refrigerated, this dressing may be stored for up to 1 week.

CITRUS VINAIGRETTE

MAKES 1 CUP

2 pink grapefruit, peeled and cut into sections

2 navel oranges, peeled and cut into sections

¼ cup citrus juice (from sectioning grapefruit and oranges)

1 tbsp lime juice

2 tbsp rice wine vinegar

2 tbsp sherry vinegar

½ tsp pink peppercorns

2 tsp chopped cilantro

1 tbsp honey

1 tbsp fish sauce

1 tsp minced ginger

1 garlic clove, minced

3 tbsp minced green onion

Dash Tabasco sauce

¼ cup vegetable oil

2 tsp olive oil

2 tsp sesame oil

Stir together the grapefruit and orange sections, citrus and lime juices, vinegars, peppercorns, cilantro, honey, fish sauce, ginger, garlic, green onion, and Tabasco in a small bowl. Slowly whisk in the oils. Refrigerated, this dressing may be stored for up to 1 week.

ASIAN VINAIGRETTE

MAKES 1 CUP

⅓ cup Vegetable Broth (page 295)

3 tbsp rice wine vinegar

2 tsp reduced-sodium soy sauce

2 tsp minced shallot

2 tsp whole-grain mustard

1½ tsp minced garlic

⅓ cup peanut oil

1 tbsp chopped chives

Combine the broth, vinegar, soy sauce, shallot, mustard, and garlic in a medium bowl. Slowly whisk in the oil. Stir in the chives. Refrigerated, this dressing may be stored for up to 1 week.

ANCHOVY-CAPER DRESSING

This creamy dressing has a briny flavor from capers and anchovies. **MAKES 2 CUPS**

½ cup part-skim ricotta cheese

1 cup plain nonfat yogurt, drained

¼ cup red wine vinegar

½ cup capers, rinsed, drained, and chopped

1 anchovy fillet, mashed

3 tbsp minced shallot

2 garlic cloves, minced

2 tbsp chopped chives

2 tbsp chopped parsley

2 tbsp chopped basil

½ tsp kosher salt

¼ tsp freshly ground black pepper

1. Purée the ricotta in a food processor or blender until smooth.
2. Transfer the ricotta to a large bowl and whisk in the yogurt, vinegar, capers, anchovy, shallot, garlic, chives, parsley, and basil. Season with the salt and pepper. Refrigerated, this dressing will thicken and may be stored for up to 1 week.

BASIL OIL

You can use the technique here to make any herb-flavored oil you like: chives, tarragon, oregano, or chervil, for instance. With the exception of basil and parsley, it is not necessary to blanch the herb leaves first. To use this flavored oil, pour a few drops on top of each bowl of soup. The heat will release the aroma and flavor of the herbs. **MAKES 1 CUP**

1 cup packed basil leaves

¼ cup packed parsley leaves

1 cup extra-virgin olive oil

1. Blanch the basil and parsley leaves in salted water for 20 seconds. Drain the basil and parsley in a colander, rinse in cold water until cool to the touch, and drain once more. Transfer to paper towels.
2. Purée the blanched herbs with half the oil in a blender until very fine. Add the purée to the remaining oil. Let the oil rest for at least 12 hours. Strain the oil through a coffee filter or cheesecloth into a clean storage container or squirt bottle. Keep chilled. Use within 5 days.

CHICKEN BROTH

Some stores sell packages of necks and backs that may be used to prepare broth. This broth may also be made with the carcasses of roasted birds. Save the bones from three birds after all the meat has been pulled or carved away (freeze the bones if you will not be making the broth within two days of removing the meat). **MAKES 2 QUARTS**

4 pounds chicken bones, cut into 3-inch lengths

12 cups (3 quarts) cold water, or as needed

¾ cup coarsely chopped onion

½ cup coarsely chopped carrot

½ cup coarsely chopped celery

1 Spice Sachet (page 285)

1½ tsp kosher salt

1. Place the chicken in a large pot. Add water to cover the chicken by at least 2 inches. Bring to a boil over medium heat, skimming any foam that rises to the surface.

2. Reduce the heat to cook at a slow simmer. Cover partially and simmer for 2 hours, skimming foam from the surface as needed.

3. Add the onion, carrot, celery, sachet, and salt and continue to simmer, skimming as necessary, until the broth is flavorful, about 1 hour more. Taste and season with salt, if needed.

4. Remove any meaty parts and save for another use. Strain the broth and discard the solids. Skim the fat from the surface or cool in an ice bath, chill, and lift away the hardened fat. Store the broth in the refrigerator for up to 5 days or in the freezer for up to 3 months.

Variations

BEEF BROTH: Replace the chicken with 4 lb bony beef cuts such as short ribs or shank. Brown the beef and vegetables, along with ½ cup tomato purée, in a 350°F oven for 45 minutes. Proceed as directed, increasing the simmering time to total 4 to 4½ hours and adding 1 leek, chopped, and ¼ cup celery leaves along with the vegetables.

FISH OR SHELLFISH BROTH: Replace the chicken with 5 lb bones from mild-flavored, lean white fish or shrimp, crab, and/or lobster shells. Replace the carrot with a coarsely chopped leek. Sauté until the onion and leek are translucent, then add the bones or shells. Cover and cook over low heat until the flesh on the bones is opaque or the shells turn bright red, 5 to 6 minutes. Add the water and simmer until very flavorful, 30 to 45 minutes.

VEGETABLE BROTH: Replace the chicken and vegetables with 1 onion, 1 celery stalk, 1 leek, 1 carrot, 1 parsnip, 1 cup broccoli stems, and 1 cup fennel, all thinly sliced. Sauté until starting to release juices, then add the water. Cover the pot and stir occasionally, 10 to 12 minutes. Simmer for 1 hour.

VELOUTÉ-STYLE SAUCE

MAKES 5 CUPS

3 tbsp cornstarch

4 cups Chicken Broth (page 294; or see Variations below)

1 cup evaporated nonfat milk

½ tsp kosher salt

¼ tsp freshly ground white pepper

1. Combine the cornstarch with enough of the broth to form a paste.

2. Bring the remaining broth to a boil in a medium sauce pot. Add the cornstarch slurry and the evaporated milk to the boiling stock, stirring constantly, until the sauce has thickened, about 2 minutes. Season with the salt and pepper. The sauce is ready to season, finish, and serve, it may be used in another preparation, or it may be cooled and stored in the refrigerator for up to 1 week.

Variations

FISH VELOUTÉ: Use Fish or Shellfish Broth.

VEGETABLE VELOUTÉ: Use Vegetable Broth.

BÉCHAMEL-STYLE SAUCE: Replace the broth with an equal amount of skim milk. Simmer gently; do not allow the milk to come to a full boil.

GINGER SAUCE

This simple sauce is an excellent accompaniment for grilled and broiled meat and fish. **MAKES 2 CUPS**

1 tbsp minced shallot

2 tbsp minced ginger

¼ cup lime juice

½ cup dry white wine

1⅔ cups Jus Lié (opposite)

½ cup heavy cream

¼ tsp kosher salt

¼ tsp freshly ground black pepper

1. Simmer the shallot, ginger, lime juice, and wine in a small saucepan over medium heat until the mixture has reduced by half.

2. Add the jus lié and heavy cream and continue to simmer until reduced enough to coat the back of a spoon. Season with the salt and pepper.

CREAMY MUSTARD GRAVY

MAKES 2½ CUPS

2½ cups Velouté-Style Sauce (page 295)

1 tbsp Dijon mustard

¼ tsp freshly ground black pepper

Bring the sauce to a simmer over low heat. Add the mustard and pepper and stir until smooth. Return to a simmer and serve at once.

JUS LIÉ

This thickened sauce adds excellent flavor enhancement to dishes. Other herbs and spices may be added. For classical dishes, add fines herbes (chives, chervil, tarragon, and parsley) to the sauce. For Asian cuisine, add lemongrass, tamarind, and ginger. **MAKES 1 QUART**

2 tsp olive oil

1 cup coarsely chopped carrot

1 cup coarsely chopped celery

1¼ cups coarsely chopped leeks

1¼ cups coarsely chopped onion

¼ cup tomato paste

1 tsp minced shallot

1 garlic clove, minced

1¼ cups red wine

1 bay leaf

1 sprig thyme

6 cups water or Vegetable Broth (page 295)

⅓ cup cornstarch

1. Heat the oil in a large pot over medium heat. Add the carrot, celery, leeks, and onion and caramelize, 10 to 12 minutes. Add the tomato paste, shallot, and garlic and continue to cook until the tomato paste is rust colored, about 5 minutes more.

2. Deglaze the pan with the wine, adding it in thirds. Allow the wine to reduce until reduced by two-thirds after each addition.

3. Add the bay leaf, thyme, and water. Simmer over medium-low heat until reduced by half, skimming the surface of foam as necessary.

4. Strain the sauce into a large bowl, pressing the solids to release all the juices.

5. Combine the cornstarch with 2 tablespoons of the broth to form a paste. Bring the remaining broth to a boil in a small pot over medium-high heat. Remove the broth from the heat.

6. Gradually add the cornstarch slurry to the broth and bring the mixture back to a boil over medium heat, whisking constantly, until the sauce has thickened. The jus is ready to use, or cool and store in the refrigerator for up to 2 weeks.

TOMATO-BASIL JUS

MAKES 1 QUART

3 lb turkey bones from turkey carcass, separated at joints

¼ cup tomato paste

¾ cup chopped onion

½ cup chopped carrot

½ cup chopped celery

1¼ cups white wine

1 bay leaf

12 cracked peppercorns

5 sprigs basil

3 parsley stems

4¾ cups Beef Broth (page 295)

5½ cups Chicken Broth (page 294)

⅔ cup Jus Lié (opposite page)

1 tbsp cornstarch (optional)

3 to 4 large basil leaves

½ cup chopped tomatoes (peeled and seeded), juices reserved

1. Preheat the oven to 375°F.

2. Roast the turkey bones, tomato paste, onion, carrot, and celery in a large pan until browned, about 30 minutes. Add the wine to the pan and stir well to release any drippings. Simmer over low heat until reduced by half. Transfer the mixture to a large soup pot. Add the bay leaf, peppercorns, basil, parsley, and broths and simmer over medium-low heat for 2 hours.

3. Strain the sauce through a fine-mesh sieve into a clean pot and return to low heat. Continue to simmer for 45 minutes, or until the sauce coats the back of a spoon. Add the jus lié, stirring until lightly thickened. If desired, thicken the sauce with a cornstarch slurry: Blend the cornstarch with 1 or 2 tablespoons cold water until smooth and add to the simmering sauce. Simmer for another 2 or 3 minutes to thicken completely. The sauce is ready to finish, or it may be cooled and stored in the refrigerator for up to 2 weeks.

4. To finish the sauce, tear the basil leaves into the sauce and add the tomatoes. Simmer long enough to heat the tomatoes, about 5 minutes. Serve at once.

ROASTED SHALLOT SAUCE

MAKES 1 CUP

2 tbsp unsweetened pineapple juice

1 tbsp lime juice

2 tsp white wine vinegar

¾ cup shredded roasted shallots (page 284)

1¼ cups Jus Lié (opposite page)

1 tbsp chopped cilantro

¼ tsp freshly ground black pepper

1. Bring the pineapple juice, lime juice, and vinegar to a simmer in a saucepan over medium heat. Continue to simmer uncovered, stirring occasionally, until the mixture has reduced by half.

2. Add the shallots and jus lié and return the sauce to a simmer long enough to develop a good flavor and consistency (it should lightly but evenly coat a spoon).

3. Add the cilantro to the sauce. Taste and adjust seasoning with pepper, if needed.

TOMATO COULIS

Serve this flavorful sauce over grilled fish such as swordfish, or to dress pasta or vegetables. **MAKES 3 CUPS**

2 tbsp olive oil

1 tsp minced garlic

3 lb chopped plum tomatoes (peeled and seeded)

5 basil leaves

Kosher salt and freshly ground black pepper, as needed

1. Heat the oil in a saucepan over medium heat. Add the garlic and sauté until aromatic, about 30 seconds. Add the tomatoes and basil, bring the sauce to a simmer, and cook gently, stirring frequently, until the liquid released by the tomatoes has cooked away, about 15 minutes.

2. Remove and discard the basil leaves. Purée the coulis through a food mill fitted with the coarse disk or with a handheld blender. Simmer the coulis a little longer over medium heat if it is too thin. Season with salt and pepper.

3. The sauce is ready to serve, or it may be rapidly cooled and refrigerated for later use.

Variation

TOMATO-GINGER COULIS: *Heat the oil in a small saucepan over medium heat and add 2 teaspoons minced ginger. Remove the pan from the heat and steep for at least 15 minutes. Strain, discarding the ginger. Continue following the original recipe, using the infused oil in place of plain oil.*

YELLOW TOMATO COULIS

MAKES ABOUT 2 CUPS

1 tsp olive oil

1 cup minced onion

1 tsp minced garlic

1¼ cups quartered yellow tomatoes

¼ tsp kosher salt

1 tsp sugar

2 bay leaves

½ tsp Tabasco sauce

Heat the oil in a large skillet over medium heat until smoky. Add the onions and garlic and cook until the onion is translucent, 4 to 5 minutes. Add the tomatoes, salt, sugar, bay leaves, and Tabasco and simmer until the mixture is dry, about 30 minutes. Remove the bay leaves. Purée the mixture in a food processor or blender until smooth. Strain through a large-mesh sieve.

RED PEPPER COULIS

MAKES ABOUT 2 CUPS

2 tbsp olive oil

2 lb red peppers, seeded and diced

2 tbsp minced shallot

¾ cup dry white wine

¾ cup Vegetable or Chicken Broth (page 295)

¼ tsp kosher salt

1. Heat the oil in a sauté pan over medium heat. Add the peppers and shallot and sauté until they are tender, 3 minutes.

2. Add the wine to the pan and stir to release any bits stuck to the bottom of the pan. Simmer over low heat until reduced by half, about 5 minutes.

3. Add the broth and reduce to approximately half the original volume.

4. Purée the mixture in a food processor or blender until smooth. Season with the salt.

ROASTED RED PEPPER COULIS

This sauce may be served as is or used to flavor tomato-based sauces, soups, or braised or stewed foods. This recipe is easily multiplied and keeps frozen for up to two months. MAKES 2 CUPS

4 red peppers, halved and seeded

2 tbsp oil, or as needed

½ cup Chicken or Vegetable Broth (page 294)

¼ cup evaporated nonfat milk

¼ tsp kosher salt

¼ tsp freshly ground black pepper

1. Preheat the oven to 450°F. Rub the peppers lightly with the oil and place cut side down on a baking sheet. Roast the peppers until very soft, 15 to 20 minutes. The skin should darken and pucker.

2. Transfer the peppers to a plastic bag and twist shut; set aside to cool for several minutes. Pull off the skins and discard.

3. Purée the peppers in a food processor or blender, slowly adding the broth until the sauce is quite smooth and thin enough to pour easily.

4. Strain the mixture into a saucepan and add the milk, salt, and pepper. Simmer for 2 to 3 minutes.

5. The coulis can be used immediately or stored in the refrigerator, covered, for up to 1 week.

PESTO

This pesto recipe doubles or triples easily. If you are making a big batch, leave the Parmigiano-Reggiano out of the portion you want to store, transfer to a clean jar, and cover with a thin layer of olive oil to prevent the sauce from darkening and drying out. Cover tightly and keep refrigerated for up to two weeks. MAKES 2½ CUPS

2 cups basil leaves, tightly packed

¼ cup pine nuts, toasted

3 tbsp extra-virgin olive oil

1 garlic clove, minced

1 tbsp water

⅓ cup grated Parmigiano-Reggiano

½ tsp kosher salt

¼ tsp freshly ground black pepper

1. Purée the basil, pine nuts, oil, and garlic in a blender or food processor until a coarse paste forms.

2. Gradually add the water with the machine still running and continue to purée until the paste is smooth.

3. Transfer the pesto to a bowl and fold in the cheese by hand. Season with the salt and pepper.

SPINACH-ARUGULA-TOMATO PESTO

MAKES 1 CUP

1¼ cups packed spinach leaves

1 cup packed arugula leaves

3 tbsp chopped basil

1 tbsp chopped cilantro

2 tsp chopped mint

1 garlic clove, minced

½ tsp extra-virgin olive oil

⅓ cup Vegetable Broth (page 295)

⅓ cup Tomato Coulis (page 298)

Purée the spinach, arugula, basil, cilantro, mint, and garlic in a food processor or blender until a coarse paste forms. Gradually add the oil, broth, and coulis with the machine still running and continue to purée while until the paste is smooth.

BARBECUE SAUCE

MAKES 3 CUPS

1⅓ cups tomato purée

½ cup white vinegar

⅓ cup tomato paste

¼ cup brewed coffee or water

¼ cup packed brown sugar

2 tbsp Worcestershire sauce

4½ tsp paprika

4½ tsp chili powder

4½ tsp dry mustard

1 tsp kosher salt

¾ tsp cayenne

Combine all the ingredients in a saucepan and whisk to mix thoroughly. Bring to a simmer over low heat for about 5 minutes, or until the sauce is flavorful. The barbecue sauce is ready to use, or it maybe stored in a covered container in the refrigerator for up to 3 weeks.

GREMOLATA

MAKES 6 TABLESPOONS

1 garlic clove, minced

2 tbsp grated lemon zest

1 tbsp chopped parsley

1 tbsp chopped sage

2½ tsp chopped rosemary

2 anchovy fillets, chopped

½ tsp freshly ground black pepper

Combine all the ingredients in a small bowl, stirring to blend evenly. The gremolata is ready to use, or you may store it in a covered container in the refrigerator for up to 24 hours.

HARISSA

Harissa, the traditional condiment for couscous, is a fiery hot red pepper sauce from North Africa. **MAKES 1 CUP**

4 dried habaneros

2 chopped red chiles (seeded)

¾ cup sun-dried tomatoes

3 garlic cloves, crushed

3 tbsp ground turmeric

1 tsp ground coriander

1 tsp ground cumin

1 tsp caraway seeds

1 tsp lemon juice

2 tbsp olive oil

1. Toast the habaneros in a small sauté pan until the skin darkens and a small amount of smoke rises, about 15 seconds on each side. Place the habaneros in a small bowl and cover with warm water. When they are soft and hydrated, remove the stems and seeds.

2. Purée the habaneros, chiles, tomatoes, garlic, turmeric, coriander, cumin, and caraway in a blender until smooth.

3. Adjust consistency with the lemon juice and oil. The harissa is ready to serve, or it may be refrigerated for later use.

MUSTARD

Supermarket shelves are full of a variety of mustards flavored with dried fruits, wasabi, honey, and wine. This version is simple to prepare, and you can fine-tune the amount of "kick" to suit your tastes. Allow the finished mustard to rest for several days to a week in the refrigerator to fully develop its flavor. **MAKES 2 CUPS**

⅓ cup dry mustard

1 tbsp sugar

¾ tsp kosher salt

3 large eggs

⅔ cup malt vinegar

1 tsp honey

½ tsp Tabasco or similar hot pepper sauce

1. Bring about 2 inches of water to a boil in the bottom of a double boiler, and reduce the heat to low.

2. Whisk the mustard, sugar, salt, and eggs together in the top of the double boiler. Add the malt vinegar and mix well.

3. Continue whisking the mixture over the simmering water until the mustard has thickened. It should fall from the whisk in ribbons that remain visible on the surface for several seconds. Take care not to let the mixture boil or it will curdle.

4. Remove the mustard from the heat, and stir in the honey and Tabasco. Cool to room temperature, then place in a clean bowl or jar, cover tightly, and chill thoroughly before serving. The mustard may be stored in the refrigerator for up to 2 weeks.

Variations
GREEN PEPPERCORN MUSTARD: Add 1 to 2 tsp of crushed green peppercorns.

HORSERADISH MUSTARD: Add 1 tablespoon (or more, if desired) grated fresh or drained bottled horseradish and ½ teaspoon freshly cracked black pepper.

MANGO-BOURBON BARBECUE SAUCE

This barbeque sauce is slightly sweet, sour, and spicy. A single mango will yield more than a cup when diced. Add the extra fruit to a green or fruit salad. **MAKES 4 CUPS**

1 tbsp vegetable oil

1 onion, minced

4 garlic cloves, chopped

1¾ cups ketchup

1 cup Chicken Broth (page 294)

1 cup diced mango (peeled and seeded)

½ cup hoisin sauce

½ cup cider vinegar

¼ cup bourbon

2 ancho chiles, seeded and chopped

2 tbsp lightly packed brown sugar

2 tbsp lemon juice

1 tbsp Worcestershire sauce

1 tsp grated lemon zest

½ tsp Old Bay seafood seasoning

¼ tsp freshly ground black pepper

Pinch cayenne

1. Heat the oil in a saucepan over medium-high heat. Add the onion and garlic, and sauté until the onions are tender and aromatic, about 6 minutes.

2. Add the ketchup, broth, mango, hoisin, vinegar, bourbon, chiles, sugar, lemon juice, Worcestershire, lemon zest, Old Bay, and peppers and simmer for 1 hour.

3. Cool slightly, about 10 minutes. Purée the sauce in a blender until very smooth. Use at once or cool and store in the refrigerator for up to 2 weeks.

APPLE BUTTER

Tart, juicy apples make a flavorful apple butter that doesn't get too sweet. Choose a single variety, such as McIntosh, or a variety of apples. Use a saucepan with a heavy-gauge bottom to prevent the apple butter from scorching as you cook it. A flame diffuser, if you have one, also keeps the heat even and gentle as the apple butter simmers. **MAKES 2 CUPS**

12 cups sliced apples (peeled)

1½ cups apple cider

½ cup sugar

½ cinnamon stick

½ tsp ground cardamom

½ tsp grated lemon zest

¼ tsp kosher salt

1. Combine the apples and apple cider in a saucepan and bring to a slow simmer over medium heat. Reduce the heat, cover, and simmer, stirring occasionally, until all the apples are soft and pulpy, about 30 minutes.

2. Remove from the heat and purée with a food mill or push through a sieve into a clean saucepan. Add the sugar, cinnamon, cardamom, lemon zest, and salt and simmer over low heat, stirring frequently, until very thick and deep brown, about 2 hours. Remove and discard the cinnamon.

3. Transfer the apple butter to a bowl set in an ice bath and cool, stirring from time to time. Once the apple butter has reached room temperature, it is ready to serve or store in a covered container in the refrigerator for up to 3 weeks.

DRIED CHERRY AND APPLE CHUTNEY

Serve this chutney with roasted or grilled chicken, duck, pork, or ham. It is also delicious spread over hearty whole-grain breads. **MAKES 1½ CUPS**

3 tbsp vegetable oil

½ cup minced onion

1 Granny Smith apple, peeled, cored, and diced

½ cup dried cherries

2 tbsp sugar

½ orange, peeled, chopped, and seeded

2 tbsp sherry vinegar

2 tbsp water

½ tsp kosher salt, or as needed

Pinch cayenne

Pinch freshly grated nutmeg

1. Heat the oil in a medium sauté pan over high heat. Add the onion and sauté until golden brown, 7 to 8 minutes.

2. Add the apple, cherries, sugar, orange, vinegar, and water and bring to a full boil.

3. Reduce the heat to low and simmer for 7 to 8 minutes, or until the chutney thickens just slightly.

4. Remove the sauté pan from the heat. Add the salt, cayenne, and nutmeg and cool to room temperature. Serve immediately or store in clean jars in the refrigerator for up to 2 weeks.

Variation

Dried pineapple, apricots, blueberries, or cranberries can be substituted for the cherries.

RED ONION MARMALADE

This marmalade is a delicious garnish for roasted meats, fish, and poultry. It could be made with Vidalia or other sweet onions. MAKES 1 CUP

2 medium red onions, thinly sliced

2 tbsp dry red wine

2 tsp sugar

2 tsp grenadine

2 tsp cider vinegar

¼ tsp kosher salt

¼ tsp freshly ground black pepper

1 tsp chopped fresh thyme or ½ tsp dried

1. Combine the onions, wine, sugar, grenadine, vinegar, salt, and pepper in a saucepan over medium-low heat. Simmer until most of the liquid has evaporated.

2. Remove the pan from the heat and add the thyme.

3. The marmalade may be served immediately or cooled and stored. To store, transfer the room temperature marmalade to a clean jar or bowl. Cover tightly and refrigerate. The marmalade will keep, refrigerated, for up to 10 days.

CORN RELISH

This lightly spiced, sweet-and-sour relish is a classic choice to accompany grilled hamburgers or steaks, hot dogs, or sandwiches. Serve it on a bed of lettuce with other sliced, shredded, or diced vegetables, such as cucumbers, carrots, jícama, peppers, celery and radishes, to make a more substantial salad. The recipe can be doubled, tripled, or even quadrupled. MAKES 1½ CUPS

2 ears corn, husked and silk removed

¼ cup diced red pepper

1 small jalapeño, seeded and finely chopped

1 green onion, thinly sliced

2 tbsp tightly packed brown sugar

3 tbsp cider vinegar

2 tsp dry mustard

Dash Tabasco sauce

1 tsp Worcestershire sauce, or as needed

½ tsp kosher salt, or as needed

1. Steam or boil the corn for 3 to 5 minutes, until the kernels are just tender. Cut the kernels from the cob and place in a bowl. Add the peppers and green onion.

2. Heat the sugar, vinegar, mustard, Tabasco, Worcestershire, and salt in a skillet over high heat and bring to a boil. Add the corn mixture and toss just until even coated.

3. Serve the relish warm, or allow it to cool to room temperature. Place it in a clean bowl or jar, cover tightly, and store in the refrigerator for up to 10 days.

TOMATO SALSA

Tomato salsa complements a variety of Southwestern or Tex-Mex dishes such as fajitas, burritos, enchiladas, grilled meats, fish, and poultry. Add more jalapeños or Tabasco or cayenne for a hotter salsa. Try other ingredients such as chopped parsley, celery, jícama, celeriac, and sweet peppers. **MAKES 1½ CUPS**

1½ cups chopped tomatoes (peeled and seeded; see Note)

½ jalapeño, seeded and minced

½ cup minced red onion

2 tbsp chopped cilantro

2 tbsp lime juice

¼ tsp freshly ground black pepper

½ tsp kosher salt

Combine all the ingredients in a large bowl. Cover and refrigerate for several hours, allowing the flavors to develop. Taste and adjust seasoning as needed.

NOTE Although fresh tomatoes are the best choice, good-quality canned plum tomatoes may be substituted. The seeds and juice of the tomatoes may be reserved and used as a flavor enhancement in braised dishes.

SALSA VERDE

Some recipes for salsa verde, or green sauce, use mainly herbs to flavor the salsa. This recipe uses tomatillos, which have a slightly sweet-and-sour flavor that complements many Latin American dishes. **MAKES 2 CUPS**

1¾ cups quartered tomatillos (husked and washed)

2 serranos, stemmed

¼ cup chopped cilantro

1 cup chopped onion

1 garlic clove, chopped

1 tbsp vegetable oil

1½ cups Chicken Broth (page 294)

½ tsp kosher salt

¼ freshly ground black pepper

1. Bring a medium pot of salted water to a boil. Add the tomatillos and serranos and boil until tender, 10 to 15 minutes. Drain.

2. Purée the tomatillos, chiles, cilantro, onions, and garlic in a blender until almost smooth.

3. Heat the oil in a medium skillet over medium-high heat. Add the purée and stir constantly for 4 to 5 minutes, until the purée is darker and thicker. Add the broth and bring the sauce to a boil. Reduce the heat to medium and simmer until thick enough to coat a spoon, about 20 minutes. Season with the salt and pepper.

4. Serve immediately, or cool rapidly and refrigerate for later use.

PAPAYA-MANGO SALSA

This salsa is great for grilled meats and fish, or on its own with tortilla chips. **MAKES 2 CUPS**

2 medium mangoes, peeled, seeded, and diced

½ medium papaya, peeled, seeded, and diced

½ canned chipotle, minced

3 tbsp orange juice

Juice of 2 limes

1⅓ cups thinly sliced green onion, split lengthwise

⅓ cup pine nuts, toasted

Combine all the ingredients in a medium bowl and toss. Let the salsa rest at room temperature for at least 20 minutes before serving to allow the flavors to develop.

PARSLEY AND TOASTED ALMOND SALSA

This salsa is a great condiment for Mediterranean-inspired dishes or for adding a bit of flavor to a simple grain pilaf.
MAKES ABOUT ¾ CUP

2 tbsp diced shallot

1 tbsp red wine vinegar

½ cup sliced toasted almonds

3 tbsp chopped parsley

2 tbsp chopped basil

1 tbsp extra-virgin olive oil

2 tsp capers (rinsed and chopped)

Marinate the shallots in the red wine vinegar in a small bowl for 20 minutes. Combine the shallot mixture with the remaining ingredients. Serve immediately or refrigerate for up to 2 days.

HALF-SOUR PICKLES

This snappy pickle can be served any time as a low-fat and low-calorie snack, but it is a classic accompaniment to sandwiches of all sorts. **MAKES 25 PICKLES**

1 tbsp pickling spice

½ cup cider vinegar

¼ cup kosher salt

12 garlic cloves, crushed

25 small pickling cucumbers

3 sprigs dill

1. Combine the pickling spice, vinegar, salt, garlic, and cucumbers in a deep nonreactive pot. Add enough water to cover the cucumbers and bring it to a boil over high heat.

2. Remove the pan from the heat. Remove the garlic. Add the dill.

3. Allow the pickles to marinate in the brine at least overnight. Serve when the flavor is fully developed. To put up the pickles, see the Note.

NOTE To put up the pickles, return the pickles and brine to a simmer. Remove the pickles and the dill with a slotted spoon and pack into hot sterilized jars to within 1 inch of the top. Return the liquid to a full boil, and pour it over the pickles to within ½ inch of the top of the jar. Seal the jars with sterilized lids, and place them in a boiling water bath for 15 minutes. Remove the jars and cool at room temperature; label and date the jars, and store in a cool, dry place.

PICKLED BEETS AND ONIONS

This pickle can be served as part of a relish tray on a buffet or as an hors d'oeuvre plate to nibble with cocktails or apéritifs. **MAKES 6 SERVINGS**

24 baby beets, tops trimmed (see Note)

3 medium red onions, julienned

3 tbsp sugar

½ cup white vinegar

1 tbsp kosher salt

1 cup water

1. Place the beets in a pan and add enough cool water to cover by at least 2 inches. Simmer the beets over medium heat until just tender, about 15 minutes. Drain and rinse under cold water; drain well. When the beets are cool enough to handle, slip off the skins and set the beets aside in a bowl.

2. Combine the onions, sugar, vinegar, salt, and water in a saucepan over high heat and bring to a boil. Lower the heat and simmer, uncovered, for 5 minutes.

3. Pour the hot onion mixture over the beets and allow to cool to room temperature. Cover the beets well and chill completely for several hours or overnight before serving. The pickled beets may be stored in the refrigerator for up to 5 days.

NOTES Twelve medium beets can be substituted for the baby beets. Cut into wedges or slices after they are fully cooked.

Make pickled eggs by adding peeled hard-boiled eggs to the marinade after it has cooled to room temperature. The eggs should marinate in the refrigerator for at least 24 hours. They can then be quartered and served with the beets as a salad, or eaten whole.

Index

A